Introduction

This guide offers a very personal selection of sites based on over 40 years experience visiting French campsites using tents, caravans and a motorhome as accommodation. The sites included in this guide have been chosen because they all have something unique and special about them:

- their location in the grounds of châteaux, or facilities located in converted old buildings
- their proximity to beaches, lakes, rivers or mountains
- the warm friendly atmosphere created by the owners

We have stayed on the majority ourselves over the years and constantly inspect them to make sure that they maintain their standards. We have chosen a variety of sites, ranging from very small intimate ones with limited services but good facilities to large, more commercial sites which are suitable for those holidaying with older children or who simply prefer a lively atmosphere with plenty of entertainment. Couples on their own have different requirements to families with children seeking new distractions every day, and we hope that our selection has something for everyone.

We are particularly keen to promote the "Green Credentials" of the sites in this guide who are members of organisations below.

Clef Verte
www.laclefverte.org

The Green Key is a label awarded to tourist accommodation providers for running their establishment in an environmentally friendly manner. Several sites in our guide have been awarded this label.

Via Natura
www.campings-la-via-natura.com

A small association of campsites whose aim is to encourage the observation and appreciation of nature in superb natural surroundings. They are committed to offering assistance in understanding and interpreting the environment and its cultural heritage, giving information on the fauna, flora and insects in several languages, promoting regular outings to discover nature and to placing emphasis on education about the environment. Like Clef Verte, the group are very keen on sustainable tourism, in particular recycling waste, and using resources such as water and electricity in a responsible manner. Five of the twelve sites are in our guide.

European Eco-label
www.ecolabel-tourism.eu

The EU Ecolabel is an official sign of environmental quality that is both certified by an independent organisation and valid throughout Europe. The European Ecolabel was originally created to reward tourist accommodation services and tourists that respect the environment. In 2004, the European Commission also established criteria for camp site services. Since 2005, camp site services can apply for the European Ecolabel. The European Ecolabel signals environmental good performance as it is an added quality value when consumers are choosing a resort. Enterprises bearing the Flower Logo have officially been distinguished as being amongst the most environmentally friendly in their area. At least two sites in our guide have eco-labels.

Reserving in advance

We recommend that you reserve in advance for the high season mid-July to mid-August or even longer on some sites. Very large outfits should consider booking at all times. You can book direct or reserve a package including ferry crossing through Eurocamp Independent, Select Sites, The Caravan Cub or The Camping and Caravanning Club.

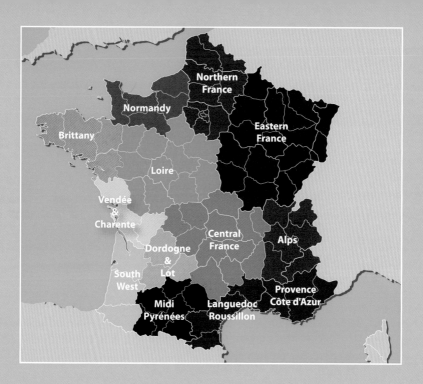

Contents

Star Ratings

We have included star ratings for all these sites. These are **not** our ratings, but those allocated by individual local authorities in France. In theory they are rated according the number of facilities provided per camper and do not necessarily reflect the quality of the installations nor the quality of maintenance. Consequently many 3-star sites can actually provide better quality services than some of the 4-star ones.

Campsite chains

A large number of sites have now joined chains to improve their marketing. There are so many different chains and sites sign up and leave quite frequently. The only chain we have mentioned is the Castels, as the majority do fulfil our remit of situation in a unique location. Most, but not all are part of large estates in the grounds of castles and manor houses.

About This Guide

Each site included in this guide has a full page description. An explanation of the details included for each site is listed below. The site descriptions have been set out in 13 different tourist regions with a sypnosis of tourist attractions for each area. We have also featured information on travelling and holidaying in France, including:

What to do Before you Travel
Staying on a Campsite in France
Checklist of Items to Take

All the sites welcome caravans, motorhomes, tents and trailer tents. We have indicated where pitches would be totally unsuitable for large outfits. Generally most of them have pitches about 100m², so do bear in mind that motorhomes 11m long or tents measuring 9m x 9m plus car will have difficulty fitting on a pitch. If you have a particularly large caravan, motorhome or tent, we recommend contacting the site before arrival even in the low season to check that there are pitches available which can accommodate your outfit. Often we say that a pitch is grassy, but do remember that by end of a busy season of heavy use, there may be very little green grass left and the pitch will be very dry and sometimes muddy or dusty. The further south you are, the more this is likely to be the case. Also when we indicate that pitches are gently sloping, we recommend levelling blocks for caravanners and motorcaravanners.

Electricity, water & drainage
220 volt electricity is generally available although the amperage provided varies from site to site. Not all sites offer pitches with water & drainage and on many sites only a limited number are equipped with this facility.

Motorhomes
Sites which are specially suitable for motorhomes because of their proximity to a town have been highlighted. This helps identify the sites where you will not need to take your outfit off site too often.

Swimming pools
The majority of sites have swimming pools and paddling pools. Only the larger sites employ attendants, so generally they are not supervised. Increasing numbers have installed indoor pools or cover the outdoor ones in low season. Although many sites advertise heated pools the temperature of the water does tend to vary. On some of the larger sites you will be obliged to pay a deposit, refundable on departure, for a wristband which permits entry. Most sites now forbid Bermuda shorts in their pools. Only trunks allowed.

Activities On Site
These vary from site to site. Some offer an enormous range of activities including tennis, all weather sports pitches, mini-golf, trampolines, paintball, adventure parks, canoe hire etc. Others only have a children's playground and a boules piste. **Boules** or **Pétanque** is the French game played with heavy steel balls thrown to be nearest the cochonnet, often played in teams. It is airborne bowls and the skill comes from reading the bumps, holes and cracks on the stony uneven surface.

Entertainment
Again this varies dramatically and is usually only available from the beginning of July to the end of August. Some sites offer no organised activities at all. The majority offer some daytime entertainment and the occasional evening concert in high season. Most sites now employ an "animateur" to run a children's club. Many sites organise sporting competitions such as tennis or volleyball tournaments and some of the bigger sites have a programme of organised activities all day long, even in the low season. Many sites offer organised excursions including guided walks. Discos are run every evening by some of the larger sites only.

Sanitary facilities

A description of the facilities is given for each site and includes details such as whether showers have temperature control and if there are sufficient hooks. Some sites do not provide toilet paper and even on those that do, don't forget it may run out at peak times! Most sites provide separate sinks for washing clothes (bac à linge) and for washing up (bac à vaisselle). It is important to take your own bowl as plugs are not always provided or tend to "disappear" during the season. Most sites have washing machines, dryers, usually operated by a token system obtained at the reception. They may be in high demand in the high season, so aim to use them early in the morning or late in the evening. Free ironing facilities are also usually available.

Services

Most sites have shops that sell only basics and generally open in the morning and in the evening from 16:00 to 19:00. Restaurants and take-aways tend to offer fairly limited menus. Do bear in mind that the chef is usually only employed for the season.

Opening times of services

These vary on most sites depending on the season. The reception on a large number of sites is closed at lunchtime from 12 - 2pm, particularly in the low season and on smaller sites they may be shut for 3 or 4 hours. Similarly other services like the shop, bar, take-away and restaurant may have more limited hours in low season or may only operate in high season. Some sites are now giving full details of the opening times on their website. If you want to be sure that something is open, either email or telephone in advance. Most proprietors or receptionists speak English well enough to respond to your queries.

Internet & Wi-Fi

All but a few sites offer an internet service and most now also offer Wi-Fi. Some offer Wi-Fi for free and others make a charge.

Barbecues

Barbecues are not allowed on all sites, particularly wooded ones, and may be banned altogether during prolonged dry periods. Gas barbecues are allowed on most sites. Some sites ban the use of electric barbecues. Open fires on the ground are banned on all sites.

Accommodation

Nearly all sites now have their own mobile homes and/or chalets available for rent. Some also have gites or rooms for rent. We have not inspected the accommodation available and have not included any specific information about them. Refer to the site's own web for further details.

Tour Operators

We have indicated as far as possible the number of British tour operators present as this obviously reflects the atmosphere of the site. It means that there will be other British children for your own to play with, but equally the number of French and other nationalities will be considerably reduced.

Opening Dates & Pricing bands

The opening dates and prices are those advised to us at the time of going to press. We do not accept responsibility for any variations in these details. Tariffs are decided entirely by the site owner. To some extent, but not always they reflect the quality of the services and the position of the site. Do remember that the majority of sites also add on "taxe de séjour", which can vary from about 0.20 euros to 0.55 euros per head per night.

Contacting the site

The postal address, email and telephone number of each site is provided.

Directions

Directions are given to the site from the most popular routes with an indication of the location of the site. The GPS coordinates are also given.

Websites

It is always a good idea to look at the campsite's website. A few are brilliant and provide good images and excellent information. The majority have enough pictures to give you an idea of what to expect, but the quality of the information is poor. However the quality of the web does not necessarily reflect the quality of the campsite.

Overnight Stops

We have added a number of good quality sites near to the ports or on main through routes which are suitable for overnight stops.

Preparing for your stay in France

Passports

Ensure that your passport is valid. If you do not have one or your previous one has expired, apply for one at least one month before departure. All children now have to have their own passports, including babies.

Forms are available from the Post Office, and on line at: www.ips.gov.uk
or tel 0870 521 0410 for further advice.

EHIC

The European Health Insurance Card is the size of a credit card and each member of the family has to have their own card. The EHIC entitles all UK residents to reduced cost (sometimes free) health care, if it becomes necessary when travelling in most European countries. It is issued by the Prescription and Pricing Authority and is free of charge. The quickest way to get an EHIC is to apply online at www.ehic.org.uk and you should receive it within 7 days. You can apply for your spouse/partner and any children up to age of 16 (or 19 if they are in full time education) at the same time as applying for your own. You will need to provide your name and date of birth and NHS or National Insurance number (CHI no.in Scotland and Health & Care no.in N.Ireland). You can also apply by calling 0845 606 2030 and it will be delivered within 10 days or pick up a form from the Post Office.

Insurance

Check the details of all your insurance cover before you leave. Remember that most travel insurance policies have a limit of £200/£250 on individual items. Your home contents policy will normally cover you for valuables and expensive camping equipment. All sites have a valuables deposit box at reception. It is essential that you take out a personal insurance policy to cover you for any unforseen circumstances such as cancellation, travel delays and most especially hospitalisation benefits that are not fully covered by the EHIC. An air ambulance can cost as much as £5,000. Car and caravan/trailer breakdown insurance is also essential.

The Green Card

This is still highly recommended although no longer obligatory for those travelling in EC countries. Unfortunately some British insurers only give minimum third party cover abroad, unless you take it out. It is rarely printed on a card and isn't usually green.

Camping Carnet

Although this is not essential, we strongly recommend that you take one with you, as it is another document giving proof of identity and can be left at the site reception instead of your passport.

Taking Money With You

Take enough euros to cover emergencies and to see you through the first few days (for motorway tolls, food etc.) particularly if you are travelling at weekends. It is probably better not to carry too much cash - if you lose it or it is stolen there is no easy way of replacing it. Travel insurance usually only covers loss of money up to £200.

Travellers' Cheques is the safest and best way of taking money abroad. Order them in advance from your local bank. Before exchanging travellers cheques on the campsites, ask the receptionist to confirm the exchange rate as it may be less favourable than at the local banks. You will need your passport or photographic identification to cash them. British driving licences are only acceptable if you have one with a photograph. Keep a note of the numbers of the travellers' cheques in case of loss. Credit Cards such as Mastercard and Visa (Carte Bleue), can be used for making payments in various establishments, and for drawing money from the bank in emergencies. There is always an extra charge per transaction. In France Visa is the most commonly used credit card and is widely accepted at motorway service tolls and in many large shops and petrol stations. Be wary when trying to use your credit card at fuel stations in rural France and in supermarkets at night. Many are fully automated outside opening hours and do not accept debit cards on UK accounts. Cash is not an option either, so have a good reserve in your tank when leaving major routes.

Car and Caravan/Trailer Tent

Do make sure that you have your car and caravan thoroughly serviced before departure. Please remember that for vehicle recovery insurance policies, you are required to service your vehicle in accordance with the manufacturer's recommendations. Carry a simple spares kit (available from the AA, RAC or local dealer) and a temporary plastic windscreen. Take a spare wheel and tyre for your caravan - failure to pack this causes many spoiled holidays. Do check tyre pressures on car (and caravan or trailer). Also check wiper blades and exhaust system. Adjust your headlights so that the dipped beam does not light the wrong side of the road. This can be achieved by deflectors or beam convertors, which can be purchased from AA or RAC offices and retailers selling car accessories. A good hook-on wing mirror is essential for each side of a vehicle towing a caravan or wide trailer.

Taking your Dog/Cat Abroad

In order to take your pet abroad, it has to have its own passport. You need to plan this very carefully and make the necessary arrangements well in advance. You will also have to book an appointment with a vet in France to arrange for flea and tick treatments between 48 and 24 hours prior to return on the ferry. For further information, contact your local vet or go to:
www.defra.gov.uk and click over 'pet travel scheme' or phone 0870 241 1710 for a free information pack.
www.dogsaway.co.uk or phone 08450 171073 - locates a convenient vet in France for a modest fee.

You also have to pay for your pet to cross the channel and for a nightly stay on most campsites. The dog will have to remain in the car throughout the ferry crossing, so a short crossing or night crossing is recommended. It is essential that your dog is kept on a leash while staying on the site.

Setting Off

It is a good idea to take a large shoulder bag for documents, camera, guides, money etc. as well as plenty of drinks, food in an insulated bag and games for the children. Pack a separate overnight bag if spending the night on the ferry or in a hotel.

Before You Leave Home:

- Have the car/caravan/trailer/motorhome serviced
- Turn off major electrical appliances, except fridges and freezers.
- Lock all doors and fasten all windows.
- Cancel newspapers and milk.
- Give neighbours contact address and telephone no and leave spare house key with friends or relatives.
- Make necessary arrangements for your pets.
- Water plants

Before Driving Off in a Motorhome or Towing a Caravan/Trailer check:

- Gas is turned off
- Water and waste bottles and toilet have been emptied
- Indicators and lights (car /caravan motorhome)
- Roof lights, hatches and windows are closed
- Fridge door is secured, it is changed to car setting
- Hob and sink covers are secured
- Rear View mirrors are fitted and correctly adjusted
- Steadies are up and caravan handbrake is off
- Coupling and safety chain
- Caravan electrics cable is not touching the ground
- Jockey wheel has been raised.

Catching the Ferry

Most companies are now issuing Ticket on Departure. Keep reference number handy. You must arrive at the port about one hour prior to sailing. If you should miss your ferry, your ticket is usually valid for any sailing, but only subject to availability. Ferry companies reserve the right to make an amendment charge at the port if you do not travel on the sailing booked, particularly if you change your price band, or if your vehicle is longer or higher than that shown on the ticket. It may mean applying to the ticket office and queuing to await any cancellations particularly if you have an overheight vehicle, such as a caravan or motorhome, as overheight vehicle space is limited on long sea routes. On arrival at the port, you go through ticket control and passport control together.

For holidaymakers with caravans and motorhomes it is possible to pull up for the night at the following ports - Roscoff, Cherbourg, Caen and Dunkerque. You can also stay overnight at Poole and Plymouth. This is particularly useful if you arrive at the port from one of the late afternoon or evening sailings or wish to get an early morning crossing.

There are also a good number of overnight sites near all the ports.

In most disembarkation lounges, there are toilets, disabled facilities and baby-changing facilities along with refreshments in cafés/bars or vending machines.

Ferry Loading Procedure is usually in accordance with a pre-determined plan depending on length, height, width and weight as well as to comply with security regulations. Sometimes, therefore, you may have to wait longer than others. Disabled passengers should let the staff at the check-in desk know if they need to be parked next to a lift to get from the vehicle deck to the passenger decks. They will then inform the loading staff who will make sure that you are parked in the correct position and give any assistance needed. You are also expected to ensure that your car alarm is not activated which means locking the car manually or deactivating the alarm. Access to the vehicle decks is prohibited during the crossing, so take everything you need from the car with you.

Take note of the number or letter of your vehicle deck to help you relocate your vehicle when it comes to disembarkation.

If you have sleeping accommodation booked, claim this as soon as you have boarded.

If you require accommodation ask at the information desk for availability. If you have a cabin, you will be woken up early in the morning, to allow you to breakfast. Listen carefully to all Public Address announcements and once you have rejoined your vehicle for disembarkation, do not start your engine until told to do so. This avoids polluting the air on the vehicle decks.

On board there are usually a cafeteria, restaurant, shops, bar, telephones, games rooms with electronic games and a play area for small children. Films are usually screened in the cinema on long-sea crossings.

Eurotunnel travellers on arrival at the terminal at Folkestone, report directly to the Check-in point for Tickets purchased in Advance where you will receive boarding instructions. When you have loaded leave the windows open so that you can hear announcements during the journey. Please stay in or near your vehicle and ensure that children are supervised at all times. Toilets are located in every third wagon. There are no refreshments on board, so it is a good idea to take some drinks and light snacks with you in the car. The train will enter the Tunnel a minute or two after leaving the platform and normally arrives 27 minutes later in France. Cars powered by LP gas, caravans and motorcaravans with fixed gas bottles are banned from travel.

Things to remember:

- European Summertime is One Hour ahead of British Summertime.

- The Michelin Road Atlas for France is highly recommended, as it is very detailed. The price is about £15.

- Mobile phones do not automatically work in France. They have to be dual band and calls are more expensive.

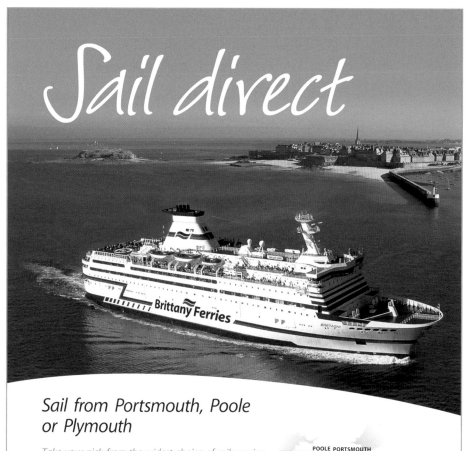

Motoring in France

Driving on the right should present no difficulties. Obviously you drive anti-clockwise round a roundabout, and may find the front passenger useful when overtaking. Road signs are easy to understand conforming to international designs common in the UK, although often they are positioned lower down at a junction and can be hidden by a passing vehicle. They are often on the junction rather than just before.

Legal Requirements

- All drivers must be over 18 years of age.
- Seat belts must be worn by the driver and front and back seat passengers.
- Under-10's may not travel in the front.
- A red-warning triangle is compulsory for all drivers in case of breakdown
- Spare light bulbs and a medical kit are compulsory.
- Beams must be adjusted for right hand drive, easily effected by sticking on black tape.
- The vehicle registration document should be carried.
- G.B. sticker or number plate with GB.
- Don't drink and drive.
- Don't overload your car, caravan or trailer.
- Carrying a Reflective Jacket to put on in case of breakdown. The AA recommends that each vehicle has at least two jackets or vest one for the driver and one for a passenger who may have to assist changing a wheel.
  They must conform to EUstandard: BS EN 471:1994 class 1 or 2.
- It is forbidden for the driver to use hand held mobile phones.

Legal requirement for caravans and large trailers

- Any vehicle towing a caravan must be fitted with two clip on wing mirrors.
- Maximum dimensions are 2.5m wide and 11m long (for vehicle and trailer max length is 18m)
- No passengers may be carried in a moving van.
- Outside built-up areas, the driver of the towing vehicle is required by law to keep a distance of 50m between him and the vehicle ahead.
- Vehicles towing caravans are not allowed to drive in the centre of many large cities or the outer lane of 3-lane motorways. On narrow roads, you must enable vehicles to overtake by slowing down or pulling into the side where possible.
- In case of breakdown, even if the caravan has hazard warning lights, you must display a red warning triangle at least 30 metres behind.
- If the vehicle or caravan is borrowed you must have written authorisation from

Road Categories

A	=	Autoroute (Motorway)
N	=	Route Nationale (Major Trunk Road)
D	=	Route Départementale - often less busy than N roads and of quite acceptable standard. Sometimes they 'cut corners' but be wary, distances on winding roads can be deceptively long.
V	=	Chemin Vicinal (Local by-road, not used by through traffic)

Speed Limits

Motorways:	130 kph (80mph)	110 kph (70 mph) in wet weather
Free Motorways:	110 kph (68mph)	80 kph (50mph) in wet weather
Ordinary road outside towns:	90 kph (56 mph)	
Roads in built-up areas:	50 kph (31 mph)	

Reclassification of French road numbers

The French government is currently transferring the administration of approximately 18,000 kilometres of national roads to local authorities, resulting in the significant re-classification and re-numbering of French roads. This will take several years to complete and road numbers are likely to change slightly. For example the N404 will become the D1404. Be prepared for the road numbers not to correspond with your maps, even if they are new!

Motorways in France

France has over 8,000 km of motorways. A toll system is in operation on most motorways, indicated by a **péage** sign before you go on. Most operate on a punched card system, which you take as you enter the toll booth by pushing the distributor button and which is handed in as you leave to assess payment. Credit cards can be used to pay tolls in the manned booths and unmanned turnstiles. There is 2m height restriction at these **carte de crédit** only exits. On shorter stretches, the toll may be paid in euro coins thrown into automatic machines. Short stretches of motorway round cities are usually free. There are several different companies running the motorway system so prices per km vary. **www.autoroutes.fr** provides both tariffs and route planning. A car and caravan count as Category 2 - you pay half as much again for the caravan as a rule. Trailer tents are generally charged at the same rate as caravans.

You will find orange emergency telephones every 2km, parking and resting areas every 10km and 24-hour petrol stations approximately every 40km. Petrol stations have many amenities including good toilet facilities. The service areas and **aires de repos** often indicated by a **P** provide excellent spacious stopping points and picnic areas. Toilets and water are also available.

Traffic Congestion

If heading south, the worst traffic problems occur each weekend throughout July until the middle of the August and then returning each weekend from mid August until the first weekend September. It is a good idea to avoid these days for travelling - Friday pm and Saturday outward and Saturday and Sundays on the return.

Breakdown on the Motorway

Park on the hard shoulder and put out the warning triangle. Do not contact your own insurance company in the first instance. Use one of the orange emergency telephones. This puts you in touch with the police who will send a mechanic to assist you. The fee fixed by government for attendance is about £50. If the mechanic can repair your car within 30 minutes, you pay this fee plus parts; otherwise the car will be towed to the nearest garage where you should contact your vehicle recovery insurance company who will make further arrangements on your behalf. Ensure you get a receipt for any charges for insurance purposes. Motorway information on the radio is FM107.7

Other Roads

A toll system is also in operation on some bridges including le Pont de Tancarville near Le Havre, Le Pont de Normandie and the Viaduc de Millau. The bridge from La Rochelle over to the Ile de Ré is subject to a toll.

Please note that on the main roads there are fewer petrol stations per distance covered in France than in Great Britain and they rarely open after 20:00 hours except on Autoroutes and near hypermarkets, so be wary of letting your tank run too low. **Bison Futé** or **Itinéraire Bis** is the term used for the road system recommended to guide traffic round congested areas on to more relaxing, scenic routes, and they are indicated by green or yellow arrows. Bison Futé maps, showing recommended routes are readily available free of charge at roadside offices marked Bison Futé. They may also be available at the channel ports. There are 59 Bison Futé centres open during the peak period giving free information on traffic conditions and recommended itineraries.
www.bison-fute.equipement.gouv.fr
Other traffic information
www.infotrafic.com

Traffic Lights

These are often positioned well to the side of the road or are suspended overhead in the middle of the road. Care is needed as they are not always repeated on the other side of the junction. They also change from red straight to green. At many junctions during off peak times, the traffic lights may only show one flashing orange light, which indicates that nobody has priority, although giving way to the right usually applies.

Emergencies and Accidents

In the event of an accident, keep calm, do not move your car initially. If somebody is injured, call the emergency services. If you have taken out a Car Breakdown and Recovery Insurance, telephone the emergency number stated in your insurance details to get advice. On a motorway, you are obliged to use their own services unless told otherwise. The police need only be called if someone is injured or your vehicle represents a dangerous hazard. Get receipts for everything to be able to make an insurance claim.

Cars towing a caravan

If the weight of the trailer exceeds that of the car, the speed limits are lower: 65kph if the excess is less than 30% and 45kph if the excess is more than 30%.

Travelling with a motorhome

A Motorhome Charter issued by a motorhome builders' committee in conjunction with the French Government issues certain guidelines to motorhome owners. The most important point is to be considerate about parking, not to impede the view of shops or any other businesses in a town, to avoid upsetting the flow of traffic and to park where possible in an area which is not heavily populated. Overnight parking of motorhomes is controlled in certain towns and cities, but where allowed, public areas should not be monopolised and they should not create any sort of problem for local residents. Evacuation of water etc. must be done in the appropriate places provided and not in any drains or rivers.

Vehicle Weight in France

Motorcaravans, caravans and trailers must not exceed the maximum authorised laden weight written on the vehicles registration certificate. Police can weigh any vehicle thay they suspect is overladen and issue a fine up to 1,500 euros.

Parking your caravan or motorhome

Overnight parking in a lay-by is not permitted on any road in France. However, in cases of driving fatigue, you can and should pull off the road for a while. Motorways are well-equipped with rest areas but should not be regarded as alternative campsites. On some roads and motorway parking areas, you will find facilities for caravans to take on fresh water, empty toilets and make extended stops. Similarly some towns allow caravans

to park on the road. However, you will also find towns forbidding caravans to park: these will have places where you may stop for provisions. The local tourist office will always provide important information.

Foreign Office advice recommends that you spend the night on a designated campsite as there has been a number of mugging incidents at the more isolated rest areas, those without petrol stations and cafés. There have also been several incidents even in well-lit service areas where ether has been pumped into the van to allow the perpetrators to carry out an easy burglary in caravans and motorhomes.

Take the middle lane in towns as there is often a filter on the right. When negotiating your way round towns, if there is any doubt follow the signs for all directions **Toutes Directions** which usually guide the driver round the town rather than straight through it. Caravans and large motorhomes are often banned from town centres as the roads may be too narrow. Follow signs for HGVs.

Petrol & Diesel

Unleaded and diesel are available throughout France. LPG is widely available at over 1,700 filling stations in France, particularly in motorway service areas.

Useful translation of road signs:

éteignez vos phares	switch off headlights
travaux/chantier	road works
chaussée déformée	bad road surface
route bombée	bad road surface
route mauvaise	bad road surface
nids de poules	potholes
gravillons	loose gravel
déviation	deviation
route déviée	deviation
route barrée	road closed
voie sans issue	no through road
sens unique	one way street
hauteur limitée	height restriction
cedez le passage	give way
serrez à droite	keep to the right
tenez votre file	keep in your lane
avertissez	sound your horn
rappel	remember
toutes directions	all routes
virages sur x km	bends for x km
entrée	entrance
sortie	exit
sortie d'usine	factory exit
véhicules lents	slow vehicles
vent violent	strong wind
stationnement interdit	parking forbidden

Planning your Journey

Many drivers undertake long journeys in, or through, France. Care should be taken to plan journeys and take sufficient breaks, approximately 15 minutes for every two hours driving. Roads in France particularly motorways are an excellent standard.

Speed Limits

Although speed limits are higher than in UK, the accident rate is also higher. Speed cameras are now much more common in France particularly on motorways and roads round large towns.   Procedures are being put in place for the DVLA in the UK to chase up fines. Severe penalties for road traffic infringements have recently been introduced in France. These include a sentence of up to 10 yrs imprisonment and a fine of 150,000 euros for causing death whilst over the alcohol limit; a sentence of 7 yrs and fine of 100,000 euros for causing death by dangerous or negligent driving; a sentence of up to 2 years, a fine of 30,000 euros and seizure of vehicle and device for using any radar detecting device, even if the device is switched off. Please note that on the spot fines (as much as 1,500 euros) for speeding and drinking and driving are very common in France. Drivers who break French driving laws can also have their driving licences confiscated by French police. The drink driving limit is 50mg alcohol per 100ml of blood, equivalent of one glass of beer.

Remember that if an oncoming driver flashes their headlights it is to indicate that he/she has priority and not the other way around.

Arriving and Staying on Site

When you arrive at a campsite, go to the reception. Your pitch is reserved from mid-afternoon to mid-morning. Most camp offices close about 20:00, sometimes earlier in the low season, except for some of the sites near the ports. During the summer months, there is usually somebody in the site office who understands English.

Campsite Rules

When staying on an individual site, you are their paying guests and should abide by its camp rules. Many camps close their gates at 22:00 or 22:30, after which entry with a car is not possible, and you will have to park your car outside, return to your caravan/tent on foot and collect it in the morning. More and more sites are installing barriers operated by a magnetic card. If this is the case, you should expect to pay a refundable deposit of about £10 on arrival. The gates are often firmly locked during the night and open about 07:00 or 08:00. If you wish to leave earlier than this, pack the car the night before and leave it outside. Do not leave any valuables in it. If you have a caravan or trailer, it will be virtually impossible to make a really early departure, unless previously arranged with the site manager.

Serious breaches of campsite regulations can result in the offenders being asked to leave the site. Each site has its own code of behaviour and you will be given a set of the site rules on arrival. On most sites noise should be kept to minimum after 22:00 and some camp proprietors are firm about maintaining peace and quiet after this time. One common and strictly enforced rule is that young children should be accompanied to toilet blocks by their parents, to ensure that they are properly used and to prevent children playing around them.

Speed of Cars

This is restricted to 10km or 5km per hour. Please respect this rule for everybody's safety. Cyclists should also respect the site rules and remember that those on foot have priority.

Waste Water

should be emptied in specified places, not on open ground or hedges.

Vegetation

Respect vegetation. Do not climb over hedges! Some sites do not allow washing lines to be tied to trees either for aesthetic or protective reasons.

Dogs

Dogs must be kept on a lead at all times and exercised well away from the pitches, often in special areas.

Security

There are remarkably few problems with security on campsites. To be on the safe side, however, it is a good idea to keep valuables locked up in your car or caravan, well out of sight of casual passers-by. Virtually all campsites have a safe-deposit box and many also have a night watchman on site. Great care is needed at beach car parks, where "professionals" often operate, so do not leave anything valuable in your car during the day, even in the boot.

Adaptors

It is essential to have a 2-pin adaptor plug. It is often necessary to use a couple of extra fittings particularly in France, i.e the French-to-CEE17 connector and the reverse polarity connector, available from most caravan dealers and some electrical shops. The French connection is often plugged inside a locked connection box which only site staff can unlock. If you have a motorhome, this may mean that you have to leave the unplugged lead on the pitch. Try to drape the lead above the ground when left unhooked. You should also be equipped with 30 - 40 metres of cable to ensure that it is long enough to meet most eventualities.

Shopping in France

Even if you have difficulty communicating in French, shopping is no problem. There are many self-service stores and large hypermarkets on the outskirts of large towns. Ask at the camp reception for full details. Most shops have longer hours than in the UK often opening at 08:00 and closing at 19:00, although, with the exception of hypermarkets, generally close from 12 noon until 14:00. Many food shops open for a short time on Sundays, particularly bakers. In some areas, there is often restricted opening on Mondays. Shops in holiday resorts have different opening times which fluctuate according to the seasonal trade.

Local Markets/Marchés

A real pleasure to visit. You can buy fresh fruit, vegetables, cheeses, eggs, meat, poultry, fish and near the coast a variety of delicious "fruits de mer" or seafood. Check with site reception for details of local markets.

Large Supermarkets/Hypermarkets

usually operate a deposit system for the trolley, so it is a good idea to have a euro piece handy.

Gas

Camping Gaz is widely available and is sold by most large campsites or can be acquired from a local supermarket or hypermarket. Garages in the main holiday areas often sell Camping Gaz, Butagaz and Propane. Red Antargaz bottles are also widely available, but suppliers are unable to refill the standard British bottles. Also the adaptors which fit European bottles do not conform to British standards. If you are not using Camping Gaz, we advise you to take as much gas as you require for your trip or be prepared to pay hefty deposits on the French Butagaz or Primagaz bottles.

Banks

Opening times vary but are generally open from 09:30 to 12:00 and 14:00 to 17:00. Banks close early on a day before a bank holiday and are often closed on Mondays.

Credit cards Visa and Mastercard are widely accepted in most establishments, provided they are for amounts above 8 euros. There are numerous ATMs in most towns.

Post Office/PTT

Normally open from 08:00 to 12:00 and 14:00 to 18:00 Monday to Friday and until 12:00 on Saturday.

Doctors and Pharmacies

The location of the nearest surgery can be provided by the site reception. They are usually happy to make an appointment for you. In an emergency go to the Accident & Emergency Dept of the nearest hospital. There is wide network of chemists in most towns which operate the same opening hours as shops. They can easily be identified by a large green cross outside. There is always one on duty at weekends.

Types of Shop

- Boulangerie: Bakers, best place to find fresh bread and croissants.
- Pâtisserie/Confiserie: Cake shop and sweet shop often combined with a boulangerie.
- Boucherie: Sells fresh meat, a butchers.
- Charcuterie: Literally a pork butcher's, but it is also the equivalent of our delicatessen, selling cold meat pâtés, prepared salads, sausages and pizzas.
- Alimentation/Epicerie: Small shops selling most items of grocery including vegetables & cheese.
- Poissonnerie: Fishmongers, fish is plentiful and reasonably priced in coastal areas.
- Pharmacie: Chemists, usually distinguished by a green cross.
- Quincaillerie/Droguerie: Hardware shop/Ironmongers.
- Maison de la Presse: Newsagents.
- Papeterie: Stationers.
- Librairie: Bookshop (a library is un *bibliothèque*)
- Fleuriste: Florist. Interflora facilities as in U.K.
- Le Tabac: Tobacconists sells cigarettes, tobacco, post cards and stamps.
- Coiffeur/coiffeuse: Hairdressers.
- Station d'essence: Petrol station.
- Hypermarchés: Hypermarkets found on the outskirts of town often on the industrial estates stay open till 21:00 or even 22:00 hours Monday to Saturday.

Cycling in France

The regulations are similar to those for Great Britain, except of course that you cycle on the right hand side of the road. You must use cycle lanes and paths whenever available. Do take out adequate insurance cover for your bicycles. French towns are actively promoting the use of bicycles. Already Rennes, Strasbourg and Nantes have increased the number of cycle paths, created or equipped parking space for bicycles as well as cycle shelters next to bus shelters. For any further information, please contact: The Touring Dept. Cyclists Touring Club, Parklands, Railton Road, Guildford GU2 9JX Tel: 0844 7368450 email:cycling@ctc.org.uk

French Tourist Offices

There are 5,000 tourist offices across France - they stock leaflets on all the tourist activities in their area and usually employ assistants who speak good English and are very helpful.

Useful websites:

www.franceguide.com
www.france.com
www.mappy.com (route planner)
www.viamichelin.com (route planner)
www.auto-routes.fr (information on motorways)
www.meteo.fr French weather forecstcast

Emergency telephone numbers
Also from mobile phone:
General 112,
Ambulance 115,
Police 117,
Fire 118.

Activities

The list below is to help identify which sites are the best locations to enjoy the popular activities listed. These activities can of course be pursued from other campsites. The ones listed offer the best opportunities due to location and information available at the campsites.

Walking

www.ffrandonnee.fr/
http://rando29.free.fr/
www.gr-infos.com/
The site listed below are in areas renowned for their walking or have a selection of good walking circuits directly from the site.

Le Grand Large	Page 45
Les Abers	Page 56
La Venise Verte	Page 81
Les Gorges du Chambon	Page 82
Le Noirrupt	Page 127
La Pergola	Page 130
La Ribeyre	Page 138
Le Peyrelade	Page 142
Camp de Florence	Page 148
Le Moulin	Page 149
Pyrénées Natura	Page 150
Airotel des Pyrénées	Page 152
La Colombière	Page 158
L'Oustalet	Page 159
La Grange au Frêne	Page 160
L'Escale	Page 161
Le Coin Tranquille	Page 163
De Martinière	Page 164
Champ du Moulin	Page 166
Au Joyeux Réveil	Page 167

Fishing

www.federationpeche.fr/
All rivers in France require a licence unless they are tidal when fishing is free. Most sites allow free fishing on lakes which belong to them however do check before you start fishing.

River Fishing

Le Ty Nadan	Page 61
La Vallée de Ninian	Page 67
La Venise Verte	Page 81
Les Gorges du Chambon	Page 82
La Vallée des Vignes	Page 105
La Citadelle	Page 106
Le Paradis	Page 115
Le Port de Limeuil	Page 116
Le Capeyrou	Page 117
Le Soleil Plage	Page 118
La Forge de Ste Marie	Page 126
Le Val de Bonnal	Page 129
Château de l'Epervière	Page 131
Les Iles	Page 139
L'Ardèchois	Page 140
Le Peyrelade	Page 142
Le Moulin	Page 149
Le Pré Lombard	Page 153
Le Camp du Verdon	Page 175
Les Pêcheurs	Page 176

Lake Fishing

Les Ormes	Page 52
Le Château du Deffay	Page 68
Le Pin Parasol	Page 76
La Garangeoire	Page 77
Domaine des Forges	Page 78
La Barbanne	Page 92
La Rive	Page 94
Château de Chanteloup	Page 102
Etang de la Brèche	Page 103
Domaine des Alicourts	Page 109
La Val de Bonnal	Page 129
La Pergola	Page 130
Le Château de Poinsouze	Page 136
Château de Leychoisier	Page 137
La Ribeyre	Page 138
Le Caussanel	Page 143
Le Moulin de Ventre	Page 174
Le Futuriste	Page 192

Canoeing

The sites below have canoes available directly from the site or within walking distance.
They are usually canadian canoes or sea kayaks.

L'Orangerie de Lanniron	Page 58
Le Ty Nadan	Page 61
La Venise Verte	Page 81
Les Gorges du Chambon	Page 82
La Rive (lake)	Page 94
Le Paradis	Page 115
Le Port de Limeuil	Page 116
Le Capeyrou	Page 117
Le Soleil Plage	Page 118
Le Val de Bonnal (lake and river)	Page 129

Sailing & Windsurfing

These sites are the best suited for taking your own sailing boat or windsurfer.

Power Boats

A certificate of competence is required for power boats over 6hp (4.5kw) and for Jetskis. The sites listed below are good for boating and water-skiing with your own boat. Other sites on the coast offer opportunities, but mooring for boats is not as easy.

Horse Riding

The following sites have their own stables.

Cycling

The following sites have prepared cycle routes from the site or are in areas with good cycle tracks.

Road Cycling

The following have mountain bike (VTT) routes from the site or are particularly well placed.

Surfing

www.globalsurfers.com;
www.brittany-ferries.co.uk/surf/france
Use the websites above to check the best locations for surfing. The two sites below are walking distance from beaches where there is usually good surf.

Skiing

The following sites are open in the winter and are close to ski-lifts.

Check List of Items to Take
*Items Asterisked are Obligatory

1. Documents
- Passports, Camping Carnet*
- Ferry crossing reference no.*
- Insurance certificates*
- EHIC card*
- Car Registration Document*
- Driving Licence*
- MOT certificate where applicable
- Car Manual
- G.B.sticker
- Written authority to drive car from owner if it is not owned by you
- Certificate of ownership for boats
- Written permission from parents if taking another family's child

2. Car accessories
- Red Warning Triangle*
- Reflective jackets x 2*
- Spare Parts Kit
- Spare bulbs and fuses*
- Cycle Rack
- Tyre Pressure Gauge
- First Aid Kit*
- Spare set of car keys
- List of foreign service agents
- Tool kit and Tow Rope
- Deflector tape for lights
- CDs or Ipod
- Car repair manual
- Towing mirrors
- Tow bar cover

3. Books and Guides
- Maps
- Any guides to area (e.g Michelin)
- French Dictionary
- Phrase Book
- Personal Reading books
- Address Book

4. Linen
- Sleeping Bags or similar
- Pillows
- Tea Towels
- Towels for shower and beach

5. Clothes
- Light clothes (T-shirts, shorts, skirts, sandals etc)
- Sundresses and sunhats
- Sweaters and jeans (for cool evenings)
- Track suits
- Swimming costumes, goggles etc.
- Beach shoes,
- Cagoules and wellingtons
- Canvas shoes or rubber shoes for rivers/lakes
- Walking boots for rambling
- Nightwear

6. For the Children and Sport
- Buckets and spades, Plastic balls, football etc.
- Games, Comics, Books
- Tennis rackets, Dinghy, Windsurfer, Bicycles
- Table tennis bats and balls, Binoculars and compass

7. Food
- Tea bags,Coffee, Sugar, Salt and Pepper
- Breakfast Cereal, Fruit Squash.
- Favourite foods so that you don't have to shop as soon as you arrive.

8. Camping/Caravanning Equipment

- Tent/Awning, groundsheet, gazebo
- Pegs and Mallet (strong pegs for hard ground when very dry or stony)
- Step for caravan
- Gas cylinders, Spanner for gas cylinders
- Table and chairs
- Adaptor Plug for hook-up with 50m of cable
- Water Carrier, Bucket
- Waste water container
- Spare guy ropes, elastics, "D" rings
- Levelling aid or spirit
- Levelling blocks or chocks for caravan/ motorhome
- Spare Wheel/Tyre for caravan/trailer
- Chemical fluid
- Polarity tester
- Fire extinguisher
- Caravan door keys
- Barbecue (check if allowed on site)

9. Kitchen Items

- Washing up bowl, Washing-up liquid
- Washing powder, Dishcloth/Scourer
- Kitchen cleaner
- Broom, Dustpan and brush
- Clothes line and peg, airer
- Cooking pans/frying pan
- Kettle/Teapot
- Chopping board, Knives (incl bread knife)
- Cutlery, Plates, bowls, Cups, Mugs, Glasses
- Measuring jug, Mixing bowl, Colander/Sieve
- Tin opener/bottle opener, Cork screw
- Kitchen roll, Tinfoil and Clingfilm wrap
- Plastic Waste Bags, Scissors
- Cool box, Plastic Food Containers

10. Medicine, Toiletries etc

- Toilet Paper not always provided on sites
- Basic First Aid Kit
- Aspirin, Paracetemol, Travel Sickness Pills
- Personal medicines and pills
- Antiseptic cream, Plasters
- Insect Repellent, Ant Powder
- Fly and Insect Spray
- Sun Screen and After Sun cream
- Soap, Toothpaste, Toothbrush
- Razor, Shaving Cream, Shampoo
- Hair Dryer, Mirror, Brushes and combs
- Cotton Wool, Tissues
- Toe clippers and scissors, tweezers

11. For the baby

- Disposable nappies/trainer pants
- Potty
- Changing bag, wet wipes, creams
- Feeder mug, baby foods
- Bottles and sterilising unit
- Buggy/backpack, travel cot and high chair
- Sunshade for pushchair
- Sunhat and sleep suits
- Armbands, plastic sandals

12. Other Items

- Matches, Torch, Tissues
- Travel Plug (for razors and hairdryers)
- Travel Iron, Coat hangers
- String, Rubber bands, insulating tape
- Thermos, Alarm clock
- Mobile phone and charger
- Camera (video, digital and still) films, discs
- Binoculars, Spare Batteries
- Sewing Kit, Shoe cleaning Kit
- Beach items, parasol, windbreak
- Sunglasses (essential for driving)

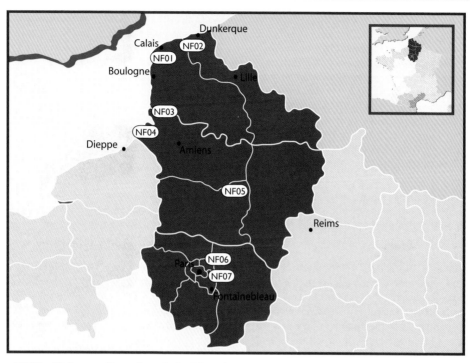

Picture opposite - Bâteau-Mouche on the Seine

Places of Interest - North and Ile De France

The **Nord/Pas de Calais** region just two hours from London, Brussels and Paris has 120km of sandy beaches, sand dunes and cliffs dotted with pretty fishing villages like Audresselles and Wissant as well as famous resorts like Le Touquet. Many of the towns have managed to preserve all the charm of their original early 20th century architectural styles. It is an area full of cycle routes and can be easily visited both by bicycle and on foot. The hundreds of small cemeteries full of white crosses are a poignant reminder of the enormous loss of life suffered during the bitter battles of World War I.

Dunkerque is France's third largest port and a dynamic city which looks out on to the busiest shipping lanes in Europe. Its famous lighthouse is open to the public.

Calais is regarded as "The Gateway to Europe" and it is the busiest port in Europe. The main shopping streets are Boulevards Jacquard and Lafayette. The huge Auchan hypermarket on the outskirts of the town, exit 14 from A26, is worth a visit to stock up with French wines and goods before returning home.

Cap Blanc Nez

Cap Gris Nez and **Cap Blanc Nez** are two enormous cliffs that offer magnificent views over the busiest navigation channel in the world. On a clear day the British coastline is visible.

Boulogne-sur-Mer a charming old town perched on a hill, has cobbled streets, ramparts, a beautiful cathedral and a superb château museum.

Nausicaa France's National Sea Centre is an amazing high-tech exhibition including a shark ring, touch tank and sea lion area, with the emphasis on ecological management of the sea.

Picardy is a region of rolling wooded countryside full of pretty villages and lovely old towns like Amiens, Abbeville and Beauvais with their Gothic architecture and traditional markets. Laon, Senlis, Chantilly and Soissons are also worth a detour. It is wonderful walking, riding, cycling and golfing country. The acres of woods and forests are home to a remarkable range of wild flowers and animals. Majestic white chalky cliffs mark the southern end of the Picardy coastline while to the north splendid sand dunes border the beaches.

The River Somme meets the sea in the spectacular Baie de la Somme, classified as one the most beautiful bays in the world and home to France's largest colony of seals.

Le Parc Marquenterre d'Ornithologie is a unique bird sanctuary situated in this bay near St Valéry. It is full of wild birds and magnificent fauna. A minimum of 2 hours is recommended for a visit, more if you are a keen ornithologist.

The Great War Like the Pas de Calais, the entire region of Picardy is dotted with battlefields and memorials to the brave soldiers who died in the Great War. The Historial de la Grande Guerre museum in the old ramparts at Péronne gives a fascinating analysis of the First World War.

Châteaux The region's spectacular castles such as Compiègne, Pierrefonds and Chantilly reflect the royal glory of the 14th, 15th and 16th centuries.

Cycling in Northern France

Paris is one of the most attractive cities in the world. Not only is there a wealth of glorious architectural heritage to explore, but the city has an exciting, enchanting atmosphere which inspires visitors to return time after time. it is a city to explore on foot, strolling along the Boulevards, discovering side streets, window shopping in the top stores or relaxing in pavement cafés. You can also visit by bus, métro and boat along the Seine. Like all beautiful capital cities you could explore Paris for weeks and not visit everything. The main tourist attractions not to be missed are listed below.

Grand Palais Paris

Eiffel Tower Climb the steps to the 2nd floor (120m) or take a lift to the top (280m) to be rewarded by exceptional views of the city.

Notre Dame Cathedral situated on the Ile de la Cité and reached via the famous Pont Neuf was completed in 1345 and is a wonderful example of Gothic architecture. The three dimensional stone carvings on its façade depict the scriptures and legends of saints and biblical kings. The nave rises to a height of 35m and is famous for its dazzling stained-glass window. You can climb the 69m twin towers to view the gargoyles and celebrated bell tower.

Sacré Coeur on Montmartre Hill is a beautiful white basilica featuring small cupolas surrounding a central dome in a Neo-Byzantine style. The style of the Place du Tetre still reflects the Bohemian way of life at the turn of the 20th century.

Champs Elysées is one of the world's most famous avenues and leads down to the Arc de Triomphe, a colossal neo-Classical style monument built on the vast Place d'Etoile from which radiate 11 further avenues.

Place de la Concorde at the eastern end of the Champs Elysées, is a magnificent square adorned with sumptious fountains and the 3,300 year old obelisk which came from Egypt.

Hotel National des Invalides is an august building that was once a hospital for wounded soldiers and is now a war museum housing over half a million items from wars dating from ancient times to the Second World War. The impressive tomb of Napoleon lies in the crypt.

Musée du Louvre A former royal residence first built in the 16th century which is now one of the most famous museums in the world. An immense glass-sided pyramid which stands in its centre designed by a Sino-American architect is a testament to the creative inspiration which pervades this building.

Centre Georges Pompidou is a vast multi-purpose cultural centre made of a unique design of steel and glass piping, housing an immense collection of 20th century and contemporary art.

Château de Versailles is a grandiose palace south-west of Paris created by the Sun King Louis XIV. A visit concentrates on the royal apartments, the illustrious Hall of Mirrors, the chapel and the opera as well as its magnificent landscaped gardens.

Château de Fontainebleau is another prestigious royal residence south-east of Paris set in a forest full of game. Its magnificent architecture and gardens make it a jewel of French art.

Two theme parks not to be missed are:-

Disneyland®Resort situated at Marne-la-Vallée 40km west of Paris. It is an action packed park with over 80 attractions and rides, daily parades and regular visits from Disney characters as well as Waltdisney Studios® www.disneylandparis.com

Parc Astérix 50km north of Paris is a theme park based around the "Gaulish" world of Astérix and Obélix. It offers several adventure areas, including some amazing roller coaster rides, the Flying Chairs ride and a Dolphinarium. www.parcasterix.com.

www.parisinfo.com
www.paris.org,com
www.tourisme-nordpasdecalais.fr
picardietourisme.com

Guines, Château Camping de la Bien Assise ***

Location Calais 11km. Dunkirk 36km. Boulogne 40km. Paris 287km.

Open 3rd Apr to 26th Sept   **Pitches** 198 (144 touring)

An impressive Castels site less than a 20-minute drive from the ferry and Eurotunnel terminals, set in the spacious grounds of an 18th century manor house. The delightful gourmet restaurant and other services are housed in the attractive outbuildings of the manor house. The site is laid out with pretty trees, shrubs and flowers and is well maintained. There is always a friendly atmosphere. but it can be very busy in the high season as there are a large number of arrivals and departures each day. Possible for an overnight stop but a longer stay is highly recommended, as there is plenty to see and do in the region.

Site suitable for all age groups.

Pitches	Grassy, separated by low hedges and shrubs, some shaded varying in size but mainly generous dimensions. The majority are flat but some slope gently so levelling blocks may be required. Larger quieter pitches are given to longer stay customers.
Hook-Up	6 amps - all pitches. 10 amps - 100 pitches. Water and drainage - 4 pitches.
Motorhomes	Motorhome service point. Walking distance of Guines.
Swimming pools	Outdoor pool medium-size, covered and heated in low season. Paddling pool with medium-sized water slide.
Activities on site	Cycle hire. Minigolf. Tennis. Pool, table football and electronic games in indoor games area, sportsground. Boules pitch. Table tennis. Children's play area. TV room.
Entertainment	None.
Sanitary facilities	There are 3 unisex toilet blocks which although not especially attractive are clean and well-maintained. Tiled individual washing cubicles and showers. Toilet seats, toilet paper. Push button showers, temperature control. Adequate hooks. Disabled facilities. Baby room. Washing machines, tumble dryers. Chemical waste point.
Services	Shop - medium-sized with good range of everyday products, open in the morning and late afternoon. Bar with snacks. Take-away. All housed in attractive stone buildings with terracotta tiled roofs. Excellent restaurant - La Ferme Gourmande. Barbecues allowed. Dogs accepted. Internet and Wi-Fi in bar and on terrace.
Accommodation	Wooden chalets and mobile homes in separate area. 3-star hotel, Auberge du Colombier.
Tour operators	Three companies with mobile homes and tents.

Excursions/Places to visit

Guines is where Henry VIII of England met Francis I of France on the Champ du Drap d'Or. A monument in the Forest of Guines also marks the landing of the first cross-Channel balloon flight in 1785. There are 300km of well maintained and signed paths in the area, which are accessible on foot, by bicycle and on horseback.

Directions

From Calais Ferry Terminal. Follow signs for the A16 in the direction of Boulogne. Leave the motorway at junction 40 and follow in the direction of Fréthun "Gare TGV". At the next roundabout take the 3rd exit and then take the next right signposted for St Tricat on D246. Continue through the villages of St Tricat and Hames Boucres. You arrive at the roundabout on the outskirts of Guines and the site has its own exit. The site is south west of the village on the D231 towards Marquise.

€ Prices 2010	High	Mid	Low
Pitch + 2	27	22	19
Hook Up 6A	4.5	4	4

Address 62340 Guines

GPS N 50° 51 59' E 01° 51' 25

www.camping-bien-assise.fr
email castels@bien-assise.com
Tel 03.21.35.20.77

Eperlecques, Château du Gandspette ***

Location Calais 31km. Dunkirk 38km. St Omer 12km.

Open 1st Apr to 1st Oct

Pitches 167 (100 touring)

Your first view on arrival is of the attractive 19th century château, still inhabited by the friendly owners. Its creamy stone-faced walls and grey slate roof dominate the wooded park where some of the beautiful trees are 100 years old. You can't fail to be impressed by the pretty outbuildings and courtyard. The site is well maintained and has a very verdant, spacious feel, which complements the warm friendly atmosphere. Its proximity to the ports means that it can be very busy in high season as there are a large number of arrivals and departures each day. Possible for an overnight stop but a longer stay is highly recommended.

Site suitable for all age groups.

Pitches	Flat and grassy, separated by pretty flowering shrubs and trees. At least 100m², some as large as 150m². Suitable for caravans, motorhomes and tents. Larger quieter pitches are given to longer stay customers.
Hook-Up	6 amps - all pitches. Water & drainage - none.
Motorhomes	Motorhome service point. Walking distance of village.
Swimming pools	Two heated outdoor pools, medium size. No pool for very small children. Generous sunbathing area.
Activities on site	Tennis (free). Pool, table football and electronic games in indoor games area. Table tennis. Children's play area. Boules pitch.
Entertainment	Small programme of organised activities in high season only.
Sanitary facilities	There are two modern well-lit toilet blocks, maintained to a high standard. Tiled individual washing cubicles and showers. Toilet seats, toilet paper outside cubicles. Push button temperature control showers with adequate hooks. Disabled facilities. Baby room. Washing machines and tumble dryers. Chemical waste point.
Services	No shop on site as there is there is a supermarket in the village 1km away,left out of site towards Watten. Baker comes to the site each morning from 1/5 to 30/9. A delightful wooden-beamed bar and restaurant, which serves very reasonably priced meals. Take-away. Barbecues allowed. Dogs accepted. Internet and Wi-Fi.
Accommodation	Two types of mobile homes.
Tour operators	None.

Excursions/Places to visit

Blockhaus of Eperlecques, planned as a launch pad for the V2 rockets during the war. St Omer and its fine Gothic cathedral 12km. The site lies in the heart of the Audomarois National park, a delightful area of marshland and canals where you can hire canoes or rowing boats and go cycling, fishing or horse riding in forest. Nausicaa sea life centre 55km.

€ Prices 2010	High	Mid	Low
Pitch + 2	23	17	13
Hook Up 6A	4	4	4

Directions

From Calais N43 in the direction of St Omer. After the village of Nordausques turn left in the direction of Eperlecques on to D221 and then D207 signposted to site. On motorway A26 take Paris direction and come off at exit 2 Nordausques and continue as above. From Dunkirk take A16 in the direction of Calais and come off at the St Omer exit on the D600 and then onto D300 following signs to site.

Address 133 Rue du Gandspette, 62910 Eperlecques

www.chateau-gandspette.com
email contact@chateau-gandspette.com

GPS N 50° 49 08' E 02° 10' 40

Tel 03.21.93.43.93

Nampont-St-Martin, La Ferme des Aulnes ***

Location Nampont 2km. Abbeville 27km. Calais 96km.

Open 1st Apr to 1st Nov

Pitches 120 (40 touring)

As the name suggests, the site enjoys a rural setting on an old farm. The stone-faced buildings with their pretty tiled roofs are built round a courtyard and house all the services including the welcoming reception area. The covered swimming pool is in the heart of the courtyard. The site is divided by a small quiet road. Most pitches are behind the reception, mainly occupied by mobile homes. The majority of touring pitches are on the other side of the road. We have chosen the site for its quiet attractive setting and warm friendly atmosphere. Musical soirées with the site owner are an unexpected pleasure.
Clef Verte

Site suitable for families and couples.

Pitches	Grassy, flat pitches divided by hedges. They vary in shape and size up to 100m².
Hook-Up	6 amp or 10 amp - all pitches. Water & drainage - 20 pitches.
Motorhomes	Motorhome service point but not walking distance of town.
Swimming pools	An average sized covered and heated pool with jacuzzi. Shallow area for toddlers but no separate baby pool.
Activities on site	Good children's play area. Basket ball and volleyball court areas. Boules pitch. Spa, sauna room in chalet. Gym. Indoor table tennis. Large indoor games room with archery. TV room. Large room for daytime and evening entertainment - all in farm outbuildings.
Activities Nearby	Fishing (free) 2km, tennis (free) 8km, 2 x 18 hole-golf courses 2km.
Entertainment	Children's club in July/August. Musical evenings in the bar where owner, who once played with Jacques Brel, sings and plays sometimes with other invited musicians. Cabaret, karaoke, couscous and paella evenings.
Sanitary facilities	Two heated unisex toilet blocks on either side of the road. They are not particularly well appointed, although they are kept clean and respectable. Push button showers, no temperature control. Individual wash cubicles, toilet seats with toilet paper. Disabled facilities. Baby room. Washing machine, tumble dryer. Chemical waste point.
Services	Small shop next to reception – order bread the day before. Small restaurant and large bar area in beautiful room with low beamed roof and open fireplace. Barbecues allowed. Dogs accepted. Internet and Wi-Fi.
Accommodation	20 chalets and mobile homes to rent, 40 privately owned in separate area of site.
Tour operators	None.

Excursions/Places to visit
Abbeville 30km, Berck-Plage 18km, Fort-Mahon Plage 18km. St. Valéry, Baie de la Somme, Marquenterre Ornithological Park. Le Touquet.

Directions
From A16 take exit 25. At 1st roundabout take 1st exit onto D303 to Arras and Montreuil. At next roundabout take 1st exit onto D901 towards Abbeville. At Nampont turn right following signs to the site and continue for 2km.

€ Prices 2010	All Dates
Pitch + 2	21
Hook Up 6A	6

Address 1 rue du Marais, 80120 Nampont St Martin

www.fermesdesaulnes.com
email contact@fermesdesaulnes.com
Tel 03.22.29.22.69

GPS N 50° 20' 10 E 01° 42' 45

St. Valéry, Domaine du Château de Drancourt **** Map Ref NP04

Location 4km south of St Valéry. Calais 125km. Abbeville 14km.

Open 1st Apr to 1st Nov

Pitches 356 (196 touring)

A Castels site set in the beautiful grounds and outbuildings of an attractive brick-built château, where the abundance of trees and flowering shrubs gives the site a welcoming feel. It is well placed for visiting the Somme battlefields and Marquenterre wildlife sanctuary. There are plenty of activities on offer for the children and there can be a bustling atmosphere in the high season. Although the quality of services can be a bit erratic at busy times, this will not detract from your enjoyment of the site which is well maintained and has a spacious feel.

Site suitable for all age groups, but tends to be lively in high season as there are large number of Tour operators. Not ideal for those seeking a quiet atmosphere.

Pitches	Level, grassy and individual. Spacious up to 150m².
Hook Up	10 amps - all pitches. Water & drainage - none.
Motorhomes	Motorhome service point but not walking distance of town.
Swimming pools	Good size outside pool with small two lane waterslide and children's pool. Small heated pool with retractable cover which creates an indoor area. Small bar and sun terrace which is not very generous.
Activities on site	Cycle and mini go-kart hire. Pony riding. Tennis. Practice golf and 12-hole mini-golf (all free in low season). Cinema. Fishing in small lake. Billiards, table football and electronic games in indoor games area. Football pitch. Table tennis. Children's play area. Boules pitch.
Entertainment	Programme of activities daytime and evening in high season only including children's club, sporting competitions and concerts. Satellite TV.
Sanitary facilities	Three heated toilet blocks. Separate ladies and gents. Attractively tiled individual washing cubicles and showers. Toilet seats, toilet paper outside cubicles. Push button showers, no temperature control, wash cubicles have single tap with warm water. Hooks and shelfs in most showers. Disabled facilities. Baby room. 3 washing machines and 3 tumble dryers in block near reception. Chemical waste point.
Services	Shop. 3 Bars - a poolside bar, a lively cinema bar and a quieter one in the château reserved for adults. Restaurant and take-away housed in converted outbuildings. Barbecues allowed. Dogs accepted Internet and Wi-Fi.
Accommodation	2- and 3-bedroomed mobile homes.
Tour operators	Three British companies with own mobile homes and tents.

Excursions/Places to visit
St Valéry-sur-Somme, medieval walled town 4km. La Marquenterre a 500-acre bird sanctuary 17km. Aqualand waterpark and the Bagatelle Theme Park at Berck Plage 40km. Abbeville 18km, Amiens 50km.

Directions
From Abbeville. Take the D40 signposted to St Valéry. Then join the D940 ringroad around St Valéry in the direction of Cayeux. The campsite is indicated to your left at the first junction. Turn left here and fork left again almost immediately. Continue along this road until you reach the campsite. From A16 take exit 24. Take D32 to Rue, then join D940 towards Le Crotoy and follow signs to St Valéry, then continue as above.

€ Prices 2010	High	Mid	Low
Pitch + 2	32	25	18
Hook Up 6A	3	3	3

Address BP 80022, 80230 Saint-Valéry-sur-Somme

GPS N 50° 09 09' E 01° 38' 08

www.chateau-drancourt.com
email chateau.drancourt@wanadoo.fr
Tel 03.22.26.93.45

Berny-Rivière, La Croix du Vieux Pont ****

Location Soissons 10km. Compiègne 24km. To A26 41km. To A1 40km.

Open All year

Pitches 520 (120 touring)

A very large and very well maintained site situated on the banks of the gently flowing river Aisne. The site owners have created an outstanding holiday complex where the abundance of trees, shrubs and colourful flowers enhance the spacious environment. There are three lakes, one for fishing, one for pedalos and one with a beach for bathing. One of the best appointed sites in the area with plenty of activities to keep the whole family occupied. You can enjoy staying in a rural location and still visit Disneyland and Paris. Possible for an overnight stop but a longer stay is highly recommended.

Site suitable for all age groups. Very busy in high season so less suitable for couples in July/August.

Pitches	Grassy, flat, well defined, some by hedges. They vary in shape and size and are a minimum of 100m². Suitable for caravans, motorhomes and tents. The best pitches overlook the third lake but are some distance from the sanitary facilities.
Hook-Up	6 amps - all pitches. Water and drainage - 50 pitches.
Motorhomes	Two motorhome services points. Recommended for motorhomes as walking distance of Berny Rivière.
Swimming pools	Two heated outdoor pools, one for children with good sunbathing area. Large indoor pool, baby pool with excellent waterslide (all open Apr - Oct).
Activities on site	Two tennis courts. Archery. Fishing. Mini-golf. Billiards, table football and electronic games in indoor game area. Table tennis (outdoor & undercover) several excellent outdoor children's play areas. Trampoline. Boules pitch. Beach on middle lake. All weather sports pitch for football, volleyball and basketball.
Entertainment	Site has own coach and organises day trips to Paris, Disneyland Paris and Parc Astérix.
Sanitary facilities	Eight modern, attractively tiled and well maintained toilet blocks. Toilet seats, toilet paper outside cubicles. Push button showers, no temperature control. Several blocks have cubicles with showers and washbasins together. Adequate hooks. Disabled facilities. Baby rooms. 8 washing machines. 8 tumble dryers. Chemical waste point.
Services	Well-stocked shop with separate bakery. Rustic style restaurant with wooden beams Take-away. Bar and spacious terrace with large screen TVs. All are housed in white stone faced farm buildings with pitched red roofs. Beauty parlour with sauna, hammam, jacuzzi and personal massages. Horse-riding and pony club 2 minutes from site. Car and caravan washing point. Barbecues allowed. Dogs accepted. Internet and Wi-Fi. Services open 27th March to 31st October.
Accommodation	Gites, superb wooden chalets, tree houses.
Tour operators	Seven companies with own mobile homes and tents separate from touring pitches.

Excursions/Places to visit

Coaches to Disneyland and Paris are organised several times a week leaving 07:50. Parc Astérix, forest of Compiègne with its Royal Palace. The cathedrals at Amiens, Beauvais, Soissons and Reims are all within an hour's drive.

Directions

Leave the A1 at exit 10 (or 9 if coming from south) to Compiègne. As you approach Compiègne take the ring road to the south signed for Soissons. After approximately 22km turn left to Vic-sur-Aisne. Cross over the Aisne river, go up the hill to the centre of the village and take the second road to the right after the central square. The site is on your right hand side after 500m.

€ Prices 2010	2 Pers	3 Pers	4 Pers
Pitch	22.50	29	32
Hook Up 6A	2.50	3	3

Address 02290 Berny-Rivière, Aisne

www.la-croix-du-vieux-pont.com
email lacroixduvieuxpont@wanadoo.fr
Tel 03.23.55.50.02

GPS N 49° 24' 21 E 02° 44' 02

Jablines, Camping Base de Jablines ***

Location 15 mins from Disneyland Paris. Paris 32km. To A1 35km. To A104 18km.

Open 27th Mar to 24th Oct   **Pitches** 150 (120 touring)

A municipal site in a very spacious quiet location where you can be sure of warm welcome from the friendly site managers. Attractively landscaped with trees and shrubs it is an ideal three or four night stopover, to visit Disneyland or Paris. There is good parking by the reception and access to the site is through a secure electronic gate with entry code for campers. It is part of a large municipal outdoor leisure complex, open during daylight hours June to September and weekends the rest of the year. It has a boating and sailing lake nearby, easily reached on foot or by car. A regular bus service operates between the site and the Disneyland resort.

Site suitable for all age groups, families in particular due to proximity to Disneyland.

Pitches	Good sized, flat, grassy pitches at least 100m² with hardstanding for caravans and motorhomes. Lmited shade but well defined by low wooden fences. Good strong pegs are needed for tents and awnings.
Hook-Up	10 amps - all pitches. Water and drainage - 60 pitches.
Motorhomes	Service area. Not near town or village but regular bus service just outside site.
Swimming pools	No swimming pool (see below).
Activities on site	Table tennis and children's play area.
Activities nearby	Beach with supervised bathing. The watersports centre offers sailing, windsurfing, canoeing and kayaking. Pedalos, waterski cable way. Riding lessons for all ages. 8 tennis courts, an all weather football pitch. Cycle hire, mini-golf, archery and fishing.
Entertainment	None.
Sanitary facilities	Two recently revamped toilet blocks with sensor lighting, separate mens and ladies, which are well maintained and clean. Push button showers, no temperature control with hooks, shelf and rail. Some individual wash basins, toilets with seats but no toilet paper. Disabled facilities. Baby room. Washing machines and tumble dryers. Chemical waste point
Services	Small shop – basics only, need to order bread in advance. Pizza delivery service. There is a café and self service restaurant in the adjacent leisure park (5 mins from site), July and August only. It is a good spot for short walks and picnics, but often very busy at weekends with local visitors. Barbecues allowed. Dogs accepted. Internet point.
Accommodation	2 bedroomed mobile homes.
Tour operators	None.

Excursions/Places to visit

Disneyland® Resort Paris 15 min by car. Centre of Paris 40 min train ride from Marne la Vallée railway station, next to Disney. Parc Astérix 40 min drive.

Directions

From the A104 Paris Est exit towards Marne-La-Vallee. At junction 6 take the exit for Claye-Souilly on the N3. The 'Base de Jablines' is signposted after 8km. Follow the D404 for 3km until you reach the roundabout and take the 3rd exit along the D45. Cross over the Marne river and follow signs to the 'Base de Jablines'. At the gates, inform the security guards that you wish to check into the campsite and follow signs to the camping and caravanning area.

€ Prices 2010	High	Low
Pitch + 2 10A Incl	26	23
Water & Drainage	2	2

Address Camping de la Base de Loisirs, 75450 Jablines,

GPS N 48° 54' 48 E 02° 44' 03

www.camping-jablines.com
email welcome@camping-jablines.com
Tel 01.60.26.09.37

Crèvecoeur, Les Quatres Vents ***

Location Paris 50km. Disneyland®Europe 20km. Provins 39km.

Open 1st Mar to 1st Nov   **Pitches** 200 (114 touring)

This site has been included because of its quiet atmosphere and proximity to Disneyland Paris (15 mins) and to the city itself (40 mins). Although just off the main road, there is a pleasant rural feel to the site. It is attractively laid out with well trimmed trees and shrubs. The pleasant reception area is dominated by a wealth of flowering plants and you can be sure of warm welcome from the Georges family who own the site. It is recommended for a maximum stay of three or four nights.

Site suitable for all ages. Attracts lots of young children because of proximity to Disneyland®Resort

Pitches	Flat, grassy well manicured pitches, very generous in size about 150m^2 and laid out in straight lines. They are divided by low hedges with wide lanes between the trees so there is a very spacious feel to the site.
Hook-Up	6 amps - all pitches. Water & drainage - none.
Motorhomes	Motorhome service point, although not walking distance of any towns or villages.
Swimming pools	Small round swimming pool, with no real shallow end and not heated. No sunloungers and not particularly attractive but ideal for a dip after a busy day at Disneyland®Resort.
Activities on site	Good well maintained children's play area with seating area for parents to supervise. Volleyball pitch. Huge undercover indoor games area with 4 table tennis tables, 2 table football games. Large boules area for competitions.
Entertainment	There is no organised entertainment.
Sanitary facilities	The 3 toilet blocks are functional but not particularly attractive with green corrugated iron roofs and basic fittings. There are no individual wash basins in two of the blocks, push button showers with no temperature control, which have a tendency to be a little tepid and have high water pressure, so be wary of getting clothes wet. There are hooks and shelves in some. Toilet seats but paper on wall outside. The blocks are not well lit at night. Chemical waste point.
Services	No shop on site, although bread and croissants are available in the morning if pre-ordered. In July/August a small snack bar serves food and drinks at entrance to site. Barbecues allowed. Dogs accepted. Internet and Wi-Fi near reception and bar area, which is free.
Accommodation	6 of their own chalets and 80 privately owned mobile homes in a separate area.
Tour operators	None.

Excursions/Places to visit
Disneyland, Paris, château at Vaux le Vicomte 32km, Provins 39km, Fontainebleau.

Directions
From A4 take exit 13 to Provins. Follow D231 in the direction of Provins. After 13km turn right onto D143e towards Crèvecoeur-en-Brie. On arrival follow signs to the campsite which is to the west of the village.

€ Prices 2010	All Dates
Pitch + 2	27
Hook Up 6A	Incl

Address rue de Beauregard, 77610 Crèvecoeur-en-Brie

www.caravaning-4vents.fr
email contact@caravaning-4vents.fr
Tel 01.64.07.41.11

GPS N 48° 45' 02 E 02° 53' 48

Le Pont Alexandre

NORMANDY

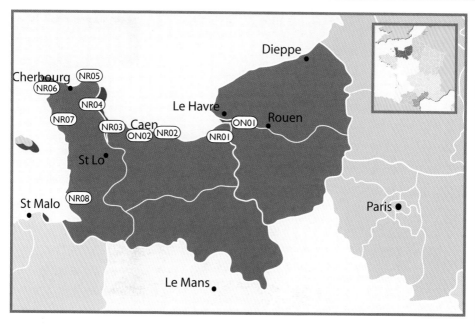

Picture Opposite - Le Mont St Michel

Places of Interest - Normandy

A verdant region of lush meadows, wooded valleys, cider orchards and 600km of magnificent coastline, it is full of famous tourist attractions. Home to four of the major Channel ports, Dieppe, Cherbourg, Le Havre, and Caen and only a 3-hour drive from Calais.

Caen The old town is made up of narrow streets, a castle and two magnificent abbeys. The wonderful Caen Memorial Museum uses audio visual and computer technology to tell the story of World War I, the dark years leading to World War II and features the D-Day landings including stunning archive films of the Allied preparation before Operation Overlord. www.memorial-caen.fr

D-Day landing beaches, famous for their strategic role in the 2nd World War stretch due west of the port of Ouistreham round to Carentan. Airborne divisions of Operation Overlord under the supervision of Montgomery and Eisenhower landed at the two extremes of the invasion front Ste Mère Eglise and Bénouville. Meanwhile beach-heads were established in the Anglo-Canadian sector under the names Gold, Juno and Sword beach and in the American sector under Omaha and Utah. Visitors to these beaches can now see commemorative monuments, war museums and cemeteries.

D-Day Cemetery

Bayeux only a few minutes from the landing beaches has an exceptional architectural heritage including streets lined with attractive slate-roofed houses and a magnificent cathedral. The town owes it fame to the unique Bayeux tapestry, an embroidery in wool on a linen background 70m x 0.5m, a pictorial account of the events leading up to the military invasion of England by William the Conqueror.

Lisieux is not only famous as an important shrine with a basilica erected in honour of Ste. Thérèse, but is also worth visiting to see its pretty town centre with half-timbered houses.

Falaise birth place of William the Conqueror is dominated by an immense castle which has been of strategic importance since the Middle Ages.

Honfleur is a delightful little fishing port and yachting harbour with pretty narrow streets of timber framed houses, homes once occupied by famous Frenchmen, including Baudelaire and Monet.

Jumièges

Deauville, Trouville and **Cabourg** have all become fashionable resorts. Deauville is full of expensive hotels, designer boutiques and is well known for horse-racing, regattas and car rallies.

Rouen is the capital of Normandy, famous for its flamboyant Gothic cathedral and the Rue du Gros Horloge with its large 14th century clock tower spanning the street with a golden clock face on either side.
Route des Abbayes runs through the Seine valley.

The majestic ruins of the Benedictine abbeys of **Jumièges** and **Saint Wadrille** are worth a visit along with **St Martin de Boscherville,** a jewel of Norman architecture. Spanning the valley you cannot fail to be impressed by the gracious bridges of Pont de Tancarville and Pont de Brotonne. The Pont de Normandie joins Le Havre and Honfleur.
Along the Alabaster coast, **Fécamp** and **Etretat** are both worth a detour.

The western area of Normandy called La Manche (channel) runs the length of coastline immediately opposite Great Britain and stretches from Cherbourg in the north to le Mont St Michel in the south. Bricquebec and Valognes in the north of the region are worth viewing.

Giverny

Coutances almost due south of Cherbourg is the religious centre of the Cotentin peninsula and is best known for its beautifully preserved cathedral.

Granville offers the visitor the chance to experience a lively seaside resort, sailing centre and commercial fishing port with the highest tides in Europe. You can also climb up to the fortified city above.

Villedieu-les-Poêles as the name suggests has an ancient craft tradition for making copper pots and pans which stretches back almost 800 years. You can still witness it today at the Copper Workshop as well as visiting a museum of modern furniture and the Lace Making museum.

Avranches the city of flowers is a bustling town overlooking the Bay of Mont St Michel.

Traditional Norman House

Le Mont St Michel is one of the most stunning attractions in Europe. Although actually in Normandy it borders Northern Brittany and is regarded by some as the 8th wonder of the world. Mont Saint-Michel and its Bay are listed by UNESCO as a World Natural and Cultural Site. It is probably the most visited tourist attraction in France outside Paris. Rising out of an ever-changing environment of sand and sea, the mount exemplifies man's ingenuity when faced with the challenge of time and the elements. Perched on the uppermost point of a solitary rock in a landscape smoothed by the passage of the winds, the abbey reminds us of the daring ambition of the builders and those who, since 708, desired to make this isolated place a meeting point for all. Viewed from its heights, everything takes on a special allure: the wonders of medieval architecture, the force of nature, the quality of the light. Built in the 8th century as a simple oratory, it has been the destination of pilgrimages ever since. Richard I, Duke of Normandy, started building the impressive abbey on top of the mount in 966, but sections were added right up to the 16th century, so it is now a quite an extraordinary mix of architectural styles. The movement of the tides in the bay is fascinating and the difference in sea level between high and low water can be over 12m, the highest in France. As the sea bed is flat, the sea retreats a long way exposing 15km of sand. The tide comes in very rapidly and combined with numerous currents can spell danger for the unwary.

Honfleur

Not only is Normandy a wonderful holiday destination, but it is also renowned for its delicious cuisine. Moules à la crème, truite au cidre and the creamy sole normande are all highly recommended. It is also famous for its cheeses: Camembert, Pont l'Evêque, Livarot and the Pavé d'Auge. The countryside is dotted with orchards that produce local cider and the famous Calvados liqueur. The cider is much lighter and dryer than British cider and has a gentle fizz. Calvados is distilled from apples according to ancient methods and matured in centuries old cellars. **La Route du Cidre** and **La Route du Fromage** are two well signposted routes you can follow to fully appreciate these specialities.

www.normandy-tourism.org

Moyaux, Le Colombier ****

Location Moyaux 3km. Lisieux 18km. Caen 83km. Le Havre 56km. Rouen 88km.

Open 1st May to 15th Sept   **Pitches** 188

As the name suggests the main focus of this site is the dovecote overlooking the pool. It is a unique site set in the beautifully laid out gardens and orchards of a magnificent château, where all the facilities are housed in attractive stone-faced buildings. Strong emphasis is placed on traditional camping in a peaceful atmosphere, enhanced by lovely verdant surroundings. It is still owned by the Charles family although now run by a manager. Some of the facilities are a little dated, but the site is well maintained and is very popular with British clients, as there are no tour operators and no mobile homes.

Site suitable for couples and families with older children who prefer a quiet ambiance.

Pitches	Flat, grassy, generous in size, individually marked out, but not defined by hedges or trees, giving a spacious open feel to the camping areas.
Hook-Up	10 amps - all pitches. Water and drainage - none.
Motorhomes	Motorhome service point. Not walking distance of town.
Swimming pools	There is only one pool on site, a good size for swimming about 25m x 12m. There is no children's pool. The area around the pool is cobbled and without sunloungers so not very suitable for sunbathing. Please note the swimming pool area is not fenced in at all.
Activities on site	Cycle hire. Tennis. 18-hole mini-golf. by bar. Children's play area. Football pitch. Badminton net. Games room with pool tables and electronic games. Small reading room and library in the lower part of the Colombier, overlooking the pool with comfortable chairs.
Entertainment	None.
Sanitary facilities	Two attractively tiled toilet blocks which are old but very well maintained as originally built to a high specification. Toilet seats and toilet paper. Individual showers and wash cubicles with hot and cold taps, hooks for hanging clothes, A good number of enamel sinks for washing up, two washing machines and two tumble dryers. Disabled facilities. Baby room. Chemical waste point.
Services	Shop, small but reasonably well stocked. Need to order bread and croissants the day before. Bar open from 8pm until midnight for over 18's only in the Le Colombier (dovecote). Take-away open from 6pm till 8.30pm. Further bar area with crêperie. It is also possible to have dinner in the château two or three evenings a week on reservation. Barbecues allowed. Dogs accepted. Internet.
Accommodation	There are a few two bedroomed caravans for hire but no mobile homes or chalets.
Tour operators	None.

Excursions/Places to visit
Moyaux 5km, Lisieux, Honfleur, Deauville, various cider and cheese factories.

Directions
From Pont-Audemer. Take the D139 to Cormeilles and then follow directions to Lisieux along the D510. The site is well-signposted along the D143 and is situated 3km to the north-east of Moyaux. From Lisieux. Follow signs to Cormeilles along the D510. The site is well-signposted along the D143. From A13. Take exit at Pont l'Evêque and follow N175 towards Rouen. After 5km turn right on D534 to Cormeilles. Then continue as above.

€ Prices 2010	High	Low
Pitch	29	22
Hook Up 10A	3	2

Address 14590 Moyaux

GPS N 49° 12' 29 E 00° 23' 19

www. camping-lecolombier.com
email mail@camping-lecolombier.com
Tel 02.31.63.63.08

Houlgate, Camping la Vallée ****

Location Houlgate 1km. Deauville 12km. Ouistreham 28km. Le Havre 70km.

Open 1st Apr to 11th Oct   **Pitches** 372 (172 touring)

The name of this site aptly describes its setting in a wooded valley with lovely views from the top over the sea. It is a large, bustling but well-maintained site just 1km from the nearest beaches and a 20-minute walk into the charming town of Houlgate, well known for its Edwardian style buildings and pretty shopping streets. The attractive flowery entrance with huge parking area complements the Norman style buildings. The mobile homes on the site tend to be higher up away from the pitches. Deauville and Trouville nearby are both worth a visit.

Site suitable for families who prefer a lively atmosphere.

Pitches	The pitches are grassy, varying in size up to 120m² and laid out on terraces. They are divided by low trees and shrubs and most slope slightly so levelling blocks are recommended.
Hook-Up	4 amps - all pitches. 6 amps + water and drainage - 60 pitches.
Motorhomes	Walking distance of town and beach. Two motorhome service points one on site and one by reception for visitors at extra charge. 12 special hardstanding pitches near reception for overnight motorhomes.
Swimming pools	Outdoor pool with paddling pool and mini slides plus separate basin for 2 waterslides. Generous sun-bathing terrace with sunloungers. New indoor pool with jacuzzi bench which is good for swimming and has an area for babies.
Activities on site	Cycle hire. Huge spacious area at back of site for games including tennis court, badminton court, volleyball, basket ball, and football pitches, boules, good children's play area. Archery. BMX cycle track. Indoor games room with pool, table football and electronic games. Undercover table-tennis area.
Entertainment	Some evening concerts during the high season only.
Sanitary facilities	Three toilet blocks of a reasonable standard with push button showers but no temperature controls, hooks in one block. Toilets with seats and toilet paper. Disabled facilities. Baby room. Separate laundry by games room. Chemical waste point.
Services	Small shop. Bar/Restaurant and take-away in old Norman building overlooking pool, open 1st May to 30 Sept. Barbecues allowed. Dogs accepted. Internet and Wi-Fi connection on most of site with a charge.
Accommodation	50 mobile homes, several other privately owned mobile homes.
Tour operators	Three British tour operators with mobile homes and tents.

Excursions/Places to visit
Houlgate 500m. Deauville 12km Cabourg 3km, Honfleur 28km, Pont l'Evêque, Lisieux. Bayeux, Normandy landing beaches.

Directions
Exit 29 from A13 Dozulé, then take road signposted to Cabourg/Dives/Mer. As you come into Houlgate turn right at first set of traffic lights and follow signs to site.

€ Prices 2009	High	Low
Pitch 4A Incl	30	21
Supplement 6A	2	2

Address 88 rue Vallée, 14510 Houlgate

GPS N 49° 17' 00 E 00° 04' 06

www.campinglavallee.com
email camping.lavallee@wanadoo.fr
Tel 02.31.24.40.69

Bayeux, Château de Martragny ****

Location Bayeux 8km. Cherbourg 108km. Caen 21km.

Open 1st May to 12th Sept   **Pitches** 160

A Castels site, owned by the de Chassey family set in the heart of the Normandy countryside. As you turn into the site you are greeted by a magnificent tree-lined avenue leading up to the elegant 18th century château. The cream stone outbuildings form an attractive courtyard and house the main facilities. The site offers a superbly verdant setting and peaceful relaxed atmosphere.

The site could do with a bit more attention at times, such as trimming and weeding but the superb surroundings in the grounds of a large estate offset this occasional lack of TLC.

Site suitable for Couples and families with young children.

Pitches	Pitches are flat, grassy but not well defined giving a spacious feel to the site. However it can seem busy in the high season and at peak times. The lack of hedging and openness appeals to the British market.
Hook-Up	10 amps - all pitches. Water and drainage - none.
Motorhomes	Motorhome service point. Not walking distance of town.
Swimming pools	Outdoor pool 15m x 8m and small baby pool. Small sunbathing area. Situated behind the château.
Activities on site	Cycle hire. Tennis. Mini-golf (not always well maintained). Children's play area. Games room. Table tennis. Fishing in attractive ornamental fishing lake behind château.
Entertainment	Occasional organised entertainment.
Sanitary facilities	2 large blocks and 1 small. Separate mens and ladies. Push button, temperature controlled showers, which are quite small. English toilets with seats and toilet paper. Double sinks and drainer for washing up. Laundry room with 3 washing machines and 2 tumble dryers. Disabled facilities. Baby room. Chemical waste point.
Services	Small shop. Bar, take-away, restaurant with basic menu. Permanent art exhibition in restaurant building. Barbecues allowed. Dogs accepted. Internet and Wi-Fi point.
Accommodation	No mobile homes or chalets, but 4 double bedrooms in château.
Tour operators	None.

Excursions/Places to visit
Bayeux (inc famous tapestry) Arromanches. Caen Memorial museum and D-Day landing beaches. Castles and farms of the Calvados region.

Directions
From Caen. Take the N13 signposted to Bayeux and Cherbourg, leaving at the exit for Martragny, drive through the village of St. Leger, as if you were going to rejoin the N13. The campsite is on your right as you exit the village.
From Bayeux direction. Take the N13 by-passing around the south of Bayeux and signposted to Caen. Leave at the exit for Martragny. Turn left into the village of St. Leger and left again, back towards Bayeux. Then continue as above.

€ Prices 2010	High	Low
Pitch	27.50	24.50
Hook Up 10A	4	4

Address 5 Rue de l'Ormelet, 14740 Martragny

www. chateau-martragny.com
email chateau.martragny@wanadoo.fr
Tel 02.31.80.21.40

GPS N 49° 14' 35 W 00° 36' 22

Ravenoville-Plage, Le Cormoran ****

Location Cherbourg 45km. St Mère Eglise 10km. St Lô 56km.

Open 3rd Apr to 26th Sept

Pitches 256 (100 touring)

A very well maintained site, 20m from a stretch of pebbly beach and 10-minute drive from St Mère Eglise where the D-Day landings started on 6th June 1944. There is a pleasant open feel to the site which is an ideal base for visiting the area.
It offers comfortable amenities and a warm family atmosphere. Local species of tree are labelled and the animal park is a great attraction for the children. A good low season choice as the pool is covered and most of the services are open.
Clef Verte

Site suitable for all ages, particularly couples and families with young children.

Pitches	Flat and grassy, defined by low trees and hedges. They vary in size but include several which are 150m².
Hook-Up	6 amps - on pitches 90 - 120m². 10 amps, water & drainage on pitches 120 - 150m².
Motorhomes	Good for motorhomes, grassy pitches or hardstanding. Some pitches suitable even for the largest outfits. Two motorhome service points. Special overnight price for 70m² pitch 6 amp elec with arrival after 18:00 and departure before 10:00.
Swimming pools	One pool 120m² covered and heated when site opens. 2 further pools 150m² and 50m² heated from 1/6 - 15/9. The baby pool has a small waterslide. The complex is attractive with good sunbathing area, jacuzzi and sauna.
Activities on site	Cycle hire and electric bike hire (40km range). Go-kart hire. Tennis, volleyball, basketball. Archery. Unique game of billiards-golf. Huge children's play area, bouncy castles, small domestic animal park. Table tennis, 2 games room. Boules pitch. Shrimping. Satellite TV.
Entertainment	Children's club and family entertainment in July and August only.
Sanitary facilities	Four toilet blocks. One block is heated for low season. Clean but three of the blocks looking dated. Toilets without seats and no toilet paper. Push button showers. Disabled facilities. Baby room. Washing machines and tumble dryers. Chemical waste point.
Services	Small well-stocked shop, bar, take-away, pizzas in high season. Barbecues allowed. Dogs accepted. Internet and Wi-Fi.
Accommodation	Several varieties of 2- and 3-bedroomed mobile homes and chalets.
Tour operators	None.

Excursions/Places to visit
Airborne Museum in St Mère Eglise 10km.
Saint-Vaast -la-Hougue 15 Km, Utah landing beach, Carentan 17km, Bayeux 65 Km, Caen 95 Km.
Good 18 hole golf course at Fontenay-sur-Mer.
Restaurant in Ravenoville and supermarket in St Mère Eglise.

Directions
From Cherbourg Port. Follow directions for Caen/St Michel on the N13, continuing past the town of Valognes. Take the Ste Mère Eglise exit and in the centre of town take the D15 signposted to Ravenoville (6km), and then follow signs to Ravenoville-Plage (3km). Then turn right onto the D421 towards Utah beach and the site is 500m further on, on your right and opposite the beach.

€ Prices 2010	Peak	High	Mid	Low	Off
Pitch +2 & 6A	32	29	28	22	20
W & Dr + 10A	7	7	7	7	3

Address Ravenoville Plage, 50480 Sainte Mère Eglise

GPS N 49° 28' 00 W 01° 14' 07

www.lecormoran.com
email lecormoran@wanadoo.fr
Tel 02.33.41.33.94

Cherbourg, L'Anse du Brick ****

Location 10km east of Cherbourg. St Lô 93km. Avranches 159km. Bayeux 104km.

Open 1st Apr to 30th Sept   **Pitches** 180 (117 touring)

A Castels site situated in a naturally landscaped area between sea and forest. It gets its name from the adjacent stark cliff face and enjoys views over a beautiful stretch of sandy beach in a sheltered cove. As it is just a 20-minute drive from the port at Cherbourg, it is an ideal spot for overnight stops and short stays. The unique hill top setting offers a lovely view from the bar/snack over the bay. The site is not that suitable for the disabled as it is quite a steep climb to top of site where pitches are laid out. Direct access to the beach via a small bridge and coastal walks are a bonus.
Clef Verte

Site suitable for for all ages.

Pitches	Flat and grassy laid out on terraces, defined by trees and shrubs, varying in size. Some have lovely views over the bay. Strong pegs are needed for tents and awnings. The new premium pitches are 150m² with 16 amp electrical hook up and water, have a sea view, garden furniture, barbecue, fridge, summerhouse for storage and free internet access at bar for an hour a day.
Hook-Up	10 amps - all pitches. Water - 23 pitches. 16amps. Water & drainage - none.
Motorhomes	Motorhome service point. Nearest shops 3km in Fermanville.
Swimming pools	Heated outdoor pool 18m x 8m with waterslide into separate basin. Baby pool. Small sunbathing area.
Activities on site	Tennis. Cycle and canoe hire. Children's play area. Boules pitch. Volleyball, badminton, table tennis, games room.
Entertainment	Daily entertainment programme including sports tournaments, dance evenings and children's club in July/August.
Sanitary facilities	One recently opened new toilet block. Separate men's and ladies. The other block needs to be renovated, although it is clean and well maintained. The toilets in the old block do not have seats, but have toilet paper and the showers are pushbutton with no temperature control but have hooks and shelf. Disabled facilities. Baby room. Washing machines and tumble dryers.
Services	Small shop, bar, take-away, pizzeria, restaurant. Dogs accepted. Internet and Wi-Fi.
Accommodation	2 and 3 bedroomed mobile homes and chalets.
Tour operators	None.

Excursions/Places to visit
Walks and cycle rides along Cotentin peninsula. Cherbourg and Cité de la Mer museum 10km, D-Day landing beaches 30mins. Valognes, St Vaast La Houge 25km.

Directions
The site is 10km east of Cherbourg. Follow the D116 coastal road through Bretteville-en-Saire. The site entrance is well sign posted to your right.

€ Prices 2010	Peak	High	Mid	Low	Off
Pitch +2 & 10A	36	31.30	26.50	21.70	19.60
Comfort Pitch	3	2.60	2.60	2.60	2.60

Address 50330 Maupertus-sur-Mer

GPS N 49° 40' 03 W 01° 29' 16

www.anse-du-brick.com
email welcome@anse-du-brick.com
Tel 02.33.54.33.57

Les Pieux, Le Grand Large ****

Location 25km south west of Cherbourg. Les Pieux 4km. St Lô 83km.

Open 10th Apr to 19th Sept   **Pitches** 226 (145 touring)

This site occupies a unique position right next to a huge stretch of sandy beach. It is a well maintained site with a friendly French atmosphere and is ideal for overnight stops in a special annex or for longer stays on the main site.

You can enjoy magnificent sunsets over the superb west facing beach and the children can spend hours playing in the sand dunes. It is a good choice for lovers of the sea. There are beautiful beach walks which lead directly from the site.

Site suitable for couples and families with young children.

Pitches	Flat, well hedged and laid out in straight lines on a mixture of grass and sand. Vary in size, some only about 80 - 90m². No trees, so no shade.
Hook-Up	6 or 10 amps - all pitches. Water and drainage - none.
Motorhomes	Motorhome service point. Not walking distance of town or village.
Swimming pools	One 20m x 8m, good-sized baby pool with mini slide. Good sun terrace overlooked by bar.
Activities on site	Tennis (free outside July & August). Large children's play area in the dunes. Games room. Table tennis. TV room.
Entertainment	Occasional evening entertainment in the high season.
Sanitary facilities	One large toilet block that was refurbished a few years ago. Separate mens and ladies. Toilets with seats and toilet paper. Push button showers. Disabled facilities. Babyroom. Washing machines and tumble dryer. Chemical waste point.
Services	Small shop with bread and basics. Bar, take-away in July and August. Barbecues allowed. Dogs accepted. Internet and Wi-Fi point.
Accommodation	Selection of 2 and 3 bedroomed mobile homes.
Tour operators	None.

Excursions/Places to visit
Cité de la Mer in Cherbourg, Gatteville lighthouse, Valognes, Coutances. St Vaast la Hague. The GR223 footpath runs along the coast by the site.

Directions
Cherbourg Port: Exit port and turn right for Cherbourg centre. At next roundabout follow signs for Caen/Rennes. Keep in right hand lane and as you climb the hill turn right on the D900 signposted Bricquebec. At next junction turn left on the D650 to Bricquebec and Les Pieux. Travel through the village of Les Pieux on the D4 and in front of the Mairie follow signs for "Plage" and Sciotot. The campsite is well signposted along this road on your left hand side. From south follow the D903 to Barneville Carteret and continue north towards Cherbourg. Turn left into Les Pieux and continue through the village towards the beach. The campsite is signposted to your left.

€ Prices 2010	High	Mid	Low
Pitch + 2	31	25	17
Hook Up 6A	4	4	4

Address 50340 Les Pieux

GPS N 49° 29' 37 W 01° 50' 33

www.legrandlarge.com
email info@legrandlarge.com
Tel 02.33.52.40.75

La Haye-du-Puits, L'Etang des Haizes ****

Location 47 km south of Cherbourg. La Haye du Puits 2km. St Lô 47km. Bayeux 72km.

Open 1st Apr to 15th Oct

Pitches 100 (60 touring)

A delightful and well-maintained little site in the grounds of an orchard. Although it has a very rural feel the site's great attraction is its proximity to the lively little town of La Haye du Puits. It is a about a 10-minute walk to its shops, bars and restaurants and has a thriving market on Wednesdays. The site has a small fishing lake that is popular with amateur anglers and a superb pool complex for the children. The friendly English speaker owner creates a warm welcoming atmosphere.

Site suitable for families and couples.

Pitches	Mostly flat and grassy defined by low trees. Standard pitches are 80/90m². The lakeside pitches and those 100m² to 130m² are a little more expensive. Several pitches have a hard standing area.
Hook-Up	10 amps - all pitches Water and drainage - none.
Motorhomes	Motorhome service point Excellent for motorhomes as walking distance of centre of La Haye du Puits.
Swimming pools	Attractive 320m² pool complex with four lane waterslide, separate swimming area and small baby pool divided by gate. Generous sun terrace, overlooked by bar terrace.
Activities on site	Cycle hire. Pedalos on lake. Carp fishing. Archery. Table tennis. Volleyball. Boules pitch. TV in bar.
Entertainment	Children's club (6-12yrs) in high season. Other organised entertainment in July/August including walks, and occasional family barbecue evenings with a disco and karaoke.
Sanitary facilities	Two toilet blocks which have both been recently renovated. Separate mens and ladies. English style toilets, but no seats. Toilet paper outside cabin. Push button showers with temperature control and hooks for clothes. Individual wash cubicles. Disabled facilities. Baby room. Washing machine and tumble dryer. Chemical waste point.
Services	No shop, but bread available in bar, which is open all day from end of May until beginning of September. Take-away and basic snacks available in bar. Good restaurants in town. Barbecues allowed. Dogs accepted. Internet and Wi-Fi.
Accommodation	20 mobile homes and chalets, plus a few privately owned ones.
Tour operators	None.

Excursions/Places to visit
10km from the sea, 30km from the D-Day sites and landing beaches, 50km from Cherbourg, 80km from Bayeux. 100km from Mont St-Michel. L'Ile de Tatihou, a small area of land off St Vaast La Houge becomes an island at high tide and is now listed by Unesco.

Directions
From Cherbourg Port. Follow directions for Caen/ Mont St Michel on the N13. Once you reach Valognes take the D2 to Ste Sauveur. Then continue on the D900 in the direction of Coutances for 7kms. At the roundabout follow the sign to La Haye du Puits and then turn right after approximately 300m. The site is well signposted from the roundabout.

€ Prices 2010	Peak	High	Mid	Low
Pitch	31	24	16	14
Hook Up 10A	6	4	3	2

Address 43 rue Cauticotte, 50250 Saint-Symphorien le Valois

www.campingetangdeshaizes.com
email info@campingetangdeshaizes.com
Tel 02.33.46.01.16

GPS N 49° 17' 58 W 01° 32' 42

St Pair-sur-Mer, Château de lez Eaux ****

Location Kairon Plage 4km. Granville 7km. Avranches 25km. Cherbourg 106km. Caen 107km.

Open 27th Mar to 26th Sep

Pitches 250 (102 touring)

A very attractive Castels site set in the spacious grounds of an 18th century château overlooking a beautiful little fishing lake. Access directly from the main road is via a pretty long tree-lined avenue. This site that has always been maintained to a very high standard and the friendly owners take great pride in the quality they offer. The services are all housed in the pretty stone-faced outbuildings. It is a safe environment for young children with a quiet atmosphere as there is no organised entertainment apart from a children's club in the high season.
Clef Verte

Site suitable for Excellent for families with young children and couples.

Pitches	Generally flat, grassy, individual pitches ranging in size from 100m² - 150m². Some may slope gently. Most are separate from the on-site accommodation. The Premium pitches are 150m² have water and drainage, as well as 10 amp electric connection. Each premium pitch also has garden furniture with a parasol and two sunbeds, a barbecue; a refrigerator and 1 hour a day of internet access included in the price.
Hook-Up	5 Amps 100m² - 30 pitches.10 Amps water & drainage 70 pitches. Premium - 2 pitches.
Motorhomes	Pitches acceptable for motorhomes, but not walking distance of a town or village. 4km to nearest supermarket. Motorhome service point.
Swimming pools	A superb indoor pool complex covering an area of 1,300m². The profusion of exotic plants, palms and banana trees makes it feel like a tropical paradise. There are two waterslides 45m and 72m long. Also a new paddling pool for toddlers and a pool for swimming exercise. The indoor pool area only opens in the afternoons in low season - times vary in high season. There is a heated outdoor pool 14m x 7m in a separate area.
Activities on site	Cycle hire. Tennis. Fishing (free). Superb children's play area. Table tennis. Games room next to bar. Football. Volleyball. Satellite TV.
Entertainment	Children's club in high season.
Sanitary facilities	Three good quality toilet blocks. Main one is light and spacious with good quality melamine doors and walls, and attractive tiling. Other blocks are older but very clean and respectable. Toilets with seats and toilet paper. Hot and cold taps in showers and wash cubicles. Disabled facilities. Baby room. Laundry. Chemical waste point.
Services	Reasonably well-stocked shop, bar with covered terrace, good take-away. Market stall visits site on Mondays. Barbecues allowed. Dogs accepted. Internet and Wi-Fi.
Accommodation	2 and 3-bedroomed chalets and mobile homes also VIP chalets with two bathrooms.
Tour operators	Three British companies with mobile homes and tents.

Excursions/Places to visit
Le Mont St Michel 46km. Beautiful sandy beaches 4km. Fortified town of Granville 7km. Avranches 25km. Villedieu-les-Poêles 30km. Champrepus Zoo 21km. 2 good golf courses 9km and 12km.

€ **Prices 2010**	Peak	High	Mid	Low	Off
Pitch 5A Incl	37	31	27	25	21
10A Water & Dr	6	6	6	4.50	4.50

Directions
From Granville. Take the D973 towards Avranches. The site entrance is well-signposted to the right about 7km from Granville. Direct access off the D973.
From Avranches. Follow the D973 towards Granville. Continue along this road for about 7km, through Sartilly and St Pierre Langers, up the hill and the main entrance to the site is on your left down a long drive. Direct access off the D973.

Address Saint-Aubin des Préaux, 50380 Saint-Pair-sur-Mer

www.lez-eaux.com
email bonjour@lez-eaux.com

GPS N 48° 47' 49 W 01° 31' 36

Tel 02.33.51.66.09

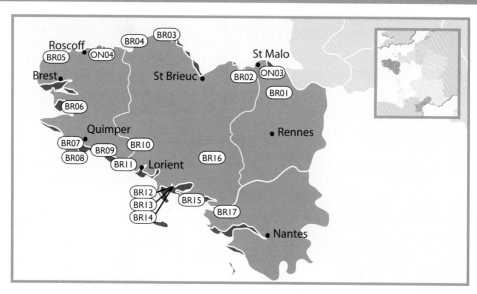

Picture opposite - Camping Port l'Epine

Places of Interest - Brittany

Brittany, a long peninsula on the Western edge of Europe, has been shaped by the swells of the ocean and the weather. The coastline is made up of hundreds of headlands, bays, coves and inlets. The north has been endowed with a magnificent hard, jagged coastline and dramatic views. The south has been blessed with a mild climate, vast sandy beaches and hundreds of islands making it a sailor's paradise. Inland the lush green gently undulating landscape is criss-crossed with woods, lakes and rivers. It is also a region full of folklore and traditions. Many signs are bi-lingual, posted in both French and Breton, a Celtic language which has strong affiliations with Welsh. The local religious festivals or "pardons" where the participants parade in traditional costumes are worth witnessing. Brittany is also renowned for its wonderful seafood and crêperies which offer both sweet and savoury pancakes called "galettes". There are 4,500km of hiking trails stretching across Brittany and many nature trails suitable for cycling.

Village Close

Northern Brittany also called the Côtes d'Armor boasts 320km of very varied coastline, starting with the amazing rock formations of the Pink Granite Coast, near the busy seaside resorts of Perros Guirec and Trégastel. South of Paimpol, the yachting marinas alternate with lovely sandy coves. Cap Fréhel with its red and grey flecked cliffs rises 70m above the sea and is full of buzzing sea birds.

Morlaix has a rich history dating back to the Romans and is characterised by half-timbered houses and a massive two-storey railway viaduct, towering 60m over the river below.

Tréguier has a Gothic cathedral and broad river quayside.

Dinan is a magical town protected by 75m high ramparts and by the Château de la Duchesse Anne which overlook the Rance river. Its medieval charm is still evident in the picturesque cobbled streets, particularly the Rue d'Horloge with its belfry and 15th and 16th century houses. The old commercial port has been replaced by a pretty yachting harbour.

Dol-de-Bretagne is a charming market town with quaint streets and shops dominated by an imposing 13th century granite cathedral.

Combourg is a pretty lakeside town with a mighty feudal castle.

Ploumanach

The Côte d'Emeraude or Emerald coastline stretches from the Mont St Michel round to Dinard offering sandy beaches and rocky outcrops. **St Malo's** old town is completely surrounded by ancient granite ramparts and is renowned for its cobbled streets and tall stone houses built by 18th century ship owners. The town's Aquarium is a good choice for a rainy day. The town looks out over the river Rance to **Dinard**, a fashionable resort with a fine sheltered beach of golden sand. The bay of Cancale east of St Malo is famous for its succulent oysters and mussels.

Quimper Fest Noz

Western Brittany where the village churches and chapels have spiky pinnacles is the most typically Breton part of the region. The further west you go, the more rugged the countryside becomes until you reach the dramatic Point du Raz. Between this most westerly point of mainland France and the Baie de Douarnenez are some of the most impressive rocks and cliffs in Brittany. The bay offers plenty of sandy beaches as well as being a major fishing area. The Crozon Peninsula just south of Brest offers a series of imposing landscapes with fabulous views of rugged cliffs and pretty fishing harbours.

Locronan is a small town of historical interest lined with granite stone houses. The rich 16th and 17th century dwellings surrounding the square have frequently been used for French film sets. Many craftsmen have set up their shops inside the old walls of the town.

Quimper the administrative capital of Western Brittany is a focal point of traditional Breton culture. It is famous for its pottery and hosts the annual "Festivale de Cornouaille" during the week preceding the fourth Sunday of July. It is a great town to explore on foot as the quays along the Odet river are dotted with numerous bridges and footbridges. At the centre is the splendid twin-spired St Corentin cathedral and the streets of the old town still keep their medieval names.

Bénodet is a picturesque seaside resort in a wooded setting at the mouth of the Odet river. It has a lively atmosphere, good cafés and bars, with excellent sandy beaches.

Beg Meil Cap Coz, La Forêt Fouesnant, Mousterlin and **Pont l'Abbé** are all coastal towns with great beaches and definitely worth a visit in their own right.

Concarneau is famous for its ancient ramparts and is still an important fishing port. The 14th century "Ville Clos" is an island in the middle of the harbour linked by two bridges.

Pont Aven is a delightful old port situated at the mouth of the Aven river known throughout the world as the town of artists. American painters set up studios here in the 1860s and were soon followed by artists of all nationalities including Gauguin and Emile Bernard.

Brittany Beach

Southern Brittany enjoys a huge stretch of gentle coastline and numerous off shore islands. It offers a mild climate and delightful sandy beaches.

La Trinité although still a thriving fishing port is Brittany's most popular marina and hosts colourful regattas during the summer months. The charming little town has a network of pretty streets. Great views over the harbour and Crac'h river can be enjoyed from the Kérisper bridge.

Carnac famous not just for its beaches but also for its ancient standing stones or "menhirs", standing 6m - 22m high in rows "alignements" or groups forming circles.

Auray has an attractive harbour and beautiful houses dating from the 15th century. The 14th century château in Josselin with four pepper pot towers is one of the most beautiful in Brittany.

La Baule is completely different from any other resort in Brittany, as its 5km curve of excellent beach is the largest in Europe. Behind the seafront, tree-lined avenues house attractive olde-worlde hotels, once frequented only by the wealthy.

Le Croisic is a busy fishing and sailing harbour and an excellent place to sample locally raised oysters and shellfish.

Guérande on the edge of the Parc Naturel de Brière is a perfectly preserved medieval town with magnificent walls and tiny cobbled streets.

Pénestin, Piriac and **La Turballe** are all worth a visit and a trip over the Pont St Nazaire spanning the Loire estuary is highly recommended.

www.brittanytourism.com

Dol-de-Bretagne, Château des Ormes ****

Location St Malo 28km. Dol 7 km. Rennes 50km.

Open 15th May to 4th Sept

Pitches 800 (100 touring)

A very large Castels site set in the lush parkland of a beautiful 16th century château with 3 lakes for fishing or canoeing and its own golf course. You cannot fail to be impressed by the magnificent setting and the beauty of the surrounding grounds. It is a very busy camp site, as there are several British tour operators with their own mobile homes and tents. It attracts a large number of teenagers and can be noisy at night. It is not recommended for those seeking a quiet French ambiance.

Site suitable for families with children of all ages, particularly teenagers. Suitable for couples in low season as services are all open.

Pitches	Majority flat some gently sloping, mostly grassy and defined by hedges, trees and shrubs. A mixture of sunny and shady. Best pitches are in the demi-lune area overlooking the cricket pitch and château.
Hook-Up	6 amps - all pitches. Water & drainage - 10 pitches.
Motorhomes	Motorhome service point. Everything you need on site, but not walking distance of any towns or villages.
Swimming pools	Three pool areas: indoor aqua parc and wave machine. Superb outdoor aqua parc with waterslides and baby pool. Good sun terrace. Further outdoor pools for swimming by piano bar/restaurant.
Activities on site	Cycle hire, mini-golf, 2 tennis courts, horse riding, pedalos & canoes, archery. Adventure course in the trees. Paintballing. Climbing wall. 18-hole golf course, pitch & putt. Lessons with qualified instructors in golf, horse riding and fishing. Huge indoor game area with electronic games, billiards, table football. Multi-sports ground. All weather football pitch. Trampoline. Huge children's play area. Table tennis. Satellite TV.
Entertainment	Entertainment programme throughout the season including children's clubs and sports tournaments during the day and concerts, live bands, quiz nights in the evening. Soundproof disco every night in the high season.
Sanitary facilities	Six toilet blocks. Best and most recently installed is next to all weather sports pitch in Bas Jardin, quite a distance from most pitches, but several large cabins with showers and washbasins combined. Push button, temperature controlled showers. Toilets, some with seats and toilet paper. Other blocks acceptable but could do with some renovation. Disabled facilities. Baby room. Two Laundry areas. Chemical waste point.
Services	Supermarket, bakers, newsagents. Bars, pizzeria, take-away. Two restaurants on site, one overlooking pool, one in golf club house. Ormizzy is an electronic credit card unique to site. It has to be purchased on arrival to allow entrance in and out of the site. Activities on site may be purchased by cash or by use of the card. Full details are on the site's web. Barbecues allowed. Dogs accepted. Internet and Wi-Fi.
Accommodation	3-star hotel rooms, Appartments, Cottages, Chalets, Mobile homes, Tree houses.
Tour operators	British, Irish and Dutch tour operators - 10 companies.

Excursions/Places to visit
The Emerald Coast, Dol 7km, Combourg 11km, Dinan 26km, Dinard, St. Malo 28km, Le Mont St Michel 37km.

Directions
From N176. Take the exit to Dol de Bretagne at junction with D4 and join the ring road to the south of the town. Follow the ringroad and turn right following directions to Combourg and Rennes on the D795. The campsite is well-signposted off the ring road. Continue for approximately 8km and the site entrance is on your left.

€ Prices 2010	High	Low
Pitch + 2	40	23.40
Hook Up 6A	4.60	3.60

Address 35120 Epiniac, Dol de Bretagne

GPS N 48° 29' 18 W 01° 43' 51

www.lesormes.com
email info@lesormes.com
Tel 02.99.73.53.00

St Cast-Le-Guildo, Château de Galinée ****

Location St Malo 33km. Dinard 20km. St Brieuc 48km.

Open 7th May to 11th Sept **Pitches** 273 (169 touring)

A Castels site situated in the spacious wooded grounds of a typically Breton 19th century manor house hidden in the countryside only 4km from the beautiful sandy beaches of the Emerald coast. The services are all housed in attractive stone outbuildings and the activities and pools are concentrated in an area near the château. An attractive verdant environment enhanced by a wealth of beautiful oak and lime trees, with a lovely indoor pool that makes this site an ideal low season choice. A quiet atmosphere.

Site suitable for all ages, although no specific entertainment for teenagers.

Pitches	The pitches are flat, grassy and divided by low hedges of flowers and shrubs. Most are separated from the rental accommodation and vary between 100m^2 and 120m^2.
Hook-Up	10 amps, water & drainage - all pitches.
Motorhomes	Motorhome service point. Not walking distance of a town or village, but accessible by bike.
Swimming pools	Outdoor pool complex with a large swimming pool ideal for doing some 'lengths', another pool with a short river section and water jets. Water slides, Childrens' pool. Superb indoor pool with large glass façade. Underwater bench with water jets and jacuzzi. Baby pool. Sauna in high season.
Activities on site	Mini-golf, 2 tennis courts. Three children's play areas, bouncy castle, mini-farm. Two small fishing ponds. Table tennis, all weather sports pitch. Volleyball pitch. Pool tables in bar. Boules pitch. Massage and aquagym.
Entertainment	In high season children's club, sports tournaments and evening entertainment twice a week.
Sanitary facilities	One large, heated family toilet block installed in converted stables. Unisex. Toilets with seats and toilet paper. Push button showers without temperature control but with hooks. Disabled facilities. Baby room. Two further very small blocks for ladies and gentlemen. Laundry facilities. Chemical waste point.
Services	Small, basic shop. Large bar, take-away, snack restaurant all housed in attractive stone outbuildings. Barbecues allowed. Dogs accepted. Internet and Wi-Fi in bar/restaurant area.
Accommodation	2- and 3-bedroomed mobile homes, some privately owned.
Tour operators	One British company.

Excursions/Places to visit

30 kms of well-signed walks along the coast. Beach at Pen Guen 4km. St. Cast, Erquy, Cap Fréhel, Dinan, Dinard. Sailing, golf and horse-riding are available nearby.

Directions

From St Malo. Take the D168 over the Barrage de la Rance towards Dinard. Continue through Ploubalay and turn right onto the D786 towards Matignon and St Cast. The site is signposted off the D786 just after the turning to St Cast-le-Guildo.

€ Prices 2010	High	Mid	Low
Pitch + 2	32	26	16.50
Hook Up 10A	5	5	5

Address 22380 St Cast Le Guildo

GPS N 48° 35' 03 W 02° 15'26

www.chateaudegalinee.com
email chateaugalinee@wanadoo.fr
Tel 02.96.41.10.56

Trélévern, Camping Port l'Epine ***

Location Location Perros Guirec 10km. Roscoff 77km. St Malo 169km. Morlaix 52km.

Open 8th May to 25th Sept   **Pitches** 160 (101 touring)

The site occupies a unique spot with direct access to a stony south facing beach that has views across the bay to Perros-Guirec and over to an archipelago of seven islands. There is a sandy beach a short walk away. It is an attractive little site, with tastefully renovated stone-faced buildings and pretty trees and shrubs. You can be sure of a warm welcome from the enthusiastic owner who is keen to maintain the site as a haven of peace and quiet. The site is also a great walking base as it is situated on the GR34 a well-known hiking route.

Site suitable for families with younger children and couples. Not suitable for teenagers as quiet should be maintained after 10pm.

Pitches	Flat, grassy, defined by hedges and flowering shrubs, 90m – 120m². Extra charge for pitches that overlook the beach and benefit from lovely views. However they tend to be smaller.
Hook-Up	16 amps - all pitches. Water & drainage - 35 pitches.
Motorhomes	Motorhome service point. Not walking distance of town.
Swimming pools	Reasonable sized pool with jacuzzi bench and "contre courant" Paddling pool with mushroom shower.
Activities on site	Good children's play area. Table tennis. Video games. Cycle hire. Coastal walks directly from site. Sea fishing and catching crustaceans at low tide.
Entertainment	None.
Sanitary facilities	One toilet block with unisex showers and washbasins, but separate WC's. Toilet seats, but no toilet paper. Push button temperature controlled showers with hooks, shelf and rail. The building is quite dated with a corrugated iron roof, but it is kept beautifully clean and the little paintings on the wall behind each toilet brighten it up considerably. Disabled facilities. Baby room. Laundry.
Services	Small shop (pre-order bread). Bar. Take-away and restaurant in high season only. Barbecues allowed. Dogs accepted. Internet and Wi-Fi in bar area.
Accommodation	Variety of 2- and 3-bedroomed mobile homes and chalets.
Tour operators	None.

Excursions/Places to visit
Trégastel, Paimpol, Lannion, Tréguier, wonderful rock formations at Perros-Guirec. Numerous coastal walks.

Directions
From Lannion take D788 to Perros-Guirec. At the roundabout south of Perros-Guirec take D6 towards Tréguier. After passing through Louannec, take left turn at crossroads for Trélévern. Go through village following "camp" signs - Port l'Epine is clearly marked as distinct from the Municipal site nearby. The site entrance is on your left when you reach the beach.

€ Prices 2010	Peak	High	Mid	Low	Off
Pitch + 2	30	27	22.50	14.50	10
Hook Up 16A	Incl	Incl	Incl	Incl	Incl

Address 10 Venelle de Pors Garo 22660 Trélévern

GPS N 48° 48' 51 W 03° 23' 04

www.camping-port-lepine.com
email camping-de-port-lepine@wanadoo.fr
Tel 02.96.23.71.94

St Michel-en-Grève, Les Capucines ****

Location Roscoff 55km. Lannion 10km. Morlaix 29km. Perros Guirec 21km.

Open 29th Mar to 2nd Oct

Pitches 100 (86 touring)

A very well maintained site, just 2km from the sandy beach at St Michel-en-Grève and very close to the pretty fishing village of Locquémeau. The beautifully trimmed trees and hedges are a real feature of the site, and there is a great feeling of spaciousness The charming owners are keen to preserve its peaceful, family atmosphere. Entertainment is organised only a couple of times throughout the season. It is an ideal centre for exploring the Pink Granite coast and a good low season choice due to its covered pool.

Site suitable for all ages, particularly young families and couples.

Pitches	Very generous grassy pitches marked out by mature trees and shrubs, mostly flat although some gently sloping.
Hook-Up	7 amps, water & drainage - 73 pitches. Camping only - 13 pitches.
Motorhomes	Motorhome service point. Not walking distance of town.
Swimming pools	Good-sized covered pool 20m x 8m. Small paddling pool outside.
Activities on site	Children's play area, mini-golf, tennis, all weather sports pitch, boules pitch. Indoor games area with table tennis, pool and table football. Library.
Entertainment	Usually only two evenings per season.
Sanitary facilities	Two very well maintained toilet blocks, separate gents and ladies. Push-button temperature controlled showers with hooks, shelf and rail. Toilet seats and toilet paper. Individual wash cubicles. Very good dishwashing facilities. Disabled facilities Baby room. Washing machines and tumble dryer.
Services	Small shop selling basics and wine (pre-order bread). Small bar, excellent take-away. Shops just over 1km away. Supermarket 5km. Barbecues allowed. Dogs accepted. Free Internet and Wi-Fi in bar area.
Accommodation	2 bedroomed mobile homes and chalets.
Tour operators	None.

Excursions/Places to visit

Beaches on Pink Granite coast with wonderful coastal walks. Pretty Breton villages, churches and monuments. Amoripark near Bégard 26km. Gallic village in Pleumeur-Bodou 20km.

Directions

From N12 take exit 22 and follow the D42 to Plestin les Grèves. In Plestin take the D786 towards Lannion until you reach St Michel en Grève. About 1km after you leave the town, remain on the D786 towards Lannion, then turn left onto a minor road and follow signs to the site. The site is situated 200 metres along Voie Romaine which has a no entry sign except for locals and campers.

€ Prices 2010	High	Mid	Low
Pitch + 2	20.30	15.80	14.40
7A Water & Dr	6.70	5.70	3.60

Address 22300 Trédrez Locquémeau

GPS N 48° 41' 35 W 03° 33' 27

www.lescapucines.fr
email lescapucines@wanadoo.fr
Tel 02.96.35.72.28

Landéda, Camping des Abers ***

Location Landéda 3.5km. Lannilis 8km. Brest 30km. Roscoff 58km.

Open 1st May to 30 Sept   **Pitches** 180 (158 touring)

The site occupies a fabulous position on the Saint-Marguerite peninsula in Western Brittany overlooking a magnificent stretch of fine sandy beach, ideal for young children. The little offshore islands are accessible at low tide. The area abounds in coastal walks and is a haven for amateur ornithologists. Generally a quiet site with excellent amenities. Although there is no pool on site, it is still a personal favourite because of its unique situation and the warm friendly atmosphere created by the Le Cuff family.

Site suitable for all ages, particularly couples and younger families.

Pitches	Grassy, flat, laid out on terraces, separated by trees and shrubs, some with lovely views over the sea. They vary in size but are generally adequate for large outfits. The best views are at the top of the site, but the pitches are less protected from the wind.
Hook-Up	10 amps - all pitches. Water & drainage - none.
Motorhomes	Motorhome service point and walking distance of restaurant.
Swimming pools	No pools, but direct access to safe swimming on beach, best at high tide.
Activities on site	Cycle hire. Children's play area. Table tennis, table football under cover. Beach volley ball. Fishing. Sailing, windsurfing, canoeing and sand-surfing from beach with own equipment. Numerous rock pools for children to explore at low tide. Three coastal footpaths directly from site. Guided walks. Riding centre nearby. An orientation table at the top of the site gives the names of the islands and places you can view.
Entertainment	In the high season a variety of family activities are organised, including art classes for children and adults, Breton dance and Breton cooking classes, sports competitions, and Fest-noz - Breton traditional night with live music and dancing. Open concerts, where singers and musicians amongst the campers are welcome to play with the site owners.
Sanitary facilities	Three unisex toilet blocks, well maintained and attractively tiled. No toilet seats, but toilet paper. Showers with hot and cold taps (small charge for token). Disabled facilities baby room. Washing machine and tumble dryer. Chemical waste point.
Services	Small shop, take-away July/August only. Restaurant within walking distance. Barbecues allowed. Dogs accepted. Washing machine and tumble dryer. Visiting masseuse and hairdresser. Internet. Wi-Fi all over site - free.
Accommodation	22 two-bedroomed mobile homes and newly built appartments.
Tour operators	None.

Excursions/Places to visit
L'Aber-Wrach, highest lighthouse in Europe, open air market and Notre Dame basilica in Lesneven. Fishermen's village of Méné-Ham. Océanopolis museum in Brest 30km.

Directions
From Lannilis. Go through the town of Lannilis and follow signs to Landéda and L'Aber Wrac'h. Drive through the centre of Landéda and turn left when you reach the coast after approximately 3km. Here follow the green camping signs which will bring you to the campsite.

€ Prices 2010	High	Low
Pitch + 2	14.70	11
Hook Up 10A	2.50	2.00

Address 51 Toull Treaz, 29870 Llandéda

GPS N 48° 35 35' W 04° 36' 11

www.camping-des-abers.com
email camping-des-abers@wanadoo.fr
Tel 02.98.04.93.35

Plomodiern, Camping l'Iroise ****

Location Plomodiern 5km. Châteaulin 19km. Quimper 28km. Roscoff 91km. Brest 60km.

Open 3rd Apr to 2nd Oct   **Pitches** 132 (87 touring)

This typically Breton site enjoys a magnificent view over the Bay of Dournanez, which is renowned for its superb beaches ideal for surfing and its rocky creeks suitable for fishing. There is a verdant spacious feel to the site enhanced by pretty flowers and shrubs. The site owner, M Garrec, takes pride in the unique position of his site, enjoys welcoming the customers and maintains it to a high standard. There is a quiet French atmosphere and easy access to the beach is a great asset.

Site suitable for all ages, particularly those who enjoy sailing and windsurfing.

Pitches	Good sized grassy pitches, about 100m² on terraces sloping up from the beach divided by low hedges. Levelling blocks are recommended.
Hook-Up	6 amp or 10 amp - all pitches, Water & drainage - 19 pitches.
Motorhomes	Motorhome service point. Perfect position for beach.
Swimming pools	A good-sized heated covered pool which can be uncovered in good weather. Paddling pool. Two waterslides going into separate basin. Sun terrace.
Activities on site	Two good children's play areas. 9-hole mini-golf, boules pitch and all weather sports pitch opposite reception. across beach road. Indoor table tennis, table football and TV room. Surf board and kayak hire 100m from site.
Entertainment	None.
Sanitary facilities	One large unisex toilet block with attractive paintings on the walls of mermaids, fish etc. that give it a bright sunny feel. Clean and acceptable. Push button showers, no temperature control, shelf, hook and hanging rail. Separate washbasins. Disabled facilities. Baby room. Washing machines and tumble dryers. Chemical waste point.
Services	Small shop selling basics. Bar/snack opposite site entrance for take-away, pizzas, mussels and chips, waffles, ice creams, etc. Restaurant on sea front. Barbecues allowed. Dogs accepted Internet and Wi-Fi free throughout site.
Accommodation	Mixture of old and new mobilehomes, some privately owned.
Tour operators	None.

Excursions/Places to visit
Douarnenez, with its three harbours 18km. Châteaulin 18km. Quimper 30km. Les Pointes du Raz et du Van 40km. Locronan 13km. Crozon 32km.

Directions
From N165 take exit at Châteaulin and follow D887 towards Crozon. After 10km turn left on D47A towards Plomodiern. Follow signs to Pors Ar Vag beach and exit from Plomodiern onto Rue de la Plage. Continue for 3.5km to Pors Ar Vag and the site entrance is on your left as you approach the beach.

€ Prices 2010	High	Mid	Low
Pitch + 2	24.90	20.90	16.90
6A	3.80	3.80	3.80

Address Plage de Pors ar Vag 29550 Plomodiern

GPS N 48° 10' 09 W 04° 17' 22

www.camping-iroise.com
email campingiroise@orange.fr
Tel 02.98.81.26.10

Quimper, L'Orangerie de Lanniron ****

Location Quimper 2km. Bénodet 16km. Roscoff 104km. Lorient 69km. St Malo 233km.

Open 15th May to 15th Sept   **Pitches** 230 (184 touring)

A delightful Castels site set in the wooded grounds of a 15th century château almost entirely rebuilt by an Englishman in 1825. You cannot fail to be impressed by the magnificent classical 17th century style gardens laid out in terraces descending to the banks of the river Odet. The site has a very verdant spacious feel and is full of beautiful trees, some over 100 years old. Attractive stone buildings house one toilet block and all the services including the new reception, bar and restaurant area at the entrance to the site. Generally a quiet secluded atmosphere, although a little road noise may be heard at night. It is a 2km walk into Quimper and a 20-minute drive to the beaches at Bénodet.

Clef Verte
Site suitable for all ages, although no specific entertainment for teenagers.

Pitches	Flat, grassy, some quite shady, laid out in rows and defined by a variety of trees shrubs and plants. They vary in size from 80-150m² and price varies accordingly. All the pitches with water & drainage are minimum 120m².
Hook-Up	10 amps - all pitches. Supérieur:120m² - 50 pitches. Supérieur confort water & drainage with min 120m² - 64 pitches.
Motorhomes	Motorhome service point. Ideal, as 500m from bus stop into medieval cathedral city of Quimper. Also possible on foot.
Swimming pools	Attractive new aqua complex 600m² with heated pools, situated behind the reception and restaurant. The 4 waterslides are tastefully built into the rocks and camouflaged by exotic plants. There are waterfalls, fountains, jacuzzi baths and an attractive sun terrace. The paddling pool has its own mushroom shower and waterslide. A further pool 17m x 8m good for swimming near the pitches. Baby pool 4m x 4m.
Activities on site	Tennis. Cycle hire. Two children's play areas. Mini-golf, 9 hole practice golf, putting green and driving range. Canoe/kayak on river twice a week. Pony riding. Fishing in Odet (no permit needed). Badminton, table tennis. Games room in bar. Boules pitch.
Entertainment	In July and August, sports tournaments, cultural activities. Children's club for 4-12 yr olds. Sundays a guided tour of the château gardens with a welcome drink. Classical music concerts two or three times during season.
Sanitary facilities	Two modern toilet blocks, well maintained and clean. Separate ladies and gents. Toilets with toilet paper. Push button showers, temperature control with shelf, hook and rail. Disabled facilities. Baby room. Washing machines and tumble dryers. Chemical waste.
Services	Shop, bar, take-away, restaurant Au Potager de Lanniron offering typical French cuisine. Barbecues allowed. Dogs accepted. Internet and Wi-Fi.
Accommodation	Gîtes in the château's park, studios, appartments, cottages, mobile homes.
Tour operators	None.

Excursions/Places to visit
Beautiful city of Quimper 2km. Beaches and port at Bénodet 15km. Concarneau, Beg Meil, Pont Aven all within 30 mins drive. Festival of Celtic music and folklore third week of July in Quimper every year.   www.festival-cornouaille.com

Directions
The site is situated to the south of the town and is well-signposted off the ring road.
Exit N165 at Quimper centre-Quimper Sud exit. Follow directions for Pont l'Abbé and Quimper until you see the exit marked Camping Lanniron on the right. At the top of the slope turn left and follow the road signs for Camping Lanniron, cross under the by-pass and take the second road on the right. Follow the road to the campsite.

€ Prices 2010	Peak	High	Mid	Low	Off
Pitch + 2	33.80	30.60	25.90	22.40	18.90
Hook Up 10A	4.80	4.50	3.80	3.20	3.10

Address 29336 Quimper Cedex

GPS N 47° 58' 43 W 04° 06' 37

www.lanniron.com
email camping@lanniron.com
Tel 02 98.90.62.02

Bénodet, Camping du Letty ****

Location Quimper 16km. Roscoff 126km. Lorient 68km. St Malo 281km.

Open 12th Jun - 6th Sept

Pitches 493 (477 touring)

In a partly wooded location with direct access to a lovely sandy beach, the site attracts a large amount of repeat business particularly from its French customers. The site has a wonderful flowery entrance and many colourful hydrangeas. Renowned for the warmth of its welcome and proximity to the centre of the town, the enthusiasm of the site owners is infectious. The site is run to an exceptionally high standard and there is always a warm welcoming ambiance. Although there is no pool, the beach more than compensates and the site fees are lower. There are no mobile homes. In spite of its size, it is not a noisy site and does not have a commercial atmosphere.

Site suitable for all ages.

Pitches	Level, grassy divided by hedges in small paddocks, most with a little shade. Easy access and reasonable size.
Hook-Up	2, 5 & 10 amps - all pitches. Water & drainage - none.
Motorhomes	Excellent for motorhomes due to position on beach, easy walking distance of Bénodet and excellent facilities on site. Motorhome service point.
Swimming pools	No swimming pool but direct access to beautiful stretch of beach. Plastic shoes are advised as the sand is coarse and their are lots of rockpools to explore. Spa area with sauna, hamman, jacuzzi and massage facilities – all with extra charge.
Activities on site	Two tennis courts, two squash courts. Table tennis. volleyball, basketball, archery, well-equipped gym, billiards, boules pitch. Children's play area.
Activities Nearby	Cycle hire, windsurfing and boat hire.
Entertainment	Day time entertainment includes sports tournaments and craft workshops. From mid-July until mid-August there is a children's club and the L'Amiral soundproof bar is a venue for shows and concerts by local bands and folk groups, as well as for a nightclub.
Sanitary facilities	There are six comfortable, well maintained toilet blocks spread throughout the site, each equipped with toilets, wash basins, showers. 60 cent charge for token for hot showers. Disabled facilities. Baby room. Two launderettes. Chemical waste point.
Services	Mini-market including fresh bread. Excellent varied take-away. 2 bars one at heart of site for a quiet atmosphere and the other for evening entertainment. Hair dressing facilities. Barbecues allowed. Dogs accepted. Internet and Wi-Fi in central area.
Accommodation	A few privately owned touring caravans for hire, no mobilehomes nor chalets.
Tour operators	None.

Excursions/Places to visit
Bénodet, Sainte Marine, Iles de Glénan by boat. Concarneau, Beg Meil, Pont Aven, Quimper.

Directions
From Quimper. Take the D34 to Bénodet. The site is situated to the south-east and is well-signposted through the town.
From the N165 expressway. Take the exit to Concarneau and then turn right, following signs to Bénodet. As you approach the town the site is well indicated.

€ Prices 2010	High	Mid	Low
Pitch + 2	22.40	20.60	17
Hook Up 10A	4	4	4

Address 29950 Bénodet

GPS N 47° 52 02' W 04° 05' 27

www.campingduletty.com
email reception@campingduletty.com
Tel 02.98.57.04.69

Raguénès-Névez, Les Deux Fontaines ****

Location Pont Aven 10km. Quimper 44km. Roscoff 139km. St Malo 268km.

Open 8th May to 11th Sept   **Pitches** 293 (100 touring)

A medium-sized family run site in a rural setting, a 15-minute walk across farmland to fabulous sandy beaches at Raguénès. There are a range of activities on offer in the high season so it is an ideal site for those who prefer a lively atmosphere. The pretty bar area overlooks the excellent aqua complex. There is generally a good blend of nationalities although there tend to be a few more British visitors. There are great coastal walks to Rospico and Port Manec'h nearby with magnificent views over the sea to the Ile Verte. The delightful artist's town of Pont Aven is only a 15-minute drive away.

Site suitable for families with children of all ages.

Pitches	Mostly flat and grassy, defined by hedges and shrubs. Some slope slightly and they tend to vary in size, with some a very good size.
Hook-Up	6 & 10 amps - all pitches 25m cable recommended. Water & drainage - 55 pitches.
Motorhomes	Special rate for overnight motorhomes in low season. Motorhome service point. 4km from Nevez and supermarket. Walking distance of beach and restaurant.
Swimming pools	Attractive aqua complex laid out with palm trees and bamboo parasols which includes a heated pool, paddling pool, jacuzzi, 4-lane waterslide and large winding slide. Good sun terrace with plenty of sun loungers.
Activities on site	Scuba diving lessons. Practice golf and 6 hole golf course. Tennis free in low season. Gym. Two children's play areas. Football, basket ball, games room. Skate park. TV room.
Entertainment	Entertainment in high season includes children's club, archery and sporting competitions, discos and karaokes in bar.
Sanitary facilities	Two blocks, one which has recently been revamped, toilet paper, push button showers no temperature control. Disabled facilities. Baby room. Separate laundry. Chemical waste point.
Services	Shop, bar, take-away, sit down snack area. Barbecues allowed. Dogs accepted. Internet and Wi-Fi in the bar.
Accommodation	One, two and three bedroomed mobile homes. Two and three bedroomed chalets.
Tour operators	4 British tour operators occupying 110 pitches.

Excursions/Places to visit
Kerascoet, Concarneau, Pont Aven, fishing port of Trévignon, Quimperlé, Pont Scorff zoo. Bénodet, Locronan, the rocky creeks and beaches of la Pointe du Raz and la Pointe de la Torche. Riding school in Kertréguier.

Directions
From Quimper. Leave the N165 at the Kérampaou exit and take the D24 towards Pont-Aven. Before you reach the town, turn right on to the D77 towards Névez. Continue through Névez to Raguénès-Plage and the campsite is signposted from the road to Port Manech.
From Lorient. Leave the N165 expressway at the Pont-Aven exit and take the D4 to Pont-Aven. Through Pont-Aven follow signs for Concarneau and then turn left on to the D77 to Névez and continue as above.

€ Prices 2010	Peak	High	Mid	Low	Off
Pitch + 2	31	28	25.50	23.60	18
Hook Up 6A	3.80	3.80	3.80	3.80	3.80

Address Raguenez 29920 Nevez

GPS N 47° 47' 57 W 03° 47' 27

www. les2fontaines.fr
email info@les2fontaines.fr
Tel 02.98.06.81.91

Arzano, Camping Le Ty Nadan ****

Location Quimperlé 15km. Quimper 58km. Roscoff 134km. St Malo 238km.

Open 27th Mar to 1st Sept

Pitches 325 (125 touring)

A Castels site occupying a unique location in the heart of wooded countryside by the river Ellé. The site is renowned for its extensive range of outdoor activities organised daily throughout the season by trained guides and entertainers. The huge indoor pool complex allows you to swim all season. An excellent choice for families as there is always something interesting to do and children will be constantly entertained. Bear in mind that there is an extra charge for most of them. The site is hidden in the countryside which is a great attraction for most people but could feel isolated for some.

Site suitable for all ages, but may be too busy for couples not interested in the activities.

Pitches	Grassy pitches separated by hedges and shrubs and mostly flat but some gently sloping, varying in size, from 100m² -160m². Some are shaded by trees. Best pitches are near the river but not close to toilet block.
Hook-Up	10 amps - all pitches. Water & drainage - 10 pitches.
Motorhomes	Motorhome service point. Not a first choice as some distance from nearest towns, although everything is provided on site and you do not need to go out.
Swimming pools	Main outdoor pool. Pool with waterslides. Good baby pool. A really good size inside pool (20m long) with warmed changing rooms and showers. Water temperature 31°C, air temperature 27°C. Baby pool with waterfall, 60m waterslide and pool reserved for swimming with hydrotherapy spa, and bench with massaging jets and jaccuzi.
Activities on site	Quad-biking. Horse riding. Mountain bike trips. Three levels of acrobatic course in the trees including zip wire. Indoor and outdoor rock climbing. Trips down the river in canoe or kayak and sea kayaking. Paintballing. Archery. Swimming lessons and aquagym classes. Prices of the activities are listed on website. Fishing with permit. To hire: Mountain bikes, pedalos, canoes, kayaks. 2 Tennis courts, Pool tables. Table tennis, football, volley and basketball field, indoor badminton. Boules. Children's play areas.
Entertainment	Children's clubs 4 - 8 yrs and 9-12 yrs. Trampoline - be wary with little ones as not supervised. Sports tournaments organised for all ages. Evening entertainment includes Breton evenings, concerts, karaokes and discos.
Sanitary facilities	Three toilet blocks. The two older octagonal shaped blocks are adequate but could do with being revamped. The largest block is modern and has some family cabins, shower and washbasin combined. Toilet seats with toilet paper. Individual wash cubicles, push button showers, no temperature control. Showers in main block tend to be a bit tepid at end of busy day in high season. Disabled facilities. Baby room. Separate laundry.
Services	Good shop, bar, take-away, restaurant. Barbecues allowed. Dogs accepted. Internet and Wi-Fi.
Accommodation	2 and 3 bedroomed mobile homes, 2 bedroomed chalets. Appartments.
Tour operators	At least 4 British companies.

Excursions/Places to visit
Les Roches du Diable (Devils rocks). Beaches 20-min drive, Quimperlé, Concarneau, Pont Aven, Le Faouët, Doëlan, Quimper, Lorient.

Directions
From N165. Take the Kerfleury/Redené exit to Quimperlé. As you come into the town, at the second set of traffic lights turn right on the D22 towards Arzano. After 8km miles turn left in Arzano signposted for Locunolé. The campsite is on your left just after crossing the river Ellé.

€ Prices 2010	Peak	High	Mid	Low	Off
Pitch + 2	46	43.70	39.70	33.10	25.30
Hook Up10A	Incl	Incl	Incl	Incl	Incl

Address Route d'Arzano, 29319 Locunolé

GPS N 47° 54' 16 E 03° 28' 28

www.camping-ty-nadan.fr
email info@tynadan-vacances.fr
Tel 02.98.71.75.47

Le Pouldu, Les Embruns ****

Location Clohars-Carnoët 7km. Quimperlé 17km. Pont Aven 19km. St Malo 239km.

Open 1st Apr to 18th Sept   **Pitches** 180 (100 touring)

Situated right in the little coastal town of Le Pouldu 250m from the nearest beach, this site is maintained to a very standard with fantastic attention to detail throughout. A small lighthouse at the entrance signals a warm welcome from the Le Guennou family. The site is landscaped with a magnificent profusion of beautiful trees, plants and shrubs including different varieties of cacti and palms. Breton artefacts adorn the site in several spots and include fishing boats full of flowers, an old cider press, pump, well and anchor. It is a real pleasure to visit, as there is something new round every corner. A personal favourite.
Clef Verte

Site suitable for all ages particularly young families.

Pitches	Good sized, spacious grassy pitches up to 120m² divided by flowering trees and shrubs.
Hook-Up	10 amps & water - all pitches.
Motorhomes	Ideal for motorhomes as walking distance of shops and beach. Motorhome service point. 12 small open pitches 80m² at back of site for motorhomes that cannot be pre-booked.
Swimming pools	A medium-sized rectangular swimming pool which is covered and heated to 28°. Paddling pool with mushroom shower outside. Good outdoor sun terrace.
Activities on site	Cycle hire. Good children's play area, 9-hole mini-golf, boules pitch, football pitch surrounded by an orchard. Under cover table tennis area and TV room. Small nature park at back of site with farm animals. Barbecue area.
Entertainment	Children's entertainment and sporting evenings daily and musical evening once a week in high season.
Sanitary facilities	Very well appointed toilet blocks with attractive tiling on floor and wooden doors kept spotlessly clean. Push button temperature control showers with hooks and shelf. There are integral bins in the wash cubicles and toilets which have seats and toilet paper. Disabled facilities. Baby room. A fabulous garden with fountain enhances the exterior of one of the blocks. Separate laundry room with washing machines and tumble dryers. Chemical waste point.
Services	Restaurant-pizzeria-bar "L'Escale Gourmande" at entrance to site opens in June. There is a mini-market "Le Filet à Provisions" over the road open all season. Barbecues allowed. Dogs accepted Internet and Wi-Fi connection throughout site.
Accommodation	A range of mobile homes and chalets to hire and some privately owned.
Tour operators	None.

Excursions/Places to visit

You are given a useful booklet on arrival with site rules and detailed information on places to visit in the area, marked out walking and cycling tracks, local markets, tides etc. Three beaches in Le Pouldu. The GR34 coastal path runs along the jagged coastline. Quimperlé, Pont Aven, Concarneau, Carnac.

Directions

From N165, exit Kervidanou/Quimperlé Ouest and follow the D16 towards Clohars-Carnoët. Continue through the village and turn left onto D24 towards Le Pouldu. Head towards the village centre and just before you arrive at a one-way section of the main street turn right and the site entrance is immediately on your right.

€ Prices 2010	Peak	High	Mid	Low
Pitch + 2	30.80	28.20	21.50	10.50
Hook Up 10A	4.50	4.50	4.50	4.50

Address Le Pouldu, 29360 Clohars-Carnoët

GPS N 47° 46' 07 W 03° 32' 41

www.camping-les-embruns.com
email. camping-les-embruns@wanadoor.fr
Tel. 02.98.39.91.07

La Trinité-sur-Mer, Camping de la Plage ****

Location La Trinité 800m. Vannes 30km. Roscoff 208km. St Malo 208km.

Open 7th May to 19th Sept   **Pitches** 200 (129 touring)

A small family-run site overlooking a beautiful stretch of sandy beach. Direct access makes it very safe for young children. The site shares its services and some activities with La Baie site 200m away on the other side of the beach road. The two sites are owned and run by two brothers and their wives. The site benefits from a unique position on the Quiberon Bay and its proximity to the wonderful sailing port at La Trinité. There are superb views over the bay from the restaurant, 200m from the site entrance.

Site suitable for all ages, but particularly young families due to direct access to safe, sandy beach.

Pitches	The pitches are flat, grassy divided by hedges and shrubs, with some shade from a variety of trees. They vary in size and shape to maximum of 100m² and access to many is difficult due to tight turning circle. Not suitable for outfits over 6.5m.
Hook-Up	6 & 10 amps - all pitches. Water & drainage - all pitches.
Motorhomes	Motorhome service point. Good position for small and medium-sized motorhomes as walking distance from centre of La Trinité.
Swimming pools	Small heated pool 12m x 6m with 2 parallel slides and one long one. Not suitable for swimming lengths. Paddling pool.
Activities on site	Jacuzzi in 2nd toilet block. Cycle hire, canoe hire. Mini-golf, two tennis courts, volleyball, basketball and boules pitch immediately opposite site and shared with La Baie. Children's play area. TV area. Games room in bar (200m). Windsurfing 500m. Quad biking 5km, Karting 8km.
Entertainment	Two children's clubs in high season. Organised activities in high season include aquagym, sports tournaments and guided walks. Occasional concerts in bar.
Sanitary facilities	Two very well maintained toilet blocks, attractively tiled. One block is built round a pretty courtyard and has some family cubicles. Individual wash cubicles, toilet seats and toilet paper, push button showers, no temperature control, hooks and shelf. Disabled facilities. Baby room. Dog shower. Laundry. Chemical waste point.
Services	Basic shop, restaurant, take-away 200m from site immediately opposite La Baie overlooking beach. Gas Barbecues only allowed. Charcoal barbecues allowed in a special area. Dogs accepted. Internet and Wi-Fi in reception and on some pitches.
Accommodation	2 bedroomed mobilehomes on 100m² pitches.
Tour operators	One British company.

Excursions/Places to visit
Walking distance of centre of La Trinité. Carnac 6km, Quiberon 15km, Auray, Locmariaquer, Vannes, Presqu'ile de Rhuys.

Directions
From the N165 expressway. Take the exit to Crach and La Trinité-sur-Mer. Follow the road through the centre of La Trinité-sur-Mer, following signs to Carnac-Plage and the campsite is well-signposted to your left as you leave the town. Care must be taken at the entrance as it is relatively sharp for caravans/motorcaravans and on a downhill slope.

€ Prices 2010	Peak	High	Mid	Low
Pitch + 2	36.50	27.5	22.5	17.50
Hook Up 6A	3.5	3.5	3.5	2.50

Address 4 rue de Kervourden, Plage de Kervillen,
56470 La Trinité-sur-mer
GPS N 47° 34' 34 W 03° 01' 47

www. camping-plage.net
email infos@camping-plage.com
Tel 02.97.55.73.28

La Trinité-sur-Mer, Camping de la Baie ****

Location La Trinité 800m. Vannes 30km. Roscoff 208km. St Malo 208km.

Open 8th May to 12th Sept   **Pitches** 170 (85 touring)

Occupying a unique position between two beautifully sandy beaches, that are sheltered by the Quiberon bay, an area renowned for its mild climate. A small coast road divides the site entrance from the beach. It is a well maintained site and only a short walk to lively sailing port of La Trinité. Owned by the brother of the owner of La Plage, the two sites share a lot of facilities and are similar except the pitches at La Baie tend to be a little more generous and the site tends to attract more couples and slightly older children.

Site suitable for all ages, but no specific actvities for teenagers.

Pitches	Pitches at least 100m² with access quite tight for very large outfits. Flat, grassy, divided by hedges and pretty flowering shrubs and laid out in long alleys.
Hook-Up	6 & 10 amps - all pitches. Water & drainage - all pitches.
Motorhomes	Motorhome service point. Good position for small and medium-sized motorhomes as walking distance from centre of La Trinité.
Swimming pools	Half-covered heated pool 12m x 6m with one long waterslide. Not suitable for swimming. Paddling pool.
Activities on site	Mini-golf, two tennis courts immediately opposite La Plage and shared with its customers. Bike and mountain bike hire. Canoe hire. Children's playground, volley ball, basket ball and boules pitch. Table tennis and table football. Games arcade with electronic games. TV room. Windsurfing 500m. Quad biking 5km, Karting 8km.
Entertainment	Children's club 6-12 yrs and sports tournaments organised in high season. Live concerts from time to time in bar opposite.
Sanitary facilities	Two well maintained toilet blocks with separate mens/ladies, toilet seats and toilet paper, individual wash cubicles, push button showers with temperature control. Well maintained facilites. Disabled facilities. Baby room. Laundry facilities. Chemical waste point.
Services	Basic shop, restaurant, take-away immediately opposite site overlooking beach. Gas barbecues only allowed. Charcoal barbecues allowed in a special area. Dogs accepted. Internet.
Accommodation	2- and 3-bedroomed mobile homes.
Tour operators	Two British companies.

Excursions/Places to visit
Walking distance of centre of La Trinité. Carnac 6km, Quiberon 15km, Auray, Locmariaquer, Vannes, Presqu'ile de Rhuys.

Directions
From the N165 expressway. Take the exit to Crach and La Trinité-sur-Mer. Follow the road through the centre of La Trinité-sur-Mer, following signs to Carnac-Plage and the campsite is well-signposted to your left as you leave the town.
N.B. As you leave the town the first turning left at the traffic lights signposted for the campsite is not suitable for caravans, please continue to the second turning left approximately 150 metres further on.

€ Prices 2010	Peak	High	Mid	Low
Pitch + 2	42.20	31.80	22.50	17.70
Hook Up 6A	3.50	3.50	2.70	2.30

Address Plage de Kervillen, 56470 La Trinité-sur-Mer

GPS N 47° 34' 26 W 03° 01' 38

www.camping-de-la-baie.net.
email camping@camping-la-baie.com
Tel 02.97.55.73.42

La Trinité-sur-Mer, Camping Kervilor ****

Location Roscoff 208km. Caen 336km. La Trinité 2km.

Open 1st May to 20th Sept

Pitches 230 (128 touring)

A family run site in a rural setting 2km from the beach and the port at La Trinité. It is attractively landscaped with trees and flowering shrubs and tends to be a quieter alternative to the two sites on the beach in the low season. In the high season it attracts older children because of its excellent aqua complex and organised evening entertainment. Pitches on this site are also more suitable for larger outfits, as it is more spacious and the alleys are wider. A free bus service runs to the beach from mid-July to about 20th August. A covered pool is planned for 2010.

Site Suitable For all ages.

Pitches	Pitches ranging from 80m² - 120m² are flat, grassy and divided by hedges. Semi-shade on most pitches. Easy access along wide alleys.
Hook-Up	6 and 10 amps - all pitches. Water & drainage - none.
Motorhomes	Motorhome service facilities. Cycling but not walking distance of La Trinité.
Swimming pools	Heated aqua complex with 2 separate sets of waterslides descending into own basins, good-sized pool for swimming and paddling pool area. Whirlpool. Good sun terrace. Covered pool plans for 2010 are on site's web.
Activities on site	Cycle hire. Tennis, mini-golf. Games room with pool tables. Children's play area. Multi-sports pitch. Boules pitch. TV in bar.
Entertainment	Children's club and some organised activities in high season including dance evenings and concert.
Sanitary facilities	Two respectable toilet blocks and a third much older one which could do with renovation. Separate men's and ladies. Toilet seats with paper. Push button, temperature control showers with hooks and rail. Disabled facilities. Baby room. Laundry. Chemical disposal point.
Services	Small shop, bar overlooking pool, take-away. Plenty of restaurants in La Trinité. Barbecues allowed. Dogs accepted. Internet and Wi-Fi in bar.
Accommodation	2- and 3-bedroomed mobile homes in separate area.
Tour operators	None.

Excursions/Places to visit
Marina and shops at La Trinité 2km, Standing stones at Carnac 3km, Quiberon 15km, Auray, Locmariaquer, Vannes, Presqu'ile de Rhuys.

Directions
From Auray. Take the D768 following signs for Carnac and Quiberon. After approximately 4km turn left on to the D186 in the direction of La Trinité. Before you arrive at La Trinité take the turning on your left in the hamlet of Kermarquer. Turn left again and the campsite is situated on the left hand side along this road.

€ Prices 2010	High	Low
Pitch + 2	28.15	21.14
Hook Up 6A	3.70	3.70

Address 56470 La Trinité-sur-Mer

GPS N 47° 36' 07 W 03° 02' 13

www.camping-kervilor.com
email ebideau@camping-kervilor.com
Tel 02.97.55.76.75

Arradon, Camping de Penboch ****

Location Vannes 8km. Arradon 2km. Roscoff 214km. St Malo 188km. Nantes 122km.

Open 2nd Apr to 25th Sept   **Pitches** 175 (100 touring)

This is a family-run site in an exceptional location 200m from a beach on the Golfe du Morbihan, a bay regarded as one of the most beautiful in the world. It is a good beach for boating and crabbing and has a small paddling area. There are also excellent beach walks nearby. The site has a rural feel and yet is only 2km from Arradon, which has a good range of shops and restaurants. It is recommended for the warm welcome from the friendly owners, the quality of its services and cosmopolitan atmosphere. The excellent indoor pool makes it is a good low season choice.
Clef Verte

Site suitable for all ages.

Pitches	Flat grassy pitches separated by trees and hedges. Some are semi-shaded in a quiet wooded area while others are on more open ground closer to the facilities. Generally a good size.
Hook-Up	6 or 10 amps - all pitches. Water & drainage - 50 pitches.
Motorhomes	Suitable for motorhomes, as close to beach and walking distance of town (20–30mins). Motorhome service point. Not recommended for outfits over 10m as access road is narrow.
Swimming pools	Good heated pool complex with 33-metre slide and smaller 4-laned slide, paddling pool with mini slide. Excellent indoor pool area with solarium, paddling pool, rapids and massage bench.
Activities on site	Mini-golf. Good children's play area. All weather sports pitch for football and basketball. Table tennis, indoor games room. Boules pitch. Windsurfing and sailing on beach. Cycle hire and tennis courts 2km.
Entertainment	Aquatic games and children's club in high season.
Sanitary facilities	Two unisex toilet blocks, one which has recently been attractively refurbished. Individual wash basins, temperature control showers with hooks and rail. Toilets with toilet paper. Integral waste basins in all the cabins in the new block. Private family cubicle with WC, shower and wash basin can be hired in the main block for an extra 5 euros a night for a minimum of 5 nights. Second block is less luxurious but respectable. Disabled facilities. Baby room. Laundry. Chemical waste point.
Services	Limited shop, bar overlooking pool. Take-away. Good shops and restaurants in Arradon. Barbecues allowed. Dogs accepted. Internet and Wi-Fi point
Accommodation	2- and 3-bedroomed mobile homes and chalets.
Tour operators	No British tour operators.

Excursions/Places to visit
Bay of Morbihan is a unique site, dotted with small islands. There are many coastal walks, with fishing and sailing also possible. Trips can be booked at the campsite to the islands in the bay. Medieval city of Vannes 5km. Sarzeau, Muzillac to the south and Auray, La Trinité, Carnac and Locmariaquer to the north.

Directions
From N165 Exit at Vannes west, take the D101 in the direction of Arradon, Ile-aux-Moines. After your third roundabout in Le Vincin, the site is well sign-posted at each junction.

€ Prices 2010	Peak	High	Mid	Low
Pitch + 2	34.80	28.80	20.50	15.90
Hook Up 6A	3.50	3.50	3.50	3.50

Address 9 chemin de Penboch 56610 Arradon

www.camping-penboch.fr
email camping.penboch@wanadoo.fr
Tel 02.97.44.71.29

GPS N 47° 37' 20 W 02° 48' 04

Taupont, La Vallée du Ninian ***

Location Ploërmel 7km. Vannes 53km. Nantes 158km. St Malo 145km.

Open 1st Apr to 30th Sept

Pitches 100 pitches (91 touring)

A peaceful little site by the Ninian river in the heart of the Breton countryside. You are in the land of Merlin the Magician and the Knights of the Round Table and are invited to make your own quest for the Holy Grail. Paul & Marylene Joubaud have created a wonderful relaxing holiday environment with the emphasis on exposing the beauty of our natural surroundings and respecting Mother Nature. The cosmopolitan atmosphere is encouraged by Paul who plays Breton folk music on his accordion round the campsite.
Clef Verte - Via Natura

Site suitable for all ages, particularly those who prefer a quiet atmosphere and appreciate Breton folk music.

Pitches	Flat, grassy pitches, 100m² - 120m² , defined by trees and low shrubs.
Hook-Up	6 amps & water - all pitches. Water & drainage - 15 pitches.
Motorhomes	Motorhome service point but 7km from nearest town.
Swimming pools	Small heated pool 12m x 7m. Good paddling pool with small water slides. Sun terrace.
Activities on site	Children's games area. Trampoline, volleyball, table tennis, boules, skittles. Large expanse of green field at back of site by river for ball games. Fishing in river.
Entertainment	The site owner organises bread and cider making sessions. There is also a campfire once a week with Breton folk music. Organised walks. A map of local cycle tracks is available at the reception.
Sanitary facilities	One toilet block, separate mens and ladies, a bit dated but kept very clean and quite comfortable. Push button showers, no temperature control with hooks. Hot and cold taps in washbasins. Toilets with seats but toilet paper outside cubicle. Disabled facilities. Baby room. Chemical waste point.
Services	Small shop selling local produce, including homemade bread and cider. Typical Breton bar with wooden beams complete with oak cider press and "Druid's magic potion". Take-away snack meals. Barbecues allowed. Dogs accepted.
Accommodation	9 mobile homes. A few privately owned ones.
Tour operators	None.

Excursions/Places to visit
Lac au Duc for fishing, sailing and supervised beach 4km, Ploërmel 7km, Josselin with its 15th century castle 7km, Broceliand forest and the legends of Merlin the magician 12kms, Gulf of Morbihan 50km.

€ Prices 2010	High	Low
Pitch + 2	14.00	11.20
Hook Up 6A	3.50	3.50

Directions
From N24 exit midway between Ploërmel and Josselin onto D169 to Guillac and Helléan. Continue through Helléan and turn right towards Taupont. The site site is well signposted with the entrance on your right after about 1km.

Address Le Rocher, Taupont 56800 Ploërmel

GPS N ° 47 58' 10 W 02° 28' 12

www.camping-ninian.com
email infos@camping-ninian.com
Tel 02.97.93.53.01

Pontchâteau, Château du Deffay ****

Location Ste Reine-de-Bretagne 2km. Nantes 59km. La Baule 33km. St Malo 194km.

Open 1st May to 30th Sept   **Pitches** 170 (100 touring)

Situated on the edge of the Brière National Park in the grounds of a 19th century château, this site has a lovely, relaxing atmosphere. The quiet but delightful wooded setting makes it a nature-lovers' paradise. The focal point is a small attractive lake suitable for fishing and boating. The site is run in a simple unsophisticated style, which could occasionally do with a little more TLC. However it is perfect for those who prefer peace and quiet and a feeling of spaciousness in a verdant setting, away from the busy coastal resorts. It is also ideal for an overnight stop going south from Caen or St Malo.

Site suitable for families and couples. No organised activities so not particularly recommended for teenagers.

Pitches	Good-sized flat pitches either in a pleasant wooded area or in a more open field divided by hedges and shrubs.
Hook-Up	6 amps - 89 pitches. Water & drainage - 13 pitches.
Motorhomes	Motorhome service point but some distance from nearest town.
Swimming pools	Main pool 16.8m x 7.7m covered in low season. Paddling pool 4.5 x 6.5m. Adequate but surrounding terrace not exceptionally well maintained.
Activities on site	Cycle hire. Occasional meals organised in the courtyard of the château. Fishing and pedalos on lake. Short fitness circuit. Tennis but court not in good condition. Excellent new children's play area. Table tennis. Boules pitch.
Entertainment	None.
Sanitary facilities	One toilet block with ladies and gents, which is clean and respectable but could do with renovation. Good number of showers and toilets for size of site. Toilet seats with paper, push button showers with no temperature control. Disabled facilties. Baby room. Laundry. Chemical waste point.
Services	Small shop with basics (order bread the night before) take-away and restaurant/bar open all season in stone-faced outbuildings of château which form an attractive courtyard. Internet and Wi-Fi in bar and restaurant area.
Accommodation	One and two bedroomed chalets and two bedroomed mobile homes.
Tour operators	None.

Excursions/Places to visit
Very picturesque villages in the Brière National Park, walled town of Guérande, La Baule 30km, Pont St Nazaire. Several international golf courses only a few minutes from the site.

Directions
Leave the N165 express road at Pontchâteau and Château du Deffay is signposted from the D33 Pontchâteau to Herbignac road, near Ste-Reine. Follow signs for "Camping du Deffay".

€ Prices 2010	Peak	High	Mid	Low
Pitch + 2	23.50	20.50	17.80	15.10
Hook Up 6A	3	3	3	3

Address BP 18, Sainte Reine de Bretagne, 44160 Pontchateau

www. camping-le-deffay.com
email info@camping-le-deffay.com

GPS N 47° 26' 17 W 020° 09' 30   **Tel** 02.40.88.00.57

VENDEE & CHARENTE

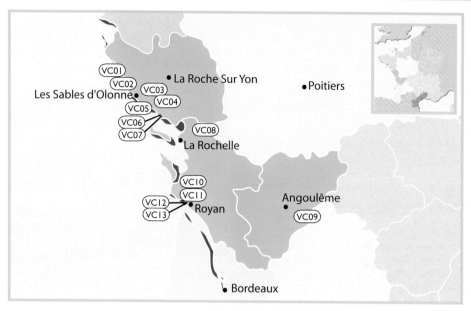

The Vendée and the Charente-Maritime are regions of sun, sea and sand with miles of flat, almost unspoilt coastline interspersed with fishing ports, marinas and lively resorts. The Vendée coastline stretches from the area near Pornic in the north to Aiguillon-sur-Mer in the south. Inland is flat and marshy criss-crossed with canals and rich in fertile pastureland, similar in appearance to the fenland regions of East Anglia. Here and there brilliant white cottages "bourrines" and windmills are dotted across the countryside. It is wonderful cycling country with numerous signed bicycle routes.

Pornic is famous for its charming beaches, its cliff-side houses, castle and port.

St Jean-de-Monts is one of the main modern resorts of the area stretching for 3km along the fine sandy beach. It is not renowned for the beauty of its architecture, but does boast well-laid out access roads and easy parking.

St Gilles Croix-de-Vie and St Hilaire-de-Riez offer two beaches on either side of the inlet of the Vie river, la Grande Plage de St Gilles and la Plage de Boisvinet. You can also see the oldest fishing port of the coast, home to over 200 boats including many tuna vessels. The beaches are some of the best known in the area and are easily accessible from the coast road.

Brétignolles-sur-Mer has good beaches, a miniature Vendée museum and a maze.

Les Sables d'Olonne is the largest town on the coast famous for its zoo and its fishing port.

Talmont St Hilaire is renowned for its château, its museum of old cars and regattas held at Port Bourgenay.

Jard-sur-Mer has a port, two beaches, a forest of large pine trees and just outside, the monastery of Notre Dame de Lieu-Dieu founded by Richard the Lion Heart.

La Tranche-sur-Mer is an attractive tourist resort renowned for its splendid beaches.

Château de la Guignardière

L'Aiguillon-sur-Mer and La Faute-sur-Mer are famous for the cultivation of oysters and mussels. At l'Aiguillon point a long sand dune runs out into the sea.

Four châteaux further inland are also worth a visit: Château de la Garnache, Château d'Apremont, Château de la Guignardière near Avrillé and Le Logis de la Chabotterie, an 18th century château and Vendée memorial museum.

Two islands off the Vendéen coast can also be visited, the Ile de Noirmoutier accessible via a road bridge or a causeway at low tide, and the Ile de Yeu reached by boat from Fromentine, ideal for visiting by bicycle due its size 12km x 4km.

Two water parks to recommend are: Atlantic Toboggan at St Hilaire-de-Riez and Parc des Attractions des Dunes at Brem-sur-Mer.

Le Puy du Fou is an enormous recreational park set well away from the coast in the direction of Cholet and is highly recommended. Set in the grounds of a magnificent Renaissance castle, the park offers a combination of culture, history and ecology. It is essential to pre-book the unique Cinescenic show which is shown only on certain Friday and Saturday evenings. It is an amazing 90 minute extravaganza of the most stunning special effects presented by local people involving 1,000 actors, 50 horsemen and firework displays. **www.puydufou.com**

Le Puy du Fou

The Charente-Maritime region is renowned for its clement climate, delightful beaches and coastal fortifications. The beaches in the extreme west of the region near La Tremblade are great surfing beaches, but can be challenging because of a strong undertow. Inland the region is full of vineyards whose grapes not only produce delicious red and white wines but also the famous local cognac Pineau de Charente served as an aperitif.

La Rochelle is a splendid Renaissance town full of quaint narrow cobbled streets and porch covered pavements. The old town is dominated by a pair of medieval towers from where you can enjoy magnificent views. The lively quayside market and Hôtel de Ville or town hall are both worth a visit. It also has the largest marina for pleasure boats in Europe, and an important boat building industry. Its famous yellow bicycles can be hired to get around the town easily.

Rochefort is well known for the admirals' houses on the Grands Boulevards and its rope making museum, La Corderie Royale, whose gardens are renowned for 1,200 varieties of begonia.

Marennes is a world renowned oyster farming capital and important seaside resort with a redeveloped waterfront and a 5 hectare bathing area.

Muscadet

The Zoo at La Palmyre 16km north of Royan is well worth a visit.

Two of the islands off the coast are also famous holiday attractions. The Ile d'Oléron, 30km long and 10km wide, is France's second largest island and oyster capital. The Ile de Ré is also 30km long but much narrower, reached from a viaduct near La Rochelle. It is famous for its white-washed green-shuttered cottages, vast sandy beaches and picturesque little harbours.

Cognac about 60km from Royan is home to some of the world's most famous cognac distilleries. Tours of the distilleries with English speaking guides are offered on a regular basis with an opportunity to sample the goods at the end of the visit. www.cognac.fr

Le Marais Poitevin is a delightful area of natural beauty now a National Park 45km east of La Rochelle. Also known as La Venise Verte or Green Venice, it is a marshy area criss-crossed by a labyrinth of canals and waterways. It is a haven for nature lovers who can explore the waterways on a flat-bottomed punt or take advantage of the excellent network of walking and cycling routes. The pretty unsophisticated town of Coulon at its heart has several bars and restaurants.

St Palais

St Palais-sur-Mer located on the Côte de Beauté gives access to 4.5km of fine sandy beaches which offer sheltered coves, sand dunes, panoramic viewpoints and legendary rock formations.

Royan is the largest of the seaside resorts on this Charente coastline and offers well supervised beaches which are good for all types of water sports including windsurfing and sailing. It has an attractive promenade, wide tree-lined boulevards and lots of open-air restaurants and cafés.

www.vendee-tourisme.com
www.france-atlantic.com

Camping La Forêt, St Jean-de-Monts **** Map Ref VC01

Location St Jean-de-Monts 6.4km. Notre Dame-de-Monts 1.5km. La Roche-sur-Yon 68km.

Open 1st Apr to 30th Sept   **Pitches 61** (38 touring)

A delightful little site renowned for its quiet peaceful atmosphere, just a 500m walk along a track through the woods and dunes to a beautiful stretch of sandy beach. It is attractively laid out with more than 50 species of trees and shrubs. Monsieur and Madame Jolivet who own the site are particularly committed to care of the environment and have won awards for their eco-friendly management. This includes low energy light sensitive light bulbs throughout the site, use of re-cycled water and regulated outflow taps, recycling, and purchase of local eco-products. Some occasional road noise.
Clef Verte

Site suitable for all ages, particularly couples and families with young children.

Pitches	A good size about 100m², flat and a mixture of grass and sand. They are divided by trees and shrubs. The turning circle for large outfits may be a bit tight as the alleys are rather narrow.
Hook-Up	6 amps, water & drainage - all pitches.
Motorhomes	Motorhome service point, walking distance of beach. Cycling distance of town.
Swimming pools	Attractive heated swimming pool 100m² at entrance to site, adequate size for number of pitches, and suitable for a swim. Paddling pool. Sun terrace with sunloungers.
Activities on site	Cycle hire. Good children's play area. Table tennis, table football. TV room with pool table. Special indoor area for toddlers with toys. Boules. Free hire of surf kayaks. Tourist information centre. The site owners are happy to recommend places to visit in the region. There are good walking and cycling tracks at the entrance to the site.
Entertainment	No organised entertainment.
Sanitary facilities	Modern toilet block which has been solidly built with heavy wooden doors and attractive tiling. The pink side is for ladies and the white for gents. Push button temperature controlled showers with deep bowls, hooks, shelf and soap dish. Hot and cold taps in wash cubicles. Toilet seats and toilet paper. The block is immaculately maintained with eco-friendly cleaning products. Disabled facilities. Baby room. Washing machine. Chemical waste point.
Services	Milk, bread and croissants are available, but need to pre-order. Soft drinks, ice creams and wine are also available. Nearest shop 1km. Take-away with good selection at reasonable prices. Barbecues allowed. Dogs accepted. Internet in reception.
Accommodation	13 mobile homes.
Tour operators	One with 12 tents.

Excursions/Places to visit
200km of cycle tracks. St Gilles Croix de Vie, Ile de Noirmoutier, Château at Talmont, Le Puy du Fou.

Directions
From Challans take the D753 to St Jean-de-Monts. Then follow ring road, the D38 towards Notre Dame-de-Monts and Noirmoutier. Continue for 6km and as you reach the outskirts of Notre Dame turn left towards Plage de Pont d'Yeu and left almost immediately into Rue Piverts which runs into Chemin de la Rive and the site entrance is on your left.

€ Prices 2010	Peak	High	Mid	Low
Pitch + 2	28	24	20	18
Hook Up 6A	3.90	3.90	3.90	3.90

Address 190 Chemin de la Rive, 85160 St Jean de Monts

www.hpa-laforet.com
email camping-la-foret@wanadoo.fr
Tel 02. 51.58.84.63

GPS N 45° 49' 06 W 03° 07' 48

St Hilaire-de-Riez, La Ningle ****

Location Beach 500m. St Jean de Monts 7km. St Gilles Croix de Vie 7km. La Roche/Yon 54km.

Open 20th May to 10th Sept   **Pitches** 150 (90 touring)

One of the smaller more intimate sites in the area run by a friendly couple who create a warm welcoming atmosphere. In a wooded setting, the site is well-maintained with an attractive reception/bar and it is just a 10-minute walk from the nearest stretch of safe, sandy beach. It attracts a large number of French families, so it is certainly not British dominated like many other sites in the area. Only a small selection of organised entertainment is provided in the high season ensuring a generally quiet atmosphere. Occasional noise from neighbouring sites and road.

Site suitable for families with young children due to proximity to beach and for couples in low season.

Pitches	Good sized pitches, most 100m² suitable for most outfits. Flat, grassy and defined by low hedges and flowering shrubs with variable shade.
Hook-Up	6 amp and 10 amps - all pitches. Water & Drainage not available.
Motorhomes	Good for motorhomes as beach and shops and other services in walking distance. Motorhome service point.
Swimming pools	Heated pool 15m x 7m with separate basin for waterslide. Pretty paddling pool with mushroom shower.
Activities on site	Cycle hire. Tennis. Children's play area. Boules pitch. Small gym. TV, billiards and video games in bar.
Entertainment	Children's club each morning from 5 yrs. Small evening parties twice a week in high season. Aquarobics twice a week in high season.
Sanitary facilities	Two toilet blocks, modern and clean but very few toilet seats and no toilet paper. Push button, temperature controlled showers. Individual wash cubicles. Disabled facilities. Baby room. Two washing machines and one tumble dryer. Chemical waste point.
Services	Pre order bread, available in reception. Bar with indoor games open July/August. Pizzas and take away food twice a week in high season. 200m away - small shop, newspapers, take-away meals, restaurant, cycle hire. Supermarket 2km. Barbecues allowed. Dogs accepted. Internet and Wi-Fi Point.
Accommodation	2- and 3-bedroomed mobile homes.
Tour operators	None.

Excursions/Places to visit
Atlantic-Toboggan Aquaparc 2km. St Gilles Croix-de-Vie 7km. Ile de Yeu. Ile de Noirmoutier 20km. Le Puy du Fou, 1 hours drive. Apremont château. Walks in forest near beach. Cycle paths starting the near the campsite and running along the Vendée coast.

Directions
From Challans take D753 through Le Perrier in direction of St Jean-de-Monts for about 10km until you reach the D38 on the outskirts of the town. Turn left on to the D38 to St Hilaire-de Riez and St Gilles Croix-de-Vie. After 6km, before Orouet, there is a right turn by the L'Oasis hotel/restaurant to Les Mouettes. After 1½km at a roundabout, turn left onto the coast road signed to St Hilaire-de-Riez. Go past two sites Les Ecureuils and Le Bois Tordu and take the next left signed to La Ningle. The site is approx 150m further on left hand side.

€ Prices 2009	High	Mid	Low
Pitch + 2 & 6A	27.80	23	17.50
Hook Up 10A	3.20	2.50	1.50

Address 66 Chemin des Roselières, 85270 St Hilaire de Riez

www.campinglaningle.com
email campingdelaningle@wanadoo.fr
Tel 02.51.54.07.11

GPS N 46° 44' 41 W 02° 00' 16

Lac du Jaunay, Le Pin Parasol ****

Location On Lac du Jaunay. La Roche-sur-Yon 28km. Coëx 5km. St Gilles-Croix-de-Vie 17km.

Open 23rd Apr to 25th Sept

Pitches 369 pitches (251 touring)

Situated on the banks of the Lac du Jaunay in the heart of the Vendéen countryside with direct access to the lake from the site down a specially created path. There is no actual beach on the lake by the site and swimming is not generally encouraged. The lake is ideal for fishing and many holidaymakers enjoy cycling or walking round the lake. It is only a 15-minute drive to the nearest beaches, but well away from the hustle and bustle of the coastal towns. The site is renowned for the warm welcome from the friendly owners and is an ideal low season choice because of the superb indoor pool. It can seem busy in high season, but the overall atmosphere is peaceful and relaxing.

Site Suitable for all ages, particularly families with younger children.

Pitches	Spacious, individual pitches 150 m² - 220 m² which are flat and grassy. The trees and shrubs in the newer area are not yet mature and afford little privacy.
Hook-Up	10 Amps - all pitches. Water & drainage - 36 pitches.
Motorhomes	A secluded setting not within walking distance of any services. Nearest supermarket 5km. Motorhome service point.
Swimming pools	Outside swimming pool 22.4 m x 8 m (1/6 - 15/9) with waterslides, heated by solar energy. Excellent children's playpool with water features, (15/6 -15/9). Superb indoor heated swimming pool 12 m x 12m. Steam room and gym.
Activities on site	Cycle hire. Tennis. Table tennis and indoor games area, boules pitch. Archery in high season. Spacious children's play areas, multi-sports ground for football, volleyball etc. BMX cycle track.
Activities nearby	Hire of canoes and pedalos on lake in July/August. Fishing in lake with permit.
Entertainment	Entertainment in high season including children's activities karaoke, bingo, and occasional visiting bands in the evening.
Sanitary facilities	4 toilet blocks. Generally well maintained, water heated by solar panels. Toilet seats but paper not provided. Individual wash basins. Push button temperature control showers. Disabled facilities. Baby room. Washing machines. Tumble driers. Chemical waste point.
Services	Shop for basic necessities and French specialities including bread which has to be ordered the day before. Bar. Take-away (high season). TV in bar. Barbecues allowed Dogs accepted. Internet and Wi-Fi.
Accommodation	84 two and three bedroomed chalets and mobile homes and 34 privately owned.
Tour operators	None.

Excursions/Places to visit

Coëx 5km, Château at Apremont, medieval ruined château at Commequiers, St Gilles Croix-de-Vie, beaches at Brétignolles 12km, Le Puy du Fou (one hour) Iles d'Yeu and Noirmoutier. Classic car museum and château in Talmont.

€ Prices 2010	High	Mid	Low
Pitch + 2	28.50	20.50	12.50
Hook Up 10A	4	4	4

Address Châteaulong, 85220 La Chapelle-Hermier

GPS N 01° 45' 25 E 46° 39' 91

Directions

From the A83 motorway south take exit 4 onto D763 and then D937 in direction of La Roche-sur-Yon. As you approach La Roche-sur-Yon take the D948 in direction of Challans to Aizenay. At Aizenay take the D6 in the direction of St Gilles. After 10km turn left to La Chapelle Hermier. In the centre of the village turn right and turn left after 2½km towards Lac du Jaunay. The site is on your right just before you reach the lake.

www.campingpinparasol.fr
email campingpinparasol@free.fr
Tel 02.51.34.64.72

St Julien-des-Landes, La Garangeoire ****

Location 2.5km north of St Julien. Brétignolles 12km. La Roche-sur-Yon 27km

Open 4th Apr to 26th Sept

Pitches 355 (136 touring)

This attractive and very well-maintained Castels site is in a rural setting 15-minutes from the nearest beaches. You are welcomed by an impressive tree-lined avenue and view of the château to an extensive estate. You can always find a quiet spot by one of the four lakes ideal also for fishing and boating. The stone faced outbuildings house the restaurant and bar. Regarded by many as the best campsite in the Vendée, there is a lot of repeat business and the customers are mostly English and Dutch. The general feeling of spaciousness is a big plus and the staff are always very helpful and efficient. In the high season, the constant stream of bikes can make the main areas feel very busy.

Site Suitable for families with children under 13 as entertainment tends not to be for teenagers.

Pitches	The generous sized pitches range from 125m² - 200m². They are marked out and individually named, with a choice of situation either in the shade of oak trees, in the meadow, sheltered by a hedge or unshaded grassy and flat. Premium pitch 260 m², Electricity 16A + Water + Drainage. Equipped with 1 table, 6 chairs, 2 sun-loungers, parasol, refrigerator, gas barbecue + internet access for 1 hr a day.
Hook-Up	8 amps - all pitches. Water & drainage - most pitches.
Motorhomes	Motorhome service point.
Swimming pools	400m² complex with waterslide and paddling pool, good for bathing but not swimming. Perhaps a little small for volume of people in high season.
Activities on site	Cycle hire. Mini-golf. Two tennis courts. Horse riding, archery, fishing for carp, perch, roach and tench in three of the lakes. Canoes and pedalos on lake. Football and volleyball fields. Boules pitch. Children's play areas. Covered table tennis and indoor games area. Walks around the lake area. Picnic tables by lakes.
Entertainment	Site run children's clubs and programme of family entertainment in high season.
Sanitary facilities	Three toilet blocks, separate ladies and gents, clean and well maintained with superb attention to detail. Hot and cold taps in spacious shower cubicles with hooks, shelf, rail and soap dish. Toilets with seats and toilet paper. Several family cabins with shower and washbasin together in two blocks. Third block is a little older but still well maintained. Disabled facilities. Baby room. Washing machines, tumble dryers. Chemical disposal point.
Services	Well stocked shop, bar, take-away/pizzeria. Attractive restaurant with childrens menus Barbecues allowed. Dogs accepted. Internet and Wi-Fi.
Accommodation	2 and 3-bedroomed mobile homes. 1- and 2- bedroomed chalets. Mobile homes specially equipped for the disabled.
Tour operators	3 British tour operators and 1 Dutch operator with own mobile homes and tents.

Excursions/Places to visit

Vendée beaches, Coëx 8km, Lac du Jaunay 5km, St Gilles Croix de Vie 12km.
Le Puy du Fou – an hour's drive.

Directions

From La Roche-sur-Yon. Take the N160 in the direction of Les Sables d'Olonne and La Mothe Achard. Turn in to the centre of La Mothe Achard after approximately 18km and follow signs to St-Julien-des-Landes. Go through the village and fork right to La Chapelle-Hermier as you exit, following signs to the site. The campsite is to your right after 2km.

€ Prices 2010	Peak	High	Mid	Low
Pitch + 2	28.50	23.00	18.50	14.50
Hook Up 8A	7.50	4.50	3	3

Address Route de La Chapelle-Hermier, 85150 St Julien des Landes
GPS N 46° 39' 49 W 01° 42' 49

www.camping-la-garangeoire.com
email info@garangeoire.com
Tel 02.51.46.65.39

Avrillé, Camping du Domaine des Forges ***

Location Avrillé 500m. Jard-sur-Mer 8km. Sables d'Olonne 20km. La Roche sur Yon 30km.

Open All year

Pitches 140 (94 touring)

A Castels site set in the spacious grounds of an attractive 16th century manor house. You cannot fail to be impressed by the pretty entrance decorated with plants. The lovely stone-faced outbuildings which house the services include a beautiful cone-shaped tower. The huge fishing lake on the right as you come into the site is a big attraction and is a wonderfully quiet spot for both angling and strolling. A fabulously peaceful spot away from the bustle of the coast, yet less than a 10-minute drive from the beaches.

Site suitable for families and couples although no entertainment for teenagers.

Pitches	Spacious pitches average 170m², some 220m², flat and grassy, divided by low hedges. Mixture of sunny and shaded pitches. Internet and satellite TV aerial connection on each pitch.
Hook-Up	32 amps, water & drainage - all pitches.
Motorhomes	Good for motorhomes as walking distance of centre of Avrillé. Motorhome service point.
Swimming pools	A good-sized pool for swimming, paddling pool. Generous sun terrace with sunloungers.
Activities on site	Cycle hire, mini-golf, tennis. Indoor games area with table tennis. Boules pitch. Fishing in lake (permit not required for campers).
Entertainment	None.
Sanitary facilities	The old toilet block has been revamped for the time being. It has been repainted and is clean and respectable, but the plumbing is old and showers are not always hot. Sinks are in rows not individual cubicles. Showers are small with push button and no temperature control. Toilets with seats and toilet paper. Laundry. Chemical waste point. A new block is planned for 2010.
Services	Pretty wooden beamed bar. Shops and restaurants in town. Barbecues allowed. Dogs accepted. Internet on all the pitches.
Accommodation	2- and 3-bedroomed mobile homes and chalets. Mobile homes for sale.
Tour operators	None.

Excursions/Places to visit
Beaches at Les Sables d'Olonne, La Tranche sur Mer, Longeville and Jard sur Mer. Renaissance Château de le Guignardière - 5 mins. Indian Advenure Forest in Le Bernard -10 mins. Moutiers-les-Mauxfaits. Le Puy du Fou - 1 hour.

Directions
From La Roche sur Yon take the D747 to La Tranche-sur-Mer and Moutiers-les-Mauxfaits. In Moutiers turn left onto the D19 towards Avrillé. As you enter the village take second turn right (next turning after Rue de l'Etang) and then right again into Rue des Forges and follow signs to the site reception.

€ Prices 2010	High	Mid	Low
Pitch + 2	27	18	16
Hook Up 32A	Incl	Incl	Incl

Address Rue des Forges, 85440 Avrillé

GPS N 46° 28' 35 W 01° 45' 18

www. campingdomainedesforges.com
email contact@campingdomainedesforges.com
Tel 02.51.22.38.85

La Tranche-sur-Mer, Camping Bel ****

Location La Tranche 400m, La Roche-sur-Yon 37km. Les Sables d'Olonne 44km.

Open 22nd May to 4th Sept   **Pitches** 200 (100 touring)

A quiet family-run site, 400m from the town centre and 300m from the beach. The owner M. Guieau has an individual approach to running his site, maintaining a high standard and creating facilities actively aimed at encouraging small children. There is a welcoming entrance housed in typical Vendée style buildings and the wealth of trees and shrubs give the site a lovely verdant feel which complements the relaxed atmosphere. No shop on site, but everything is within walking distance.

Site suitable for couples in low season and families with young children.

Pitches	Flat pitches on a mixture of grass and sand, hedged for privacy and generally a good size varying from 80m² - 120m².
Hook-Up	10 amps - free in May, June and Sept & water - all pitches. Drainage - limited number.
Motorhomes	No motorhome service point but everything accessible on foot.
Swimming pools	A good-sized adult pool, paddling pool with two mini waterslides, sun terrace and sun loungers. Covered jacuzzi for adults only. Covered aqua complex 150m.
Activities on site	Two half court tennis. Excellent children's play area. Outdoor fitness area. Indoor children's play room and kid's cinema. Games room with table tennis. All-weather sports pitch for badminton and basketball.
Entertainment	Children's club in the morning, cinema in the evening. No entertainment for adults.
Sanitary facilities	Two well maintained modern toilet blocks, painted in blue and yellow to match sun loungers. Toilets with seats and toilet paper outside. Hot and cold taps in the some of the individual wash cubicles. Push button showers, no temperature control, shelf and hook. Some family cabins. Disabled facilities. Excellent baby rooms. Washing machines and tumble dryer. Chemical Waste Point.
Services	Baker calls each morning. Bar, take-away/snack (open from end of May). Shop 150m. Bars and restaurants in walking distance. Barbecues allowed. Dogs not accepted. No internet or Wi-Fi connection on site, but free in centre of town.
Accommodation	None of their own accommodation.
Tour operators	Two British tour companies with mobile homes and tents.

Excursions/Places to visit
La Tranche, Talmont St Hilaire, Vendée beaches. Les Sables d'Olonne, La Rochelle, Ile de Ré, La Venise Verte.

€ **Prices 2010**	High	Low
Pitch + 2	24	24
Hook Up 10A	4	Incl

Directions
From La Roche-Sur-Yon. Take the D747 to La Tranche-sur-Mer. On arrival in La Tranche you come to a roundabout take the first exit. Take the second exit at the next roundabout, Rond Point des Joncs, and then turn first left into Rue Bottereau. The site entrance is on your right after 200 metres.

Address Rue du Bottereau, 85360 La Tranche-sur-Mer

No website
email campbel@wanadoo.fr
GPS N 40° 20' 47 W 01° 25' 55   **Tel** 02.51.30.47.39

La Tranche-sur-Mer, La Baie d'Aunis ****

Location 500m town centre. Sables d'Olonne 42km. La Roche-sur-Yon 37km.

Open 1st May to 18th Sept

Pitches 153 (134 touring)

You will receive a warm welcome from the friendly owners of this site which occupies a unique position 100m from one of the best beaches in the southern Vendée and a short walk from the centre of La Tranche. It is a small intimate site with a good mixture of nationalities and no organised evening entertainment. Although well-shielded from the road, there may be some traffic noise. Access to the beach is via two gates operated with a magnetic key. There is a sea-water lagoon right next to beach where you can learn to windsurf.

Site suitable for all ages, although would be quiet for teenagers.

Pitches	Flat, sandy pitches separated by hedges and varying in size up to 100m². The turning circle is tight for large outfits. Many good pitches are pre-booked by regulars so early reservation is recommended with exact details of your outfit's dimensions essential.
Hook-Up	10 amps - all pitches. Water & drainage - none.
Motorhomes	Ideal for motorhomes as site has motorhome service point and is walking distance of town and beach.
Swimming pools	Attractive pool area behind reception 20m x 10m with paddling pool divided from main area by barrier. Good sun terrace with sunloungers.
Activities on site	Two children's play areas. Table tennis. Volleyball, Boules pitch. Tennis 300m.
Entertainment	Aquagym and water polo in July/August only. Clubs and bars with music, cinema 500m.
Sanitary facilities	Two well maintained toilet blocks. The main block is modern with toilet seats and toilet paper, although there are still a couple of French style toilets in the smaller block. Push button temperature control showers with hooks and shelves. Individual wash cubicles. Disabled facilities. Baby room. Laundry facilities. Chemical waste point.
Services	Bread in the morning. Shops within walking distance. Bar/Restaurant La Paillotte just outside the gate on beach site open all season. Take-away hatch on site. Barbecues allowed. Dogs accepted in low season only, not July/August. Internet and Wi-Fi in town.
Accommodation	9 chalets and 10 mobilehomes.
Tour operators	None.

Excursions/Places to visit
La Tranche, Talmont St Hilaire, Les Sables d'Olonne, Avrillé, La Rochelle. La Venise Verte.

€ Prices 2010	High	Low
Pitch + 2	27.50	19.50
Hook Up 10A	5	5

Directions
From La Roche-Sur-Yon, take the D747 to La Tranche-sur-Mer. On arrival in La Tranche you come to a roundabout take the second exit towards the beach. At the T-junction turn right following signs to the campsite and then follow the road round to the left. The site entrance is on your left after 500m.

Address 10 Rue du Pertuis 85360 La Tranche-sur-Mer

www.camping-baiedaunis.com
email info@camping-baiedaunis.com

GPS N 46° 20' 47 W 01° 25' 55

Tel 02. 51. 27. 47. 36

Coulon, Camping La Venise Verte ****

Location Coulon 1km. A10 exit 33 20km. A83 exit 9 14km. La Rochelle 63km.

Open 1st Apr to 31st Oct

Pitches 140 (115 touring)

Situated in the heart of France's "Green Venice", an area criss-crossed by ancient waterways and canals, this spacious site is a verdant haven of peace and quiet. Le Marais Poitevin abounds in wildlife and is an ideal destination to explore by boat, by bike or on foot. The friendly owner prides herself on the site's sustainable tourism credentials and it is one of only a handful of establishments to be awarded the European eco-label for important activities such as water conservation, energy saving and waste management.

Clef Verte - Via Natura - European Eco-label

Site suitable for all ages, particularly nature lovers, cyclists and walkers.

Pitches	Flat and grassy laid out in straight alleys. There is an open feel as they are divided by occasional shrubs and trees and the majority are 80 -100m². For an extra fee there are ten 180m² pitches available. Not heavily shaded.
Hook-Up	10 amps, water & drainage - all pitches.
Motorhomes	Motorhome service point. Ideal as walking distance of Coulon and canals.
Swimming pools	A medium-sized rectangular pool with a sun terrace and a few sunloungers. Paddling pool.
Activities on site	Cycle hire. Canoe hire. Children's play area. Volleyball. Boules pitch. Table tennis. Indoor games area with pool and table football. TV area. Nearby: good selection of cycle tracks and routes marked out for ramblers. Canoeing and punting on canals. Fishing.
Entertainment	In the high season organised activities include sporting competitions, art classes and massage.
Sanitary facilities	One unisex toilet block, maintained to a high standard. Push button, temperature control showers with hook and shelf. Toilet paper on wall outside cubicle. Individual wash basins. Disabled facilities. Baby room. Laundry. Chemical waste point.
Services	Pre-order bread. A few basics available but no real shop. Bar, traditional cuisine, take-aways and snacks available in restaurant, "la Nappe à Carreaux", open all season. Barbecues allowed. Dogs accepted. Internet. Wi-Fi free throughout site. Number plate recognition entrance barrier.
Accommodation	25 mobile homes, some privately owned.
Tour operators	None.

Excursions/Places to visit
Church in Coulon, network of canals. Musée des Tumulus de Bougon 40km. Place de la Brèche in Niort, 10km. La Rochelle, Le Puy du Fou.

€ **Prices 2010**	**High**	**Mid**	**Low**
Pitch + 2 10A	24	22	18
Large Pitch	5	-	-

Directions
Exit 33 from A10. Follow signs to Marais Poitevin, join N11 and take 1st exit signposted to Coulon on D1. In town turn left on to D123 at traffic lights and then take ring road towards Arcais. From A83, take D148 towards Niort. Turn right onto D25 towards Coulon. The campsite is on the west side of Coulon and is well signposted from the town.

Address 178 Route des Bords de Sèvre, 79510 Coulon

www.camping-laveniseverte.com
email accueil@camping-laveniseverte.fr

GPS N 46° 18' 53 W 00° 36' 32

Tel 05.49.35.90.36

Eymouthiers, Les Gorges du Chambon ****

Location Angoulême 40km. Montbron 8km. Limoges 99km.

Open 24th Apr to 18th Sept   **Pitches** 120 (80 touring)

This site is a real gem as it combines fabulous views over the surrounding Charente countryside, spacious pitches, a warm welcoming atmosphere, excellent facilities and an eco-friendly environment. The Petit family have created a holiday centre where there is strong emphasis on the importance of nature and respect for our verdant surroundings. You cannot fail to be impressed on arrival by the beautiful courtyard, laid out with flowers and shrubs as an ornamental garden. The services are housed in attractive stone-faced farm buildings and the grounds are very well maintained.
Clef Verte - Via Natura - European Eco-label

Site suitable for those who enjoy the comforts of a top class site in a quiet rural atmosphere.

Pitches	Very generous sized grassy pitches up to 130m², not hedged but divided by the occasional trees and shrubs, giving a wonderful feeling of spaciousness, particularly on the pitches towards the back of the site. Some do slope gently.
Hook-Up	10 amps & water - all pitches. Water & drainage - 8 pitches.
Motorhomes	Motorhome service point. No major tourist attractions or towns in walking distance.
Swimming pools	A rectangular pool 18m x 7m so good for a swim. Small paddling pool 5m x 5m. Sun terrace with sun loungers.
Activities on site	Two free tennis courts, one on site, suitable for beginners only and a second one in good condition 100m from the site. 9-hole mini-golf. Volleyball. Pony rides with charge. Table tennis. Giant chess set. Games room with table football and electronic games. Excellent children's play area. Category 1 fishing in river with permit. Shallow area on river with pebbly beach and shade. Walks direct from the site which take between 15 mins and 40 mins. An outdoor centre next to site offers activities including kayaking, climbing, mountain biking, archery etc.
Entertainment	In high season children's club 6 - 12yrs every afternoon, family team games from 5:30pm to 6:30pm, musical evenings once a week, barbecues or theme meals once a week in restaurant. Daily walks with local nature guide, free of charge. Accompanied visits round region by car.
Sanitary facilities	Two fairly old but extremely well-appointed, unisex toilet blocks, kept immaculately clean and managed in an eco-friendly way. Push button, temperature control showers with hooks and shelf. Individual wash basins, toilets with seats and toilet paper. Very attractive washing-up area. Washing machines and tumble dryers. Chemical waste point.
Services	Small shop. Bar. Take-away and restaurant with pretty terrace also open to public, with good choice at reasonable prices. Barbecues allowed. Dogs accepted. Internet.
Accommodation	20 mobilehomes/chalets. 5 Trigano tents. 8 permanent caravans, all at edge of the site.
Tour operators	One Dutch company on 8 pitches.

Excursions/Places to visit
Golf course 6km. Piégut-Pluviers 15km.
La Rochfoucauld 22k, Nontron 28km.
Brantôme 48km.

€ Prices 2010	Peak	High	Mid	Low
Pitch + 2	27.15	23.10	18	14.60
Hook Up 6A	3.70	3.70	3.70	3.70

Directions
From N10. Leave the N10 at the Mansle exit. At Mansle follow signs for La Rochefoucauld then to Montbron. At Montbron take the D6/D91 towards Piegut-Pluviers as far as the small village of La Tricherie. As you enter La Tricherie the campsite is signposted to your left.

Address Eymouthiers, 16220 Montbron

www.gorgesduchambon.fr
email gorges.chambon@wanadoo.fr

GPS N 45° 39' 35 E 00° 33' 28   **Tel** 05.45.70.71.70

St. Just-Luzac, Camping Séquoia Parc ****

Location Marennes 5km. Royan 22km. Rochefort 20km. Saintes 40km.

Open 12th May to 5th Sept

Pitches 426 (151 touring)

A fabulously maintained Castels site set up in the grounds of a mid-19th century château. The well preserved stone outbuildings form a magnificent courtyard dominated by an imposing entrance porch. An abundance of beautiful trees, shrubs and flowers further give the site a very verdant welcoming atmosphere. Although a top quality site in terms of facilities, it is a very busy particularly in high season. It attracts large numbers of Dutch and British families and is at least a 15-minute drive to decent beaches.

Site suitable for active families seeking both daytime and evening entertainment, not for those seeking a quiet peaceful atmosphere.

Pitches	Flat, grassy, divided by hedges and generous in size varying from 120m² - 200m². The vast majority of the touring pitches are all together, away from the mobilehomes.
Hook-Up	6 amps - 128 pitches. 10 amps water & drainage - 123 pitches.
Motorhomes	No motorhome service point and need to drive to get to both beaches and shops.
Swimming pools	A huge but attractive 2000m² aqua complex which is supervised. It consists of four main pool areas, three heated, one giant slide with three lanes, a further large toboggan, a paddling pool with toddler's slide, a jacuzzi, geysers, lazy river and mini-waterfalls. Large sun terrace with sun loungers.
Activities on site	Cycle and go-kart hire. Two tennis courts. All weather sports pitch, football and volleyball fields. Boules pitch. Excellent children's play area. Table tennis, pool tables. Video games room. Massage and relaxation sessions.
Entertainment	Organised games and competitions including football and waterpolo. Two children's clubs, 4-7yrs and 8 -13yrs. Pony club with riding lessons. Entertainment every evening including concerts of traditional local folk music, rock and blues etc, cabarets, kid's theatre, open-air disco, kid's mini-disco, traditional folk dancing, quizzes and bingo.
Sanitary facilities	Three very well appointed unisex toilet blocks which are attractively laid out and usually immaculately clean. Toilets with toilet paper. Some showers and washbasins together in each block. Temperature control showers with hooks. Disabled facilities. Baby room. Separate laundry. Chemical waste point.
Services	Vival supermarket. Small shop selling regional products. Take-away, which is very busy in high season. Attractive bar/restaurant situated in courtyard of château. Barbecues allowed. Dogs accepted. Internet Point and Wi-Fi.
Accommodation	Selection of mobile homes and chalets from 4 – 7 persons.
Tour operators	9 different companies including at least 3 Dutch ones.

Excursions/Places to visit

Marennes is an oyster fishing centre. Beaches on Côte Sauvage 12km. Zoo at La Palmyre 20km. Ile de Ré and Ile d'Oléron. Cognac. La Rochelle 50km.

€ Prices 2010	Peak	High	Mid	Low
Pitch + 2 & 6A	45	33	22	19
10A Water & Dr	3	3	3	3

Directions

From A10 at Saintes take exit 35 onto N150 to Royan and Ile d'Oléron. After 2km take a right fork from N150 onto D728 in to Marennes. Continue along this road for about 33km to village of St. Just Luzac. The site is 1km on the other side of the village signposted to the right. From Rochefort. Take D733 to Marennes. At St Agnant turn right onto the D123. Continue along this road for 12km and then take a sharp left turn onto D728. The site is a short distance on the left.

Address 17320 Saint Just Luzac

GPS N 45° 48' 40 W 01° 03' 40

www.sequoiaparc.com
email info@sequoiaparc.com
Tel 05.46.85.55.55

Saint Augustin, Le Logis du Breuil ***

Location Royan 8km. Saintes 40km. Rochefort 44km. La Rochelle 74km.

Open 15th May to 30th Sept   **Pitches** 370 (310 touring)

Although a fairly large site with a large number of British visitors, it does not feel commercial at all. Situated on the edge of a pine forest in a rural setting and just a 10-minute drive from the wonderful sandy beaches of La Grande Côte, the site was once a farm and has a fabulously spacious feel. It is laid out along three sides of a grassy open field leaving plenty of space between the pitches and the converted outbuildings which house the reception, games room and other services. You can expect a warm welcome from the friendly Gagnard family who are keen to maintain a quiet, peaceful, atmosphere.

Site suitable for all ages, but does not cater for teenagers.

Pitches	Generous sized pitches up to 200m², flat and grassy, divided by the odd tree or shrub, not heavily hedged, giving nice open feel, but majority have very little shade.
Hook-Up	3 or 6 Amps (or 10 Amps low season only) - all pitches. Water & drainage - 10 pitches.
Motorhomes	Motorhome service point. Walking distance of supermarket. 5km cycle track to beach.
Swimming pools	An attractively laid-out pool complex at the entrance to the site. A good size for swimming with generous sun terrace and a handful of sun loungers. Paddling pool.
Activities on site	Cycle hire. Excellent children's play area. Tennis. All weather sports pitch. Basket ball. Volleyball. Archery. Indoor games area with table tennis. Boules pitch. Nearby: horseriding, windsurfing, sailing and fishing.
Entertainment	Aquagym. Organised meals in "salle de réunion" and excursions to Cognac and local vineyards. No other entertainment.
Sanitary facilities	Four toilet blocks, all built in a similar style. They are not especially well appointed, but are very clean and well maintained. Push button showers, no temperature control and no hooks. Water can be a bit tepid in high season and you may have to queue. Some individual wash basins and some open ones. Toilet paper outside cubicle. Laundry. Chemical waste point.
Services	Well-stocked shop. Bar, take-away, snack with attractive terraced area. Fridge hire. Gas Barbecues only. Dogs accepted. Internet and Wi-Fi Point in reception.
Accommodation	60 mobile homes. Winter caravan storage.
Tour operators	None.

Excursions/Places to visit
Beaches of La Côte de Beauté, lively bars and restaurants in Royan, zoo at La Palmyre, Cognac 40km. Rochefort, La Rochelle.

Directions
Arriving on the N150 from Saujon or the D733 from Rochefort, take the D25 Royan ringroad in the direction of La Palmyre and St Palais-sur-Mer. Continue following these signs through 3 roundabouts, following the sign for St Augustin on leaving the third one. At the next set of traffic lights fork right on the D145 in the direction of St Augustin. Go throught the hamlet of Lafont, then turn left. The campsite is situated opposite the temple.

€ Prices 2010	High	Mid	Low
Pitch + 2	21	18.65	14.85
Hook Up 6A	4.75	4.25	4.05

Address 17570 Saint-Augustin-sur-Mer

GPS N 45° 40' 29 W 01° 05' 45

www.logis-du-breuil.com
email camping.logis-du-breuil@wanadoo.fr
Tel 05.46.23.23.45

Vaux-sur-Mer, Le Val Vert ***

Location Royan 3.5km. Vaux 300m. La Rochelle 64km. Bordeaux 140km.

Open 9th Apr to 21st Sept

Pitches 166 (95 touring)

As its name suggests, this site has been chosen because of its delightful verdant setting just a 15-minute walk from the beach and 300m from local shops. You can be sure of a warm welcome from the friendly owners, who prefer to maintain a quiet atmosphere. The rural feel of the site is a pleasant surprise after the access through a small housing estate. A small stream runs next to the site with a park on the other side and an entrance just 200m away. It is an ideal spot for a relaxing stroll.

Site suitable for all ages.

Pitches	Flat, grassy pitches divided by low hedges varying in size from 80m² - 100m². Some overlook the stream running along one side of the site, but there is no direct access to the stream. Access to pitches for large outfits in high season can be difficult.
Hook-Up	6 or 10 amps - all pitches. Water & drainage - none.
Motorhomes	Good for motorhomes as walking distance of local shops and and beach. Motorhome service point.
Swimming pools	Good sized heated pool and paddling pool. Sun terrace with chairs but no sun loungers.
Activities on site	Cycle hire. Good children's play area. Table tennis outside. Volleyball court. Games room with pool, table football and video games. Boules pitch. TV for big events only.
Entertainment	In July and August one dance and one karaoke evening a week, aquagym and children's games in the morning and petanque in the afternoon.
Sanitary facilities	Three well maintained unisex toilet blocks. Toilet seats but no toilet paper provided. Push button showers, no temperature control, no hooks, just a rail. Some individual wash basins. Disabled facilities. Laundry facilities. Chemical waste point.
Services	Small shop, bar restaurant, take-away. Terrace of bar overlooks pool. Charcoal barbecues not allowed, gas barbecues permitted. Dogs accepted. Internet and Wi-Fi connection in bar only.
Accommodation	Mixture of chalet and mobilehomes in one area of site.
Tour operators	None.

Excursions/Places to visit
Beaches at Nauzan, Saint-Palais-sur-Mer, le Platin, la Grande Côte, la Côte Sauvage. Golf course. Numerous cycle tracks. La Palmyre Zoo 3km. Cognac, La Rochelle, Rochefort.

Directions
From Saintes. Take the N150 to Royan. When you arrive at the D25 ring road turn right. At the second roundabout Le Sable take the third exit. Continue along this road crossing over the Bd du Générale de Gaulle and into Rue de la Roche. Fork right after 200m into Ave Frédéric Garnier and the site entrance is on your right after 200m.

€ **Prices 2010**	**High**	**Mid**	**Low**
Pitch + 3	28.20	24.20	17
Hook Up 6A	5.00	4.50	4.50

Address 108, Avenue Frédéric Garnier, B.P. 60457
Vaux-sur-mer17207 Royan
GPS N 45° 38' 38 W 01° 03' 48

www.val-vert.com
email camping-val-vert@wanadoo.fr
Tel 05.46.38.25.51

Vaux-sur-Mer, Camping le Nauzan Plage ****

Location Vaux 800m. Royan 5km. Bordeaux 141km. Saintes 44km. La Rochelle 80km.

Open 1st Apr to 30th Sept

Pitches 235 (169 touring)

This family-run site has been chosen primarily because it offers a unique combination of proximity to the beach and verdant setting. The huge sandy beach at Nauzan is 450m away and the pretty little stream running through the site, with a tiny island in the middle and overhanging weeping willows, gives it an almost rural feel. Royan is also only a bus ride away. Although there is organised family entertainment in the high season, the site offers a quiet relaxing, ambiance.

Site suitable for young families and couples.

Pitches	Flat, grassy, divided by low hedges and some trees. They vary in size up to a maximum of 100m² and are not heavily shaded. We would recommend that large outfits book in advance.
Hook-Up	10 Amps - all pitches. Water & drainage - none.
Motorhomes	No specific motorhome service point but proximity to beach and town make it a good choice for motorhomes.
Swimming pools	A medium-sized pool with small sunbathing area and a few sunloungers. Paddling pool.
Activities on site	Cycle hire. Children's play area. Table tennis, volleyball. Boules pitch. TV Room. Fishing in stream.
Entertainment	There is a programme of activities in July and August including aquagym, games for the children, and theme evenings that always finish by midnight and do not involve amplified music. There are night clubs and a casino nearby.
Sanitary facilities	There are four toilet blocks scattered throughout the site. Although not ultra-modern, they are well equipped and maintained to a high standard. Ladies and gents are separate. Showers are push-button, temperature control, with a shelf, rail and hook. Separate wash cubicles and toilet paper provided. Disabled facilities. Baby room. Laundry. Chemical waste point.
Services	Small shop, bazaar selling beach items, bakery, bar/snack, pizzeria – open mid-June to end August. Fridge hire. Walking distance of restaurants and bars. Barbecues allowed. Dogs accepted. Internet and Wi-Fi.
Accommodation	66 mobile homes mostly situated round perimeter of site.
Tour operators	None.

Excursions/Places to visit

Beaches at Nauzan, Saint-Palais-sur-Mer, le Platin, la Grande Côte, la Côte Sauvage. 18 hole golf course. Numerous cycle tracks. Zoo at La Palmyre 3km. Cognac, La Rochelle, Rochefort. Ile de Ré and Ile d'Oléron.

Directions

From Saintes. Take the N150 to Royan. Join the D25 ring road heading west. At the second roundabout take the third exit along rue de la Roche. Turn right along Bd du Générale de Gaulle. After 300m turn left into rue Ambroise Paré which runs into Ave de Nauzan Plage and the site is 500m on your left.

€ Prices 2010	Peak	High	Mid	Low
Pitch + 2	32	24	18	17
Hook Up 10A	5.50	5	5	5

Address 39, Avenue de Nauzan Plage, 17640 Vaux-sur-Mer.

www.campinglenauzanplage.com
email camping.le.nauzan@wanadoo.fr

GPS N 45° 38' 34 W 01° 04' 19

Tel 05.46.38.29.13

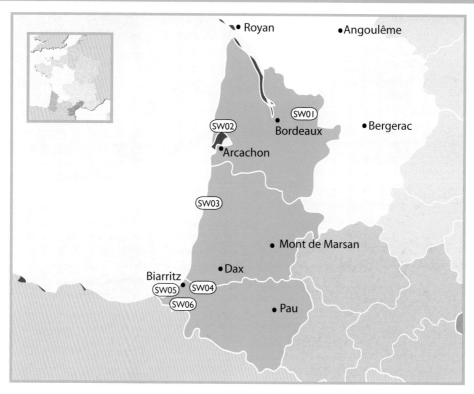

• Royan
•Angoulême

SW01
SW02
Bordeaux
•Bergerac

•Arcachon

SW03

• Mont de Marsan

•Dax
Biarritz
SW05 SW04
SW06
• Pau

Picture Opposite - Biarritz lighthouse

Places of Interest - South West France

The Gironde, Landes and Pyrénées Atlantiques form the coast of South West France. A region of wide open spaces renowned for its ocean, forests, vineyards, lakes and mountains. Together with the Dordogne and the Lot-et-Garonne, it is an area collectively known as Aquitaine. It stretches from the Gironde estuary and Bordeaux in the north to Biarritz and the Pyrénées mountains in the south. Surfers will enjoy the impressive Atlantic breakers which pound the coast while the lagoons and lakes are a paradise for watersports enthusiasts particularly windsurfers and yachtsmen.

Lakeside beach

The Gironde is the largest department in France covering an area of 6,650 sq. miles. It boasts 119km of magnificent Atlantic surf fringed with beautiful sandy beaches and its million acres of pine forest offer a wealth of cycle tracks and country walks.

The Medoc is renowned for its vineyards and impressive châteaux. Here, practically every town and village lays claim to a great vintage - a little wine tasting is highly recommended.

Bassin d'Arcachon is a vast indentation in the pine forest and has the air of a lagoon. It is subject to the tides, and is protected from the winds by the Cap Ferret headland. The "bassin" owes its unique character to the endless sandbanks uncovered at low tide. There are over 10km of sandy beaches leading up to the Dune du Pyla which is the highest sand dune in Europe: 2.7kms long, 500m wide and 104m high. There are two ways to reach the summit, either an arduous walk up the sand or to climb the 190 steps. It is certainly worth the effort to witness the views, especially the western horizon at sunset. Two spots near Arcachon which may be of interest are **Aqualand at Gujan Mestras**, which is great for children and **Le Teich Ornithological Park**, a site of international importance in terms of the conservation of endangered birds, where over 260 species have settled.

Bordeaux, the capital of the Gironde department occupies a crescent-shaped bend of the Garonne river. The marriage of Eleanor of Aquitaine to Henry II of England in 1152 meant that Bordeaux became an English dominion. The English discovery of the pale red liquid known as "claret" led to an overwhelming demand for the wine. Indeed wine was an everyday drink in England at that time. The town itself has beautiful wide avenues and esplanades bordered by elegant buildings. The old quarter with its narrow picturesque streets are enlivened by a thousand small shops and restaurants.

Basque beach

St Emilion situated in a region of vineyards and hillsides crowned with châteaux owes its unique charm to the stone ramparts, steep narrow streets, delightful little squares and houses also built of old stones.

St Emilion wines

Landes A department with over 100km of lovely sandy beaches and a variety of inland lakes but not renowned for interesting places to visit. It is dominated by the largest expanse of pine forest in Europe covering an area of over 600,000 hectares and also boasts about 2,300 hours of sunshine a year, 1,440 of those between 1st May and 31st October.

Surfers

The Beaches of the West Coast The wonderful foaming breakers of the beaches attract all levels of surfers and swimmers. It is, however, important to remember that the pounding sea can be dangerous for those who are not strong swimmers and a red flag is always displayed on the beaches when the tide is going out as there is a fierce undertow. It is foolish to ignore these red warning flags.

The lakes of **Sanguinet** and **Léon** are safe for swimming and are perfect for windsurfers, yachtsmen, canoeists and anglers. The flatness of the surrounding countryside and many long straight stretches of road make sightseeing by bicycle the perfect way to view the region - not too strenuous but a great way to keep fit. The villages and towns all have a special French charm.

Dax founded by the Romans is the largest spa in France. The hot spring itself with 2,660 cubic metres of water at 63°C is a very impressive sight and famous for its curative properties. The Gothic cathedral, the arena and archeological collections at the Borda museum are all worth a visit.

St Jean de Luz

Pyrénées Atlantiques A department which has about 30km of coast on the Atlantic Ocean, has a border with Spain and is delightfully situated in the foothills of the Pyrénées. It is also steeped in its own unique Basque culture. You are perfectly situated for quick visits across the border into Spain and for day trips into the mountains to appreciate the beautiful and dramatic scenery of the Pyrénées.

Bayonne is right on the borders of the Landes and Basque country and has a long tradition as a port. There is a wealth of medieval architecture demonstrating both Gascon and Basque influences. The walled town contains many treasures including the glorious Gothic Cathédrale Ste Marie famous for its spires and charming cloisters.

Biarritz is a beautifully elegant town famed for its hortensia flowers, and the attractive promenades along the cliffs, in particular the one starting from the Grand Plage, around the Rocher de la Vierge to the southern beaches. This is the surfing centre of France and probably Europe. It also has 4 golf courses within a 15km radius of the town.

Saint Jean-de-Luz is not only a picturesque fishing port but also one of the most fashionable and cosmopolitan resorts in France. It has a medieval background and evidence of Spanish and Moorish influence. Its beautiful white houses contrast with the green slopes of the Basque mountains and the magnificent bay is surrounded by beaches and protected by dykes. St Jean-de-Luz is a town of traditions and here you will discover all the specialities of the Basque game of Pelote.

Oloron Sainte Marie A typical Haut Béarn town just a few miles inland was an important stopping place on the Road to Santiago de Compostella worth a visit to see its cathedral.

Le Train de la Rhune A 4.2km tourist train ride up La Rhune which is 900m high and on the edge of the Pyrenean foothills, near Ascain. www.rhune.com Two caves worth visiting in the foothills of the Pyrénées are: the **Grottes de Betharram** and the **Grottes d'Isturitz et d'Oxocelhaya.**

www.tourisme-aquitaine.fr
www.tourisme-gironde.fr
www.tourismelandes.com
www.bearn-basquecountry.com

St. Emilion, Domaine de la Barbanne ***

Location St. Emilion 3km. Bordeaux 50km. Angoulême 124km. Bergerac 78km.

Open 9th Apr to 20th Sept   **Pitches** 160 (140 touring)

Just a 5-minute drive from the delightful medieval town of St Emilion, you will find the perfect site for keen anglers, wine connoisseurs and nature lovers. Situated in the heart of the vineyards on the edge of a picturesque fishing lake, the site is attractively laid out with pretty plants, shrubs and trees. An attractive pool complex is ideal for the children and a welcome dip after a busy day wine-tasting or sight-seeing. The enthusiastic owner has created a warm family atmosphere and is proud of her eco-friendly management and organisation.
Clef Verte - Via Natura

Site suitable for all ages, particularly anglers and nature lovers.

Pitches	Flat, grassy, varying in shape but generally about 100m². They are divided by low hedges and shrubs with access via wide alleys. The more mature pitches near the lake have more shade.
Hook-Up	10 amps - all pitches. Water & drainage - 10 pitches. Hardstanding - 19 pitches.
Motorhomes	Motorhome service point. Walking and cycling distance of local vineyards. Free bus shuttle to St Emilion.
Swimming pools	Attractive heated pool with a tropical theme decorated with banana trees and exotic plants. Waterslide. Good sun terrace with comfortable sun loungers and straw parasols. Paddling pool with a small slide and a clown showering water.
Activities on site	Cycle hire. Two tennis courts and BMX cycle track, 200m from site - all free. Fitness circuit. Mini-golf. Giant chess set. Fishing in lake, no permits required and good variety of fish. Canoes and pedalos to hire. Volleyball. Boules pitch. Table football, table tennis. Wooden beamed communal room with TV, microwave and washbasin. Free shuttle bus into St Emilion at 10 am and 2 pm daily.
Entertainment	Children's club 4 -12yrs in July/August. Guided vineyard walks with wine tastings. Walking and cycling tours, canoeing on Dordogne.
Sanitary facilities	Two toilet blocks with separate ladies and gents, one is quite old but well maintained with mixture of English and French style toilets. The other is more modern. Push button, temperature control taps in showers and washbasins. Hooks in both. Toilets with paper. Disabled facilities. Baby room. Laundry facilities. Chemical waste point.
Services	Small shop selling basics (pre-order bread), also sells good selection of local wines at same price as châteaux. Bar and small restaurant with a basic menu also provides take-away. Barbecues allowed. Dogs accepted. Internet and Wi-Fi next to reception and behind restaurant.
Accommodation	20 mobile homes.
Tour operators	None.

Excursions/Places to visit
St Emilion, various châteaux for wine-tasting. Bordeaux, Blaye. Spectacular festival of the proclamation of the grape harvest in middle of September.

Directions
The campsite is situated 3km north of St-Emilion on the road to Montagne and is well signposted along this road.

St-Emilion town centre bans caravans, so approach the site by taking the D243 from Libourne or from Castillion on the D936.

€ Prices 2010	High	Mid	Low
Pitch + 2	30	26.50	18
Hook Up 10A	5	4	4

Address Route de Montagne, 33330 St Emilion

www.camping-saint-emilion.com
email barbanne@wanadoo.fr
Tel 05.57.24.75.80

GPS N 44° 55' 00 W 00° 08' 31

Arès, La Cigale ***

Location Centre of Arès 800m. Arcachon 45km. Bordeaux 54km. Biarritz 202km.

Open 7th May to 26th Sept

Pitches 74 (41 touring)

A delightful little site in a wooded setting and walking distance of the centre of Arès. There is easy access to a small lagoon on the Bassin d'Arcachon and you are only a 15-minute drive from magnificent surfing beaches. It is a great area for cycling and walking. The site is beautifully maintained with pretty floral displays. It offers a quiet friendly atmosphere where the owners always make you feel welcome. You may be aware of some traffic noise from the adjacent road.

Site suitable for all ages, particularly couples and young children.

Pitches	Flat and grassy, all a minimum of 100m² divided by a mixture of hedges, small fences and flower beds. All pitches have some shade. Accommodation is on two separate areas of the site.
Hook-Up	6 or 10 amps - all pitches. Water & drainage - 15 pitches.
Motorhomes	Ideal as walking distance of town and has motorhome service point.
Swimming pools	Pretty little pools but unheated, open end May until September. Rectangular swimming pool 12m x 6m, paddling pool 8m x 4m. Sun terrace with sun loungers.
Activities on site	Football, volleyball, small children's play area. Table tennis, games room. Small animal park for the children. Nearby: Tennis and horse-riding 1.7km, mini-golf 3.5km.
Entertainment	Children's club and small programme of sporting competitions in July/August.
Sanitary facilities	One unisex toilet block, looking a bit dated now but well equipped and kept immaculately clean. A family room. Push button showers, no temperature control, hooks but no shelf. Toilets with seats and toilet paper. Some individual wash cubicles. Disabled facilities. Washing machine and tumble dryer. Chemical waste point.
Services	Bar open 08:00 to 23:00 each day serves drinks and snacks. Bread and croissants - order previous evening. Pizzas to eat in or take away July/ August only. Shops and restaurants in Arès. Barbecues allowed. Dogs accepted . Internet. Wi-Fi for 2010.
Accommodation	8 chalets and 14 mobile homes.
Tour operators	None.

Excursions/Places to visit
Cycle tracks and forest walks nearby. Atlantic surfing beaches 15 mins, Arcachon 40 mins. Bordeaux vineyards 45 mins. Teich Ornithological Park 15km, Cap Ferret 23km. Dune du Pilat 34km.

Directions
From Bordeaux. Take exit 10 from the ringroad on the D213 in the direction of Martignas. Continue on this road until you join the D106. Follow the D106 towards Arès and take the first exit to the town. In the town centre turn right towards Lège Cap-Ferret and the site is on your left after 500m. From Bayonne. Follow the A63 towards Bordeaux and exit at junction 23 onto the D5. Follow the D5 until you reach the junction with the D106. Turn left onto the D106 then continue as above.

€ Prices 2010	Peak	High	Mid	Low
Pitch + 2	30	27	22	20
Hook Up 6A	5.50	5.50	5.50	5.50

Address 53, Avenue du Général de Gaulle, 33740 Arès

www.camping-lacigale-ares.com
email contact@camping-lacigale-ares.com

GPS N 44° 46' 26 W 01° 08' 29

Tel 05.56.60.22.59

Biscarrosse, Domaine de la Rive ****

Location Sanguinet 3km. Biscarrosse 6km. Arcachon 25km. Bordeaux 70km. Biarritz 165km.

Open 1st Apr to 5th Sept

Pitches 640 (340 touring)

This large site has been selected because it is one of the best in the area and is still family-run. It has a unique west facing position on the banks of the magnificent lake Sanguinet with a beautiful sandy beach and access to a wide range of watersports. Although rather commercial in atmosphere (take a look at its website), it is very well run, well equipped and maintained to a high standard. The original pine forest has been replaced by a variety of new trees, so there is not much shade.
Clef Verte

Site suitable for active families and water sports enthusiasts.

Pitches	Flat, sandy divided by shrubs about 100m². Some pitches might be tight for large outfits. Have to be reserved for a minimum of 10 nights in July/August.
Hook-Up	6 amps - all pitches. Water & drainage - 200 pitches.
Motorhomes	Motorhome service point but need transport to get to sea. Everything provided on site.
Swimming pools	A huge aqua complex covering an area of over 2500m². Includes two outdoor basins for bathing and separate basin for waterslides, two fabulous paddling pools and good-sized covered pool plus a sun terrace. A large indoor pool with spa is planned for 2010.
Activities on site	Windsurfing, sailing, canoeing, banana sledging, water ski-ing. There are also pedalos and catamarans for hire. Jet ski is permitted from Mon - Thurs 3pm to 7pm. Cycle and pedal car hire. Skateboard park. All weather sports pitch. Bungee trampolines with small charge. Bouncy castle. Indoor games room. Two tennis courts - free low season. Table tennis. Excellent children's play area. Boules pitch.
Entertainment	A lively programme of organised activities throughout July/August including sporting competitions, children's clubs and dancing every night until midnight.
Sanitary facilities	There are four toilet blocks which are clean and respectable but nothing special. One has been modernised. Push button showers with no temperature control. Individual wash cubicles. No toilet paper. Some toilet seats missing. Disabled facilities. Baby room. Laundry facilities in all blocks. Chemical waste point.
Services	Small supermarket with a bakers. A newsagents that also sells gifts and souvenirs. Bar, restaurant, take-away. Hire shop called Locarive that hires out fridges, TVs, microwaves etc. Mooring on lake. ATM machine. Gas barbecues only allowed. Dogs accepted. Internet and Wi-Fi Point.
Accommodation	Chalets and mobile homes to hire.
Tour operators	Three British companies, inc a watersports operator, two French companies.

Excursions/Places to visit
Biscarrosse Plage 18km. Adventure Park in Biscarrosse. Aqualand at Gujan Mestras near Arcachon. Dune du Pilat. Vineyards of Médoc.

€ Prices 2010	Peak	High	Mid	Low	Off
Pitch + 2 & 6A	44	37	29.50	23.50	21.50
Water & Dr	3	3	3	3	3

Address Route de Bordeaux, 40600 Biscarrosse

GPS N 44° 27' 38 W 01° 07' 51

Directions
From Bordeaux. Exit 15 onto A63 in the direction of Arcachon. Exit 22 onto A66, then turn left onto D216 in the direction of Sanguinet and Biscarrosse. From Sanguinet take the D652 in the direction of Biscarrosse and 4km further on the site is well signposted off this road, situated on the banks of the Lac de Sanguinet on your right.

www.larive.fr
email info@camping-de-la-rive.fr
Tel 05.58.78.12.33

St Martin-de-Seignanx, Camping Lou P'tit Poun *** Map Ref SW04

Location Bayonne 7km. Biarritz 15km. Easy access from A63. Bordeaux 189km.

Open 1st Jun to 11th Sept   **Pitches** 168 (142 touring)

Hidden in the heart of the Landais countryside, staying on this site is like camping in a large garden, because of the wonderful variety of trees, shrubs and plants. The attractive entrance with a beautiful flower bed in front of the spacious reception is 200m from the main site. The site has a very verdant, spacious feel and the quiet, peaceful atmosphere is a pleasant contrast to the nearby bustling coastal resorts and beaches.

Site suitable for for young families and couples and those who prefer a quiet site away from the busy coastal resorts.

Pitches	Grassy pitches varying in size from 100m² - 130m², attractively laid out between shrubs and low hedges. Some slope very gently. There is some shade from a lovely variety of trees. If booking in advance reserve pitches on southern half of site to avoid slight noise from road. Large family pitches are also available.
Hook-Up	10 amps - all pitches. Water & drainage - 40 pitches.
Motorhomes	Motorhome service point, although would need own transport to reach towns and beaches.
Swimming pools	A medium-sized L-shaped pool overlooked by the bar, with small paddling pool. Sun terrace is part tiled and part decking with sun loungers.
Activities on site	Two children's play areas one by reception and another near bar. Half-court tennis. All weather sports pitch. Boules pitch. Games room with table tennis, table football and electronic games. TV.
Entertainment	In high season a children's club for 4 - 10 yr olds and organised evening entertainment such as folk music or dancing once a week.
Sanitary facilities	Two unisex toilet blocks. Push button showers, no temperature control, no hooks but hanging rail. Showers and washbasins closed 22.30 to 07.30. Toilet paper but no seats. Both are clean and respectable although nothing special. Disabled facilities. Baby room. Laundry facilities. Chemical waste point, but near washing up sinks.
Services	Basic items in small shop. Pre-order bread. Bar/snack in July and August only. Barbecues allowed. Dogs accepted. Internet and Wi-Fi not available. Other shops 5 - minute drive.
Accommodation	16 chalets, 10 mobile homes.
Tour operators	One Dutch company renting site's own mobile homes.

Excursions/Places to visit
Beaches and Bayonne 7km, Biarritz 15km, St Jean-de-Luz, Spain 40km.

Directions
From A63. Take exit 6 and join the D817 in the direction of Pau. The site is signed at the Leclerc supermarket. Continue on the D817 for approximately 5km and the site entrance is then clearly signed on your right off this road.

€ Prices 2010	High	Mid	Low
Pitch + 2	28.50	26.50	17.50
Family Pitch	7.50	7.50	7.50
Hook Up 10A	5	5	5

Address 40390 St Martin-de-Seignanx

GPS N 43° 31' 27 W 01° 24' 43

www.louptitpoun.com
email contact@louptitpoun.com
Tel 05.59.56.55.79

Bidart, Le Pavillon Royal ****

Location Biarritz 4km. Bayonne 18km. St Jean-de-Luz 11km. Spain 26km. A63 2km.

Open 15th May to 30th Sept   **Pitches** 303 (300 touring, 75 for tents only)

This site, named after the Royal Pavilion built in 1890 and perched on the hill next door, occupies a fabulous location overlooking a beautiful stretch of sandy beach. This beach is perfect for surfing and swimming and is accessed via a gate, operated with a magnetic card, and down some steps. It is surrounded by a pine forest and inland there are views of the Pyrénées. A long thin site laid out in attractive alleys, it slopes gently from the reception to the beach-view pitches. In spite of its size, it is a quiet peaceful site. There are also 7 golf courses within a 7km radius.

Site suitable for those who prefer a quiet site by the sea, surfers and golfers.

Pitches	Grassy, mostly flat, varying in shape and size with the majority at least 100m². There is some shade except on those nearer the beach.
Hook-Up	5 amps and water - 225 pitches. Tent only plots opposite reception - 75 pitches.
Motorhomes	Motorhome service point. Right on beach and walking distance of Bidart.
Swimming pools	A good-sized rectangular pool 20m x 10m good for swimming. Small square paddling pool. Sun terrace with sun loungers.
Activities on site	Children's play area. Indoor games area. Table tennis. Fitness room. Boules pitch. Surfing and swimming on supervised beach. Golf course next to site. Mini-golf 200m.
Entertainment	Very little organised entertainment. Music once a week in high season in the bar/restaurant.
Sanitary facilities	Four separate blocks, two for toilets alone and two for showers and washbasins. Not ultra modern, but very well maintained and clean. Mixture of English and French style toilets. Push button temperature control showers with hooks. Separate laundry. Chemical waste point.
Services	Well-stocked little shop. Bar, take-away, restaurant with terrace overlooking site, basic food but very acceptable - all open all season. Barbecues allowed. Dogs not accepted. Internet and Wi-Fi in restaurant.
Accommodation	3 chalets and 4 mini studios.
Tour operators	None.

Excursions/Places to visit
Bidart, Biarritz and its Musée de la Mer.
St Jean-de-Luz. Spain. Walking, rafting in the Pyrénées. Exploring little Basque villages.

Directions
Exit 4 from A63 on to D810 direction Bidart. Turn right at roundabout signposted to site on to D911 and then left after 500m just after pedestrian crossing. The site is well sign-posted.

€ Prices 2009	Peak	High	Mid	Low
Tent Pitch + 2	39	37	25	23
Hook Up 5A	49	45	30	29

Address Avenue du Prince de Galles, 64210 Bidart

www.pavillon-royal.com
email info@pavillon-royal.com
Tel 05.59.23.00.54

GPS N 43° 27' 17 W 01° 34' 39

Urrugne, Camping du Col d'Ibardin ***

Location Biarritz 27km. Hendaye beach 7km. Spanish border 200m. St Jean-de-Luz 8km.

Open 1st Apr to 30th Sept

Pitches 203 (135 touring)

A family-run site in the heart of the Basque countryside, literally on the border with Spain. You are welcomed by a lovely flowery entrance and the pitches are laid out in a beautiful wooded area of mature oaks. The site is just a short drive from Hendaye one of the best beaches in the area and enjoys magnificent views of the Pyrénées.
A pretty little stream runs through the middle of the site and the services are housed in attractive stone faced buildings with terracotta tiled roofs. There is a welcoming and peaceful ambiance.

Site suitable for families and couples who prefer a quiet atmosphere.

Pitches	Terraced pitches, most flat, some slope gently and vary in size up to at least 110m². Divided by hedges with good shade from oak trees. Reduction for 80m² pitches.
Hook-Up	5 or 10 amps - all pitches. Water & drainage - 100 pitches.
Motorhomes	Motorhome service point. Not walking distance of a town.
Swimming pools	Good sized rectangular shaped pool 22m x 10m, great for swimming. Good sun bathing terrace - no sun loungers. Planning new paddling pool complex for 2010.
Activities on site	Good children's play area. Tennis court. Table tennis. Area for football, volleyball and basketball. Boules. Pool table and electronic games in bar. Small animal park.
Entertainment	Some entertainment in high season. Children's club 5 – 10 yrs. Organised sports tournaments and music evenings once or twice a week.
Sanitary facilities	Two toilet blocks with separate ladies and gents. The block at the top of the site is attractively tiled and is more modern and has the Chemical waste point. Both blocks are well maintained, have push button, temperature control showers with hooks and some individual wash basins. No toilet paper. Disabled facilities. Baby room.
Services	Small shop selling basics. Pre-order bread. Take-away. Attractive bar/snack. Terrace overlooks pool. Barbecues allowed. Dogs accepted. Internet and Wi-Fi in bar.
Accommodation	42 mobile homes and 26 chalets spaciously laid out.
Tour operators	None.

Excursions/Places to visit
Coastal towns of Hendaye, St Jean-de-Luz, Biarritz and Bayonne. San Sebastian in Spain. Guggenheim in Bilbao 70 mins. Hiking in the mountains. Walks available directly from site up La Rhune the highest peak in the immediate area. The pilgrim's route to Santiago de Compostella passes nearby.

Directions
Exit 2 from A10 St-Jean-de-Luz sud, direction Urrugne, Col d'Ibardin on D810. In Urrugne turn left at roundabout on to D4. Continue for 4km and site is on your right.

€ Prices 2010	Peak	High	Mid	Low
Pitch + 2	32	25	20	17
Hook Up 5A	5.50	5.50	3.50	3.50

Address 64122 Urrugne

www.col-ibardin.com
email info@col-ibardin.com
Tel 05.59.54.31.21

GPS N 43° 20' 01 W 01° 41' 05

LOIRE

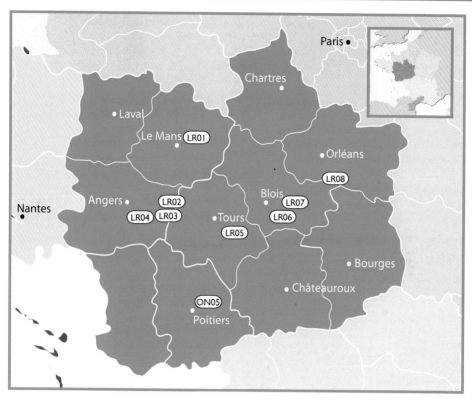

Picture opposite - Saumur

Places of Interest - Loire

The châteaux of the Loire are the main attraction of the area, but it is unlikely that the visitor would want to see more than a few of these beautiful stately buildings at one time. The valley is very attractive in its own right and offers beautiful scenery, fine food and local wines and history which pre-dates the châteaux. It is a very flat region and great for cycling, even for novices. The Loire river rises in the departement of the Ardèche and flows for more than 1,000 km before it reaches the Atlantic between Southern Brittany and the Vendée. However, it is only the stretch between Angers and Orléans that is generally thought of as the Loire Valley.

Orléans has no real château but is most famous for Joan of Arc. The stained glass windows of the Cathédrale Sainte Croix tell the story of the Maid of Orléans and how Joan raised the English Siege of Orléans in 1429.

Gien is an attractive town built on the banks of the Loire. The focal point is the delightful bridge which spans the river.

Château de Chambord

Château de Chambord is the best known and perhaps most fascinating of the châteaux of the Loire. From a distance the building looks quite symmetrical but once closer the visitor can appreciate that the 800 capitals and 365 towers, spires and turrets on each side are completely different. The exterior is intricate and impressive and the interior cavernous. One of the central features is an ingenious double spiral staircase. It was not until the 17th century that Chambord came alive. Louis XIV created a suite of linked apartments and being an absolute monarch, placed his bedchamber at the centre of the Château.

Château de Cheverny This is the most magnificently furnished château in the Loire, including a remarkable Louis XV grandfather clock, a rare Louis XIV commode, the bed used for lying-in-state in the King's bedroom, various old masters and 17th century Flemish tapestries. From the grounds of Cheverny you can take a balloon trip and experience magnificent views of the surrounding countryside. You can also visit the superb park around the château by boat and electric car.

Château de Chenonceau The unique beauty of this castle, spanning the river Cher is reflected in the water and is the region's most photographed and most graceful. Called the Château des Dames in the French history books, Chenonceau owes a large part of its charm to the women who built it. The lovely formal garden and the park add to the impression of delicate beauty and grace.

The **Châteaux** at **Amboise**, **Chaumont** and **Blois** are all worth a visit.

Between Tours and Saumur the following châteaux are definitely worth a visit.

Château d'Azay-le-Rideau, built on an island in the middle of the Indre, was constructed between 1518 and 1523 and is a perfect blend of the traditional and elements borrowed from Italian architecture.

Wine tasting at Vouvray

Château d'Ussé, also called the Castle of the Sleeping Beauty forms a magnificent white outline overlooking the Indre valley. Its unique appeal is to welcome visitors into a sumptuously decorated ancestral home which is still inhabited.

Château de Villandry This château is renowned for the elegance of its Renaissance architecture and magnificent gardens. It is the last of the Renaissance châteaux built on the banks of the Loire.

Château de Chinon The fortress of Chinon was built on the site of an ancient Celtic hill fort on a rocky spur overlooking the Vienne valley. The 14th century Tour de l'Horloge is a curiously narrow structure, 5m wide with a bell dating from 1399 that still rings the hour.

Chenonceau

Loches The fortress at Loches dates back to the XIth century. At 36 metres high, it is considered to be one of the most impressive keeps of the Norman period. The Gate House, the 14th century Governor's lodge, the Louis XIth tower crowned with its early artillery emplacements, "Cardinal Balue's" dungeon, the torture chamber together with video projections and computer generated images all combine to give first hand experience of the medieval era. The Logis Royal, built on a rocky spur, dominates the town.

Saumur is renowned for its beautiful château rising imperiously over the river. The town is also very attractive with good museums, including the Musée du Cheval where a fascinating exhibition of horses, saddle and tack from the around the world is held.

Angers Capital of Anjou and gateway to the Loire valley, Angers is distinguished as much for the richness of its heritage as for its cultural and economic dynamism. The towers of the imposing castle fortress dominate the town, and the streets, museums, gardens, shops, gastronomic restaurants, art festivals and student life give it a vibrant atmosphere.

For a different view of one or more of the châteaux, visit an evening Son-et-Lumière show. These take place regularly through the season at Azay-le-Rideau, Blois, Chambord and Chenonceau and during July and August at Amboise and Loches.

If you would like a change from visiting châteaux other places to visit include:

Zoo at Doué-la-Fontaine about 13km west of Saumur. This is open every day from the beginning of February until the beginning of November and is a wonderful natural environment for a collection of 65 species of animals.

Le Musée Cadillac 6km east of Langeais. Fifty models of this American car spanning the years from 1926 until the present time will thrill both the young and old.

Les Grottes Pétrifiantes de Savonnières 1km east of Villandry, are an underground world of waterfalls, lake, stalactites and stalagmites.

Le Mans to the north of the main area of the Loire. The circuit through the town is well known for various races, a 24-hour motor-cycle race, a 24-hour lorry race and of course the famous 24-hour car race which usually takes place in mid-June. 3,000 cars representing all the famous models Porsche, Ferrari, Bentley, Peugeot, Audi, Nissan etc. drive round the circuit, creating an amazing spectacle for car afficianados.

Cycling lin the Loire

If you want to see something of the late 20th and 21st century for a change, a full day visit to **FUTUROSCOPE**, is highly recommended. The site is full of permanent exhibitions and fascinating film show experiences. Do not miss the sound and light show staged every evening at about 10pm from the first Saturday in April until the end of August.

www.futuroscope.com
www.westernfrancetouristboard.com
www.loirevalleytourism.com

Sillé-le-Phillippe, Château de Chanteloup ****

Location Le Mans Centre 18km. Exit 7 on A11 24km. Caen 193km.

Open 1st Jun to 31st Aug

Pitches 120 (all touring)

Set in the spacious grounds of an attractive classic style château dating back to 1850, this Castels site is hidden in the heart of the French countryside. It is ideal for short stopovers as well as longer stays for those who prefer a relaxing non-commercial atmosphere. The woods surrounding the site provide plenty of space for walks. The château houses the reception, bar and indoor games. During the week leading up to the Le Mans 24-hour race the site is busy and very lively. High season activities and prices apply during this period.

Site suitable for all ages, particularly car enthusiasts during Le Mans.

Pitches	Two separate areas of pitches, some laid out in semi-circles which are not defined giving a very spacious feel, others backing on to woods are divided by low hedges. All flat, grassy and generous in dimension.
Hook-Up	6 amps - all pitches, long leads needed for some pitches. No water & drainage.
Motorhomes	Motorhome service point. Need to drive to get anywhere.
Swimming pools	An attractive little pool with semi-circle shape at one end. Paddling pool. Sunbathing terrace with parasols and sun loungers is on surrounding grass.
Activities on site	Tennis. Football, volleyball and basketball courts. Badminton. Boules pitch. Table tennis. Children's play area. Fishing in small pond. TV Room in château. Free access to "Club des Cèdres" which offers tennis, squash, badminton (15km).
Entertainment	In high season: organised sporting competitions, canoeing, horse-riding and wine tasting trips, barbecue evenings and other occasional theme evenings.
Sanitary facilities	One toilet block in outbuildings of château. Separate mens and ladies, very respectable and well maintained. Lever temperature control showers. Individual washbasins. Toilet paper. Disabled facilities. Baby room. Laundry. Chemical waste point.
Services	Shop for basics only in high season. Bread delivered by local baker in morning. Bar, take-away and restaurant in high season - need to pre-book. Barbecues allowed. Dogs accepted. Internet and Wi-Fi access.
Accommodation	Three apartments and two gîtes.
Tour operators	None.

Excursions/Places to visit
Car museum and medieval old town in Le Mans. La Ferté-Bernard, Montmirail, Asnières-on-Vègre.

Directions
From A11. Take exit 7 to Le Mans Centre and Tours, follow the D338 and then at the ringroad, take the D313 towards Le Mans, Le Mans-zone Industrielle-nord, Coulaines. After 3km exit onto the D301 towards Bonnetable. Continue for 10km past Savigné l'Evêque and the site is signposted to your right at the top of a rise after a further 2km.

€ Prices 2010	High	Low	Le Mans
Pitch + 2	28.50	21.90	36.10
Hook Up 6A	3.80	3.80	3.80

Address 72460 Sillé-le-Philippe

GPS N 48° 06' 19 E 00° 20' 27

www.chateau-de-chanteloup.com
email chanteloup.souffront@wanadoo.fr
Tel 02.43.27.51.07

Varennes-sur-Loire, L'Etang de la Brèche ****

Location Saumur 6km. A85 16km. Tours 62km. Le Mans 135Km. Poitiers 84km.

Open 12th May to 12th Sept   **Pitches** 201 (110 touring)

A delightful Castels site created in 1973 by the St Cast family in the verdant grounds of a restored manor house. The original stone fire place is still in the pool room. You will immediately be impressed by the feeling of spaciousness and the quality of the services. You can expect a warm welcome from the charming English speaking proprietor whose attention to detail makes it one of the best sites in the Western Loire. It is very popular with British and Dutch visitors, so not recommended for those seeking a French ambiance.

Site suitable for all ages particularly younger children.

Pitches	Very spacious, flat grassy pitches varying in size from 130m² - 170 m², laid out in wide alleys. Divided by plants and trees but not heavily hedged. Most have some shade with sun either in the morning or afternoon. Lovely open feel to camping area. Mobile homes are in a separate area.
Hook-Up	10 amps - all pitches. Water & drainage - 40 pitches.
Motorhomes	Motorhome service point. Need to drive or cycle to get anywhere.
Swimming pools	Attractive aqua complex: heated pool which can be covered in low season and cool weather, further pool with good waterslides, good-sized paddling pool. All with sun terrace and sun loungers.
Activities on site	Cycle, tricycle and go-kart hire. Two tennis courts. Mini-golf. 9-hole Swing-golf. Pony rides. All weather sports pitch. BMX track. Two fishing lakes - no permit required. Table tennis. Indoor games area with pool and electronic games. Bouncy castle. Excellent children's play areas. Boules pitch.
Entertainment	A variety of daytime activities are organised in the high season including a children's club, sports competitions and wine tasting. 5 cycle circuits go directly from the site.
Sanitary facilities	Three modern well-appointed toilet blocks always kept clean. Separate mens and ladies. Push button temperature control showers with hooks, shelf and stool. Some cubicles have showers and washbasins together. Toilet seats and toilet paper. Disabled facilities. Baby room. Laundry. Chemical waste point.
Services	Small supermarket which sells all essentials as well as freshly baked bread and croissants. Oak beamed bar with terrace. Take-away/pizzeria, restaurant with covered patio offering reasonably priced menus. Opening hours on sites web pages. Barbecues allowed. Dogs accepted. Internet and Wi-Fi.
Accommodation	30 of own 2 & 3-bedroomed mobile homes and 2 chalets for disabled.
Tour operators	64 pitches occupied by two British companies.

Excursions/Places to visit

Saumur 5km. Châteaux at Ussé, Azay-le-Rideau, Villandry and Le Lude. Zoo at Doué-la-Fontaine. Mushroom caves and troglogdyte villages.

€ Prices 2010	Peak	High	Mid	Low
Pitch + 2	33	25	19	16
Hook Up 10A	3.50	3	Incl	Incl

Address 49730 Varennes-sur-Loire

GPS N 47° 14' 50 W 00° 00' 02

Directions

From Saumur. Take the D952 in the direction of Tours. The campsite is situated on your left hand side 5km from Saumur.
From Tours. Exit A85 intowards Chinon on D749. At intersection with D952 turn towards Saumur and continue along the Loire. You pass a right hand turn to Varennes-sur-Loire. The campsite is on your right hand side 5km from this junction.

www.etang-breche.com.
email mail@etang-breche.com
Tel 02.41.51.22.92

St. Hilaire-St-Florent, Camping de Chantepie ****   Map Ref LR03

Location St Hilaire-St-Florent 2km. Saumur 6km. Tours 79km. Le Mans 133. Angers 44km.

Open 15th May to 11th Sept   **Pitches** 150 (106 touring)

Set amid the Anjou vineyards with magnificent views over the Loire river and valley, this site is run by an organisation that actively provides work for the disabled. They are responsible for the overall maintenance of the site, the cleaning, gardening and looking after the mini-farm. The high standard of care can be seen in the pretty displays of plants and flowers, well trimmed grass and hedges and well-kept sanitary facilities. The attractive old stone faced farm buildings form a partial courtyard and house the reception, shop and bar/snack. The site has a quiet atmosphere and a special rustic charm.

Site suitable for all ages, particularly couples and young families.

Pitches	Minimum 100m², flat, grassy and divided by plants, shrubs and small trees. Eight pitches have views of river with extra charge.
Hook-Up	10 amps - all pitches. Extra large 200m² - 220m² - 30 pitches. Water & drainage - 5 pitches.
Motorhomes	Motorhome service point but transport needed to visit area.
Swimming pools	A medium-sized L-shaped pool, good for swimming, paddling pool, tiled sun terrace with sun-loungers. Further greenhouse style covered pool.
Activities on site	Cycle hire. Mini-golf. Table tennis. Children's play area. Volleyball. Boules. Animal park with ducks, hens, goats and pigs. Walking distance from river. Fishing with permit.
Entertainment	Children's club in high season. Pony rides. Organised games and other family activities 3 times a week including a weekly canoe trip and wine-tasting from disabled organisation's own cooperative.
Sanitary facilities	One well appointed toilet block. Push button showers with deep bowls, no temperature control, hook, rail and shelf plus individual wash basins in one part, and toilets with toilet paper in separate area. Excellent disabled facilities. Baby room. Laundry. Chemical waste point
Services	Small shop for basics and wine. Bar/snack. Take-away, pizzeria. Barbecues allowed. Dogs accepted. Internet and Wi-Fi. St Hilaire has post office, bank, newsagents and a restaurant.
Accommodation	19 mobile homes, 11 Trigano tents and one chalet.
Tour operators	Dutch tour operator on 14 pitches.

Excursions/Places to visit
Saumur château 7km. Champigny vineyard 6km. Mushroom museum 1km. Cadre Noir riding school 2km. Zoo at Doué-la-Fontaine 19km. Château de Brézé 14km. Fontrevaud Abbey 18km.

Directions
Exit A85 at Saumur. Take the D347 towards Saumur Centre and after crossing the river, at the roundabout take the second exit D161 and turn slightly to the right to join the D751. Follow the road along the river for about 6km and then turn left into Rue de la Croix and left again into Route de Chantepie following signs to the site.

€ Prices 2010	High	Low
Pitch + 2	28	16
Hook Up 6A	2	2

Address Saint Hilaire-St-Florent, 49400 Saumur

GPS N 47° 17' 38 W 00° 08' 33

www.campingchantepie.com.
email info@campingchantepie.com
Tel 02.41.67.95.34

Concourson-sur-Layon, La Vallée des Vignes **** Map Ref LR04

Location Doué-la-Fontaine 3km. Saumur 26km. Angers 48km. Le Mans 140km. Tours 99km.

Open 1st Apr to 29th Sept   **Pitches** 86 (72 touring)

A delightful little site situated just outside the village of Concourson-sur-Layon amidst the vineyards and sunflowers. It is spaciously laid out in an open field and has a quiet peaceful atmosphere. You can expect a warm welcome from the charming English proprietors who also run the attractive little bar/restaurant in the evening. Inevitably the majority of visitors are British, so it is not recommended for those looking for a typically French ambiance.

Site suitable for all ages, particularly couples and young families.

Pitches	Flat, grassy spacious pitches divided by low hedges of shrubs and trees. Limited shade.
Hook-Up	6 amps, water & drainage - 48 pitches. Tents only - 24 pitches.
Motorhomes	Motorhome service point. Walking distance of small village.
Swimming pools	Pretty rectangular pool 16m x 8m open 15/5 – 15/9. Small paddling pool in high season only. Large sunbathing terrace with sun loungers.
Activities on site	9-hole mini-golf, half-court tennis, table tennis, boules pitch, basketball, volleyball. Good children's play area and sand pit. Zip wire for the older ones. Pet's corner. Fishing with permit in river Layon running along the back of the site.
Entertainment	Children's club in high season on demand. Some organised family entertainment in high season including wine tastings, barbecues, treasure hunts, boules and pool competitions. Theme nights with music.
Sanitary facilities	A well maintained unisex toilet block. Spacious showers, push button but no temperature control with hooks. Individual wash basins, toilet paper. Disabled facilities. Baby room. Washing machines. Chemical waste point.
Services	No shop, but bakery service from mid-June. Bar and Restaurant overlooking pool open every evening except Monday from 15/05 - 15/09. Bar open for drinks and snacks from 12pm during the peak season and 7pm during low season until late. A full set menu is available in the evening for dinner. Bakers, bar-tabac and church in village, 2 minutes walk. Barbecues allowed. Dogs accepted. Internet and Wi-Fi.
Accommodation	14 mobile homes, some for sale.
Tour operators	None.

Excursions/Places to visit
Zoo in Doué la Fontaine. Enormous variety of châteaux to visit nearby including Angers, Brissac, Brézé, Villandry, Azay-le-Rideau, Montreuil-Bellay and Monsoreau. Abbaye Royale de Fontevraud.

Directions
From Angers. Take N260 ringroad to the east of the town following signs for Poitiers. Go over the Loire river and take the D748 to Brissac-Quincé. In Brissac-Quincé at the end of the dual carriageway head straight on at the roundabout on D761 in the direction of Doué-la-Fontaine. At Doué-la-Fontaine take the first exit off the roundabout to Cholet and Concourson-sur-Layon. Continue through the village and just after crossing the bridge over the river Layon the campsite is signposted to your right. From Saumur. Take the D960 towards Cholet and past Doué-la-Fontaine. Then continue as above.

€ Prices 2010	High	Low
Pitch + 2	23	17.50
Hook Up 6A	4	4

Address La Croix Patron, 49700 Concourson-sur-Layon

GPS N 47° 10' 27 W 00° 20' 51

www.campingvdv.com
email campingvdv@aol.com
Tel 02.41.59.86.35

Loches, La Citadelle ****

Location Loches 500m. Tours 49km. Châteauxroux 69km. Chinon 76km.

Open 22nd Mar to 3rd Oct   **Pitches** 164 (117 touring)

This family run site has been chosen because of its unique position less than a 10-min walk along the River Indre to the centre of the royal medieval city of Loches. As the name of the site suggests it is famous for its magnificent château and ramparts. From the edge of the site, you have a view of the three towers, the Church, the Logis Royal and La Tour St Antoine. The weir and display of potted plants at the site entrance create a welcoming atmosphere and complement the lovely variety of trees around the pitches. The site could occasionally do with a bit more TLC.

Site suitable for all ages particularly couples and young families.

Pitches	Flat and grassy, divided by low hedges and split into two separate areas of 86 standard pitches 90m² - 110m² and 31 luxury pitches 130m² - 200m² . The large pitches have very little shade.
Hook-Up	10 amps - 72 pitches. 16 amps, water & drainage - 31 luxury pitches.
Motorhomes	Motorhome service point. Ideal for motorhomes as everything within walking distance.
Swimming pools	Small aqua complex on site with heated pool and paddling pool. Sun terrace with sun loungers and parasols. Large indoor municipal pool at entrance to site with charge.
Activities on site	Good children's play area. Volleyball/badminton area. Boules pitch. Table tennis. Sauna. Games room with electronic games. TV. Fishing with permit. Nearby: Cycle hire. Tennis.
Entertainment	A variety of organised entertainment in July/August including a children's club, sports activities, wine and cheese tasting. There are occasional evening concerts, and a night visit to Loches once a fortnight.
Sanitary facilities	Three toilet blocks. Push button temperature control showers with hooks and rail. Individual wash basins, toilets with seats and toilet paper. Block by swimming pool has some family rooms - showers and washbasins together. Disabled facilities. Baby room. Washing machines and tumble dryers. Chemical waste point.
Services	No shop but pre-order bread and croissants. Bar/snack which serves take-aways and pizzas open from mid-June. Shops, bars and restaurants in town. Barbecues allowed. Dogs accepted Internet and Wi-Fi.
Accommodation	28 mobilehomes, chalets and tents. 19 privately owned mobilehomes.
Tour operators	None.

Excursions/Places to visit
Loches and numerous châteaux within a 50km radius including Chenonceau, Amboise, Villandry, Azay-le-Rideau. Beauval animal park 34km.

Directions
From the North. Take the ringroad to the west of the town following signs to the campsite. From the roundabout at the south of the town head towards the town centre. The campsite entrance is on your right after about 500m and is accessed through the car park to the municipal swimming pool.

From the South. Head towards the town centre from the roundabout on the ring road and follow directions as above.

€ Prices 2010	High	Mid	Low
Pitch + 2	24.70	17.80	15.20
Hook Up 10A	4.30	4.30	4.30
Luxury Pitch	7.80	6.40	6.10

Address Avenue Aristide Briand 37600 Loches

GPS N 47° 07' 22 E 01° 00' 08

www.lacitadelle.com
email camping@lacitadelle.com
Tel 02.47.59.05.91

Cheverny, Camping Les Saules ****

Location Cheverny 1.6km. Blois 15km. Tours 77km. Orléans 74km.

Open 1st Apr to 26th Sept

Pitches 169 (149 touring)

You cannot fail to be impressed by the pretty entrance to this site with its small fishing lake overhung by the magnificent weeping willow, from which it takes its name. There is a wonderfully verdant feel to the site and a warm friendly atmosphere created by the enthusiastic family who run it. All the services are located in a converted 17th century farm house. The site is generally well maintained and further enhanced by a wealth of flowers and trees. You are in the heart of the Loire with 15 châteaux within easy reach. It is also great cycling country.
Clef Verte

Site suitable for all ages, particularly couples and young families.

Pitches	Flat, grassy up to 110m², divided by trees, not hedged so spacious open feel to site. Pitches towards middle of site are quite heavily shaded.
Hook-Up	10 amps - all pitches. Water & drainage - none.
Motorhomes	Motorhome service point. Walking/cycling distance of Cheverny and château. Shuttle bus in high season to Chambord and Blois with charge.
Swimming pools	One rectangular good-sized swimming pool and a paddling pool which are heated and surrounded by attractive sun terrace with sun loungers.
Activities on site	Mini-golf- free. Cycle hire. Two good children's play areas. Table tennis, volleyball field. Small fishing lake. TV Room. Horse riding round site. Walking track from site.
Entertainment	Children's club 10/7 – 20/8. Hot air balloon flights with charge in high season. No other organised entertainment although site has arranged discounts for its visitors with several local tourist attractions including the châteaux at Cheverny, Chambord, Blois, Beauregard and Villesavin. Cheverny Golf club 2km also has special rates.
Sanitary facilities	Two toilet blocks which have been renovated and are kept clean and well maintained. Push button showers, no temperature control, hooks. Individual wash cubicles. Toilet seats and toilet paper on wall outside. Disabled facilities. Baby room. Washing machines and tumble dryer. Chemical waste point.
Services	Small shop selling basics, pre-order bread. Bar/snack/take-away. Restaurant in attractive renovated farm building with low beams – different set menu each evening. Barbecues allowed. Dogs accepted. Internet and Wi-Fi.
Accommodation	10 chalets.
Tour operators	One Dutch company on 10 pitches.

Excursions/Places to visit
Châteaux at Cheverny, Chambord, Chenonceaux, Chambord, Blois, Beauregard and Villesavin. Numerous cycle tracks.

Directions
From A10 at Blois take exit 17 and head south over the Loire river on D956 in the direction of Romarantin and Vierzon. After 6km take the left fork on to D765 and follow signs for Cheverny. Just after Cour-Cheverny, pass in front of the entrance to the château and turn on to D102 in the direction of Contres. The site is about 2km along this road off to the right, easy to find because of the weeping willows (saules) at the entrance to the site.

€ Prices 2010	High	Mid	Low
Pitch + 2	25.50	20	17.50
Hook Up 10A	3.50	3.50	3.50

Address D102 Route de Contres, 41700 Cheverny

www.camping-cheverny.com (not in English)
email contact@camping-cheverny.com

GPS N 47° 28' 41 E 01° 27' 03

Tel 02.54.79.90.01

Muides-sur-Loire, Château des Marais ****

Map Ref LR07

Location 17km north east of Blois, easy access from A10 and D2152.

Open 13th May to 15th Sept

Pitches 300 (180 touring)

This site is included as it is located in a unique position just 500m from the Chambord estate and because of its wonderful aqua complex. It is situated in the spacious wooded grounds of an attractive 17th century manor house on the edge of the village of Muides-sur-Loire. In spite of its size it has a peaceful rural atmosphere. It also offers easy access by car or by bike to a large number of the well-known Loire châteaux.

Site suitable for all ages, although no organised entertainment specifically for teenagers.

Pitches	Flat, grassy and spacious, divided by hedges, ranging from 100m² - 120m², some quite heavily shaded.
Hook-Up	6 or 10 smps, water & drainage - all pitches.
Motorhomes	Motor home service point. Good for motor homes as walking distance of village and cycling distance of Château de Chambord.
Swimming pools	Excellent aqua complex with four separate basins, some heated. One can be covered in cool weather, one is a paddling pool, there are two sets of waterslides and a lazy river, all surrounded by an attractive sun terrace with sun loungers. A new spa centre with hammam, sauna, jacuzzi and massage area has recently been installed.
Activities on site	Cycle and 4-wheel bike hire. Tennis. Canoe/kayak hire. Table football, pool. Table tennis. Electronic games area. Volleyball area. Children's play area. TV room. Fishing in pond - free.
Entertainment	No organised entertainment in the day time. Twice weekly evening entertainment in high season.
Sanitary facilities	Three toilet blocks which are respectable and well maintained but rather dark. Push button temperature control showers with hooks. Individual wash basins. Toilets with seats and toilet paper. Disabled facilities. Baby room. Laundry. Chemical waste point.
Services	Shop for basics. Bar, take-away, restaurant with basic menu and sometimes slow service at weekends. Bakers, butchers and restaurants in Muides. Barbecues allowed. Dogs accepted. Internet and Wi-Fi.
Accommodation	20 mobile homes and chalets.
Tour operators	Three British companies with 80 mobile homes and 20 tents.

Excursions/Places to visit
Châteaux at Chambord, Chenonceau, Cheverny, Blois, Chaumont, Amboise. Beauval zoo. Vineyards for wine tasting.

Directions
From the town of Mer. Take the D112 over the river Loire in the direction of Muides-sur-Loire and Chambord. Go through Muides-sur-Loire and then straight across at the crossroads. The campsite is situated on the right hand side after approximately 150 metres. From Blois. Take the N152 to Mer, here join the D112 over the river Loire in the direction of Chambord and Muides-sur-Loire. Go through Muides-sur-Loire and then straight across at the crossroads. The campsite is situated on the right hand side after approximately 150 metres.

€ Prices 2010	Peak	High	Mid	Low
Pitch + 2	36	32	26	25
Hook Up 6A	5	5	5	5

Address 27 Rue de Chambord, 41500 Muides-sur-Loire

GPS N 47° 39' 58 E 01° 31' 45

www.chateau-des-marais.com
email chateau.des.marais@wanadoo.fr
Tel 02.54.87.05.42

Pierrefitte-sur-Sauldre, Domaine des Alicourts **** Map Ref LR08

Location Pierrefitte 5km. Orléans 49km. Tours 152km. Bourges 75km.

Open 28th April to 8th Sept

Pitches 510 (150 touring)

Although in a rather remote situation in the heart of the wooded Parc de Sologne, we have included this site because of the excellent quality of its facilities and services plus its lovely lake for swimming and boating. It caters particularly for children under the age of 15, with wonderful attention to giving them a fun-filled holiday. It is a fabulous spot just to sit back and relax but is not recommended as a centre for visiting the main tourist spots of the Loire region. Everything is provided on site, so there is no need to go out. Great cycling in the nearby woods.

Site suitable for families with children of all ages. who enjoy on-site entertainment.

Pitches	Flat, grassy and spacious about 100m², all in the same area not far from the lake. Three types of pitch with different prices. Lakeside and 'grand confort' pitches with electricity, water & drainage and standard pitches.
Hook-Up	6 amps - all pitches. Water & drainage - 42 pitches.
Motorhomes	Motorhome service point. Everything on site but not near town.
Swimming pools	Large supervised aqua complex with four pools including a paddling pool with magic mushroom, two sets of waterslides, a wave machine and islands. A spa/hydrotherapy complex has recently opened, housed in an octagonal shaped building and includes a jacuzzi, hydro-massage pebble corridor with water jets, hydro-tubs, water cannons, water-jet cabins, large beaches and terraces and outdoor solarium, all at 32°.
Activities on site	Lake for swimming with separate area for fishing. Man-made beach with parasols and canoes and pedalos for hire. Suitable for inflatables. 9-hole Golf, practice range. Cycle hire and 4-wheel bike hire. Mini-golf. Tennis court. Huge football pitch. Volleyball, basketball. Roller skate park. Mini go-karts. Archery. Table tennis, pool and video-games. Huge children's play area.
Entertainment	Baby-Paradise for children up to 3yrs - a covered playground exclusively for them, under the supervision of their parents. Organised activities for children from 4yrs to 17yrs 6 days a week including a mini-show, put on by the children every week. Further evening entertainment for all the family.
Sanitary facilities	Two very well-appointed modern toilet blocks with separate ladies and gents. One is equipped for small children with sinks and toilets for a range of heights. Some cubicles with showers and washbasins, showers are push-button temperature control with hooks, shelf and rail. Toilets with toilet paper and beautifully designed hand washing sinks outside. Disabled facilities. Baby room. Chemical waste point.
Services	Mini-market with everyday essentials and regional produce. Newspaper shop. Bar, one small one overlooking lake and one with restaurant, take-away. Barbecues allowed. Dogs accepted. Internet and Wi-Fi in the library area.
Accommodation	Range of chalets, mobilehomes and two tree houses.
Tour operators	Four British companies on 100 pitches.

Excursions/Places to visit
Great cycling in the nearby woods. Beauval zoo. Nearest town 16km.

Directions
Leave A71 at exit 3. Follow D923 to Lamotte-Beuvron. Turn right onto N20 for a short distance and then left back onto D923 towards Brinion-sur-Sauldre. After 14km turn right onto D24e at le Coudray and follow signs to the campsite.

€ Prices 2010	Peak	High	Mid	Low
Pitch + 2	42	36	22	18
Hook Up 6A	Incl	Incl	Incl	Incl

Address 41300 Pierrefitte-sur-Sauldre

GPS N 47° 32' 40 E 02° 11' 28

www.lesalicourts.com
email info@lesalicourts.com
Tel 02.54.88.63.34

DORDOGNE & LOT

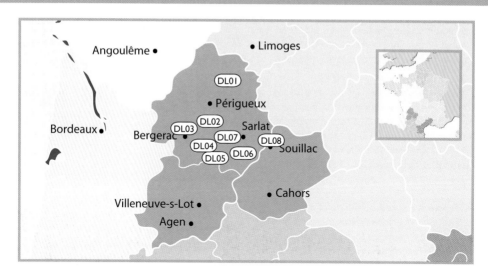

Picture opposite - Montfort

Places of Interest - Dordogne Lot

The Dordogne is the third largest "département" in France and is famous for its magnificent river winding through beautiful rocky valleys. Control of the river has always been of strategic importance and this accounts for the large number of castels and bastides to be found along its banks. It is also a region which boasts a wealth of attractive towns and prehistoric caves. The north of the département, or Périgord vert, is renowned for its delightful green countryside and is a combination of forests, meadows, streams and lakes.

Périgueux is the chief town situated along the Isle valley. The Tour de Vesone in the town, 25 metres high, is a rare example of a round temple, and you can see where the amphitheatre used to stand in the Arena Gardens. It has streets full of Renaissance houses and a lovely cathedral.

Canoeing on the Dordogne

Nontron is situated on the tip of a promontory overlooking the gorges of Bandiat. It was once a medieval fortress which fell during the French Revolution to leave only the attractive ramparts and old streets.

Château de Jumilhac a combination of 15th and 17th century architecture which overlooks the Isle valley near a Romanesque church and is a mass of imposing slate rooves, sharp pointed turrets and watch towers.

Brantôme known as the green Venice of the Périgord is one of the département's leading tourist and cultural centres situated on the banks of the Dronne river. The Benedictine Abbey founded by Charlemagne in 769 bears the marks of its repeated destruction over more than twelve centuries.

The south-east of the department is called the Périgord noir because of the chestnut tree coppices and the everlasting leaves of the holm-oak trees which form a black carpet in winter. This is the most popular region of the Dordogne as its wealth of caves offers a veritable valley of prehistory and there is a magnificent variety of châteaux to visit, dating from the 12th to 17th century.

Limeuil

Sarlat-la-Canéda situated in the heart of this region evokes the past when it was once the home of merchants, scholars, clerks and law students. Much of its charm lies in its narrow streets, secluded courtyards and old buildings, in particular the materials used to construct them: yellow ochre building stone, white limestone roof tiles or thick grey slates from the Corrèze. Today the protected town centre offers remarkable architecture like the Maison de la Boetie, the cathedral, la Chapelle des Pénitents Blancs and la Lanterne des Morts. The layout of the town lends itself to street entertainment and shows in July and August.

St. Jean de Cole is a picturesque medieval village much chosen as a location for historical films. The magnificent 12th century towers of the Châteaux de Marthorie dominate the main square of the village.

Château de Puyguilhem in Villars built at the beginning of the 16th century is undoubtedly the most beautiful of the Renaissance châteaux in the Périgord, very original and full of fine sculptures.

Lez Eyzies-de-Tayac is one of the leading world centres of prehistory, the number of its archeological findings making it unique. It occupies a pleasant position surrounded by green-topped cliffs, at the confluence of the Beune and the Vézère. The first finds were made here during the 19th century and further research uncovered 15,000 year old human remains and stunning cave paintings, drawings and carvings.

Beynac is unique because its fortress was built beneath a rock overhang halfway up a cliff and houses the Musée National de Préhistoire. The river formed the dividing line between the French and English armies during the Hundred Years War, with the French holding the highly fortified feudal fortress on the cliff top at Beynac, and the English, the gloriously situated 12th century castle at Castelnaud directly opposite. The view from Beynac is well worth the climb up from the village.

Beynac

Limeuil is one of the prettiest villages in France. It occupies a unique position on the confluence of the Dordogne and Vézère rivers and is a great spot for canoeing and swimming. As a prehistoric site, its rocky terraces overlooked the rivers making it an important defensive position. You can visit L'Eglise de Sainte-Catherine with its black virgin, the Chapelle Saint Martin which bears witness to the fact that Aquitaine was once under English rule and walk through the Marquisat gate which spans one of the narrow cobbled streets.

Rocamadour is a delightful village perched precariously on a limestone cliff. It is a shrine that tells a story of religious belief and human endeavour. Looking out over the gorge of the River Alzou, this city devoted to the Virgin Mary has remained for over nine hundred years a symbol of faith and hope.

There are numerous fascinating caves in the area:-
La Grotte de Font-de-Gaume is famous for its many multi-coloured paintings often superimposed on one another: all the drawings of horses, bison, mammoths, reindeer etc are of great artistic skill.

La Grotte de Lascaux II is a technological masterpiece: the wall relief of the original cave closed to the public due to disease caused by humidity has been reproduced in great detail and the paint colours have the same natural colourings as 17,000 years ago.

Les Grottes du Roc de Cazelle a cliff cave city is particularly good for younger children as it shows reconstructions of the life of prehistoric man in the actual places where they lived.

La Gouffre de Proumeyssac has been christened the "crystal cathedral" and is the largest cave area in Périgord.

La Gouffre de Padirac is a great chasm said to have been created by the Devil as he returned to Hell looking for souls on earth. A visit of the huge caves of stalagmites and stalactites is by boat and on foot.

St Cyprien Market

The star of the Périgord is of course the Dordogne river itself. There are a number of places where you can hire a canoe for full days or half-days. One of the best and most popular stretches to paddle is from Carsac south-east of Sarlat to Les Milandes. This will take you past **Domme** perched high above a loop in the river and then to **La Roque-Gageac**, the prettiest riverside village on the Dordogne and almost built into the cliff. The river then carries you past **Castelnaud** and **Beynac**, both châteaux much more impressive from the water. There are plenty of places to stop for a drink or a picnic on route. You will then be met at a pre-arranged point and transported back to your starting point. The Dordogne river is good for swimming but is only easily accessible and safe in a few places. Canoes can also be hired on the quieter Vézère.

www.sites-en-perigord.com
www.best-of-perigord.tm.fr

Champs-Romain, Château Le Verdoyer **** Map Ref DL01

Location Périgueux 55km. Nontron 15km, St Pardoux-la-Rivière 8km. Angoulême 63km.

Open 24th Apr to 6th Oct   **Pitches** 180 (69 touring)

We have included this Dutch-run site because of its fabulous location in the grounds of a charming 19th century château complete with fairy tale towers, its excellent pool area and attractive fishing lakes. The services are all in the converted stone-faced outbuildings set round a pretty courtyard. It is set in the unspoilt countryside of the Northern Périgord, good for cycling but a complete contrast to the central Dordogne area. It is a very Dutch orientated site and quite lively in high season. Do not expect a French ambiance. Although generally well maintained, it could do with a bit more TLC in the grounds.
Clef Verte

Site suitable for couples in low season and young families in high season.

Pitches	Mostly flat and grassy, set out in terraces, divided by hedges offering a mixture of shade and sun. A real variety of sizes, most generous ones with views at the back of the site.
Hook-Up	5 or 10 amps - all pitches. Water & drainage - most pitches.
Motorhomes	Motorhome service point but need transport to go anywhere.
Swimming pools	Excellent sized rectangular pool 25m x 8m. 37m waterslide. Paddling pool 12m x 8m. Pretty sun terrace with sun loungers with view of château behind.
Activities on site	Cycle hire. Tennis court. Mini-golf. Volleyball. Table tennis. Boules piste. Children's play area. Fishing in well-stocked lake with pontoons. Games in the bar and converted barn: pool, darts, video games, air hockey, table football. Special room above bar for the youngsters.
Entertainment	In high season: Children's club, programme of daytime activities and organised musical evenings with visiting groups and singers, karaoke evenings.
Sanitary facilities	Three unisex toilet blocks. Main one in converted barn is best. There is a new one is in a very upmarket type of portakabin. One near the mobile homes could do with renovating. All kept clean and respectable. Push button showers, no temperature control, hooks. Individual wash basins and toilets. Disabled facilities and excellent children's and baby room in main block with washbasins and toilets at different heights. Laundry. Chemical waste point.
Services	Shop-pre-order bread. Bar/snack, take-away - all in attractive courtyard. Restaurant in château. Barbecues allowed. Dogs accepted. Internet and Wi-Fi.
Accommodation	24 mobile homes and chalets. 45 privately owned mobile homes. Rooms in the château.
Tour operators	Three Dutch companies on 32 pitches.

Excursions/Places to visit
St Saud Lacoussière 3km, Nontron 15km
Piégut-Pluviers 15km, Brantôme 20km.

€ Prices 2010	High	Low
Pitch + 2	29	18
Hook Up 5A	3	3
Water & Dr.	4.50	Incl

Directions
From A20. Follow N21 in direction of Périgueux until you reach Chalus. Turn right towards Nontron on D6Bis & D85. After 20km turn left at crossroads onto D96 to St Saud. The campsite is on the left. From Nontron. Take the D707 to St Pardoux-la Rivière and turn left after 3km onto D85. After 9km turn right onto D96 and continue as above.

Address 24470 Champs Romain

www.verdoyer.fr
email chateau@verdoyer.fr
Tel 05.53.56 94.64

GPS N 45° 33' 04 E 00° 47' 43

St Léon-sur-Vézère, Le Paradis ****

Location Montignac 11km. Les Eyzies 14km. Sarlat 35km. Périgueux 68km. Limoges 136km.

Open 1st Apr to 19th Oct

Pitches 200 (160 touring)

As its name suggests this site is a paradise of luscious vegetation filled with over 100 different types of plants from banana plants to cacti to flowering shrubs. It is a beautifully maintained site run by a friendly Dutch family whose priority is to protect and conserve the environment at all costs. Since the site opened in 1967, the family have gradually created a campsite in a botanical garden. The sanitary facilities are among the best in France. It is a real pleasure to stay in such verdant surroundings and yet be only a short drive from all the main tourist attractions of the Perigord region. Clef Verte

Site suitable for all ages, particularly couples and young families.

Pitches	Flat, grassy, a minimum of 100m² and hedged with shrubs plants and trees giving a mixture of shade and sun.
Hook-Up	10 amps - all pitches. Water & drainage - most pitches.
Motorhomes	Motorhome service point but need transport to get anywhere.
Swimming pools	A very attractive complex of three pools surrounded by banana trees and other plants, a large one for swimming 25m x 10m, a medium-sized one and a paddling pool. Generous sun terrace with sun loungers.
Activities on site	Canoe hire. Bathing in river, fishing for carp, perch, pike with permit. Two tennis courts. Cycle and quad bike hire, quad bike track. All weather sports pitch for volleyball, badminton. Football pitch. Adventure park in trees. Wonderful herb garden. Floodlit boules pitch. 4 table tennis tables. Pony and horse riding. Good Children's play area. Indoor games room.
Entertainment	Children's club 4 -11yrs from June to beginning of September. In high season: sports tournaments, organised walks and mountain bike circuits, archery and climbing during the day with live entertainment in the evenings. Disco once a week.
Sanitary facilities	Two well appointed toilet blocks beautifully designed round a quad decorated with plants and flowers and well lit through glass roof and walls. Spacious family rooms with shower, washbasin and toilets together. Push button temperature control showers with hooks and shelf. Both blocks have attractive tiling and are kept very clean. Disabled facilities. Baby room .Laundry. Chemical waste point.
Services	Good shop, bar, take-away and attractive restaurant with reasonably priced menus. A small welcome booklet giving information on opening times of all the facilities is handed to each customer on arrival. Barbecues allowed. Dogs accepted. Internet and Wi-Fi.
Accommodation	21 two- and three- bedroomed mobile homes.
Tour operators	One British company on 19 pitches.

Excursions/Places to visit
Les Eyzies-de-Tayac, La Roque-Gageac, Châteaux des Milandes and de Castelnaud, Beynac, Sarlat, Grotte de Lascaux at Montignac.

€ Prices 2010	High	Mid	Low
Pitch + 2	27.50	23.50	18.40
Hook Up 6A	3.50	3.50	3.50

Address 24290 St Léon-sur-Vézère

GPS N 45° 00' 06 E 01° 04' 16

Directions
The site is located along the Vézère River, between Montignac and Les Eyzies. From Périgueux take the A89 towards Brive then the N89 towards Le Lardin St Lazare where you turn onto the D704 to Montignac. Drive through Montignac and take the D706 to St Léon-sur-Vézère. The site is on your left about 2km south from St Léon-sur-Vézère.

www.le-paradis.fr
email le-paradis@perigord.com
Tel 05.53.50.72.64

St Avit-de-Vialard, St Avit Loisirs ****　　　Map Ref DL03.

Location Le Bugue 7km. Les Eyzies 14km. Sarlat 35km. Périgueux 42km. Limoges 135km.

Open 31st Mar to 18 Sept　　　　　　**Pitches** 265 (223 Touring)

Tucked away in the heart of the Perigordian countryside this site is recommended for families who enjoy entertainment in quiet wooded surroundings. There is a fantastic aqua complex and an enormous number of activities available. All the installations are excellent quality and maintained to a high standard. The services are housed in pretty cream stone-faced buildings built in a typical local style. The glass-sided restaurant building enjoys lovely views over the pools and surrounding countryside.

Site suitable for active families.

Pitches	Grassy and sloping gently, a minimum of 100m² but varying in shape depending on the shrubs and trees that divide them. A mixture of sun and shade.
Hook-Up	6 amps - 199 pitches. Water & drainage - 100 pitches.
Motorhomes	No motorhome service point.
Swimming pools	A magnificent and attractive heated aqua complex with good sized pool for swimming, play pools, paddling pool, waterslides, crazy river rafting. Jacuzzi. Indoor tropical style pool with paddling pool. There is a generous sun terrace with sun loungers.
Activities on site	A spacious Fun Zone with practice golf, archery, quad bikes, climbing wall, grass football pitch and super trampoline for older children. Tennis. Mini-golf. Cycle hire. Gym. All weather sports pitch for football, volleyball basketball. Superb children's play area with climbing frame that looks like a tree.
Entertainment	In high season: children's club 4 – 11yrs 5 days a week, daily organised sports tournaments. Evening entertainment every night except Saturday, with bands, karaoke, shows and theme evenings that usually finish by 11pm. Organised canoe trips.
Sanitary facilities	Three modern unisex toilet blocks, all beautifully tiled and built to a high specification with opaque glass roofs, giving them a light airy feel. Double flush toilets with paper. Showers and washbasins together in large cubicles, push button temperature control showers. Disabled facilities. Baby room. Laundry in each block. Chemical waste point.
Services	Mini supermarket. Bar. Self-service cafeteria and take-away. Gastronomic restaurant which is also open to the public, so recommend pre-booking. All open for entire season. Fridge hire. Barbecues allowed. Dogs accepted. Internet and Wi-Fi.
Accommodation	Chalets and mobile homes.
Tour operators	Two British companies.

Excursions/Places to visit
Le Bugue, Les Eyzies-de-Tayac, La Roque-Gageac, Châteaux at Milandes and Castelnaud, Beynac, Sarlat, Grotte de Lascaux.

Directions
From Périgueux take the D710 towards Le Bugue. Continue on the D710 and 13km after the junction with D47 turn right towards La Combe and St Avit-de-Vialard. The campsite is well-signposted. From Le Bugue take the D710 towards Périgueux and turn left after 3km.

€ Prices 2010	High	Mid	Low
Pitch + 2	35.10	25.10	14.20
Hook Up 6A	5.30	5.30	5.30
6A + W & Dr	8.90	8.90	8.90

Address Le Bugue, 24260 Saint Avit-de-Vialard

www.saint-avit-loisirs.com
email contact@saint-avit-loisirs.com

GPS N 45° 33' 04　E 00° 47' 43　　　　　　**Tel** 05.53.02.64.00

Allès-sur-Dordogne, Le Port de Limeuil ****

Location Le Bugue 7km. Les Eyzies 14km. Sarlat 36km. Bergerac 39km. Périgueux 53km.

Open 1st May to 30th Sept

Pitches 100 (69 touring)

A beautiful little site occupying a unique position on the confluence of the Dordogne and Vézère rivers opposite the medieval hillside village of Limeuil. A short walk over the river takes you to bars and restaurants in the village. There is a peaceful relaxed ambiance. The pitches are laid out in spacious wooded alleys that slope down to the river where there is a generous beach area for launching boats and swimming. The site has its own canoes – you are taken upriver to paddle back down to the site at your own pace, a trip that is highly recommended.

Site suitable for young families and couples.

Pitches	Spacious pitches up to 150m², varying in shape and size and amounts of shade, most divided by low hedges, flat and grassy.
Hook-Up	5 & 10 amps - all pitches. Water & drainage - 20 pitches.
Motorhomes	Motorhome service point. Walking distance of Limeuil.
Swimming pools	A pretty pool complex, water not heated, reasonable size for swimming, about 100m² and floodlit. Paddling pool 80m² with mini-slide. Sun terrace with sun loungers.
Activities on site	Cycle hire, canoe hire. Mini-golf. 2 children's play areas. Football pitch. Basket ball pitch. Badminton. Table tennis. Boules pitch. Games room with pool and table football. Horse riding, tennis 1km.
Entertainment	High season only there are organised sports tournaments. Visiting circus. Wine tasting. Music in the bar.
Sanitary facilities	Two toilet blocks. The one opposite the entrance is the better of the two as it is more spacious. The showers are temperature controlled with pull-on lever, shelf and hook. Individual wash basins. Toilets with toilet paper. There may be queues at peak times in high season when showers tend to be tepid. Both kept clean and respectable. Disabled facilities. Baby room. Separate laundry. Chemical waste point.
Services	Reasonably well-stocked shop. Pretty bar/snack serving basic meals and take-aways, open from last week of May. Fridge hire. Barbecues allowed. Dogs accepted. Internet and Wi-Fi in bar area.
Accommodation	11 mobile homes and a gite to rent.
Tour operators	One British and one Dutch company on 22 pitches

Excursions/Places to visit

Limeuil 500m, Le Bugue, Les Eyzies, Beynac, Sarlat and numerous grottos including Le Grand Roc, Combarelles and le Fond de Gaume.

Directions

From Périgueux. Take the N89 towards Brive, after 12km, turn right at the roundabout on to the D710 to Le Bugue. Continue through the village to Le Buisson. After 6.5km take the first turning to the right in the direction of Limeuil on the D51. At the first junction turn left to cross over the Dordogne and the site is on your right hand side. From Bergerac. Take the D660 to Lalinde, where you cross over the river Dordogne, and continue on the D29 to Le Buisson. Take the D51 north in the direction of Le Bugue and turn left after 3km. Stay on the D51 and then continue as above.

€ Prices 2010	High	Mid	Low
Pitch + 2	25.40	17	14
Hook Up 6A	3.5	3	2.5

Address 24480 Allès-sur-Dordogne

GPS N 44° 52' 47 E 00° 53' 10

www.leportdelimeuil.com
email contact@leportdelimeuil.com
Tel 05.53.63.29.76

Beynac-&-Cazenac, Camping le Capeyrou ***

Location Beynac 500m. Sarlat 10km. Les Eyzies 24km. Bergerac 65km. Souillac 37km.

Open 1st Apr to 30th Sept   **Pitches** 120 (117 touring)

This small site has been chosen because of its unique position right on the Dordogne river and the fantastic view it enjoys of Beynac with its château perched on the rocks above the town. The site is well maintained and the French/Dutch owners create a wonderful welcoming atmosphere. For those who enjoy a quiet ambiance you have the best of everything, access to all the facilities in the town, direct access to the river with a sandy beach and very pleasant, attractive surroundings. Good mixture of nationalities.

Site suitable for all ages, particularly those who prefer a quiet atmosphere.

Pitches	Flat, grassy pitches, divided by hedges and not heavily shaded. They vary in size, average 100m², but some even more generous.
Hook-Up	6 or 10 amps - all pitches. Water & drainage - 50 pitches.
Motorhomes	Motorhome service point. Excellent for motorhomes as walking distance of centre of Beynac.
Swimming pools	Excellent swimming pool 20m x 12m and paddling pool with attractive sun terrace and sun loungers. View from pool area of château at Beynac towering above the site.
Activities on site	Cycle hire. Volleyball. Badminton. Boules pitch. Games area in bar with darts and pool. Children's play area. Canoe/kayak hire on river. Clean sandy beach for swimming in river. Tennis courts 100m. 9-hole golf course 5km.
Entertainment	Organised barbecue evening once a week with music from visiting band.
Sanitary facilities	Two unisex toilet blocks. The one nearest reception has been completely refurbished with attractive fittings and family rooms – shower & washbasin together. Second block is much older but well maintained with a couple of French style toilets. In both blocks, push button temperature control showers, some individual wash basins and toilets with seats and toilet paper. Both blocks kept very clean. Disabled facilities. Baby room. Laundry. Chemical waste point.
Services	Attractive bar on site in converted barn. Fridge hire. Vival shop, bakers, butchers/delicatessens immediately opposite site. Restaurants within walking distance. Barbecues allowed. Dogs accepted. Internet and Wi-Fi in bar area.
Accommodation	3 mobile homes.
Tour operators	None.

Excursions/Places to visit
Beynac, La Roque-Gageac, Les Eyzies de Tayac, Châteaux at Milandes and Castelnaud, Sarlat, Grotte de Lascaux.

€ Prices 2010	High	Low
Pitch + 2	18.40	13.80
Hook Up 6A	3.20	3.20

Address 24220 Beynac-&-Cazenac

GPS N 44° 50' 17 E 01° 08' 55

Directions
The site is situated by the river Dordogne to the east of Beynac.
From Bergerac take the D660 and then the D29 to Le Buisson. From here take the D703 towards Sarlat and you arrive in Beynac after 25km.
From Sarlat take the D57 to Vézac then turn right onto the D703 to Beynac.

www.campinglecapeyrou.com
email lecapeyrou@wanadoo.fr
Tel 05.53.29.54.95

Vitrac, Domaine de Soleil Plage ****

Location Sarlat 8km. La Roque-Gaegac 5km. Domme 5km. Montfort 2km. Souillac 26km.

Open 2nd Apr to 26th Sept

Pitches 226 (125 touring)

The site's fabulous location on a bend of the Dordogne river combined with top quality services makes it a very popular holiday destination. There is a pebbly beach ideal for launching canoes and a sandy beach where the river is shallow enough for swimming and paddling. The beautiful rocky backdrop makes it a truly delightful spot. The site is divided into two separate areas, with the best pitches near the river, but a short walk from all the services and activities. There is a fairly lively atmosphere in high season and a good mixture of nationalities.

Site suitable for all ages, although no special entertainment for teenagers.

Pitches	Flat, grassy and hedged, giving plenty of privacy. The majority have good shade. Most are minimum of 100m², but the narrow alleys make it unsuitable for outfits over 7.5m.
Hook-Up	16 amps and water - all pitches. Water & drainage - 45 pitches.
Motorhomes	Motorhome service point. Need transport to visit area.
Swimming pools	Attractive aqua complex with heated swimming pool, lagoon, paddling pool, waterslide, lazy river and sun terrace with sun loungers.
Activities on site	Canoe hire. Swimming in river - plastic shoes recommended. Cycle hire. Tennis. Mini-golf. Fishing with permit. Boules pitch. Fitness circuit. Table tennis. All weather sports pitch. Three children's play areas. Walking and cycle tracks direct from site.
Entertainment	In high season: programme of daytime and evening entertainment including children's club, aqua gym, sports tournaments, evening concerts and theme evenings in the restaurant.
Sanitary facilities	Two unisex toilet blocks one in each area. Block in section near reception is less modern but clean and respectable. The second block on river side is more attractive, decorated with flowers and well-lit. Most of the showers are push button, temperature control with hooks and shelf. Individual wash basins and toilets with seats and toilet paper. Disabled facilities. Baby room. Laundry facilities. Chemical waste point.
Services	Vival shop. Pretty bar. Take-away. Fabulous gastronomic restaurant offering variety of reasonably priced menus. All open from 1st May. Fridge hire. Barbecues allowed. Dogs accepted. Internet and Wi-Fi.
Accommodation	42 mobile homes, 27 chalets in own spacious area.
Tour operators	Two British tour operators on 32 pitches.

Excursions/Places to visit

Canoe trip from site highly recommended. Walking distance of château at Montfort. Sarlat, Beynac, La Roque Gaegac, Domme, Rocamadour, Gouffre de Proumeyssac, Grotte de Lascaux.

Directions

From Sarlat. Take the D46 south towards Vitrac and La Roque Gageac. In Vitrac-Port turn left onto the D703 towards Montfort. (NB the D55 has a ban on all caravans). The campsite is signposted to the right just after the golf course. Continue along this road and the site entrance is to your left after the canoe hire centre.

From Souillac. Take the D804 west from the town which becomes the D703 after 3km, signposted to Bergerac and following the river. When you reach Monfort the campsite is signed to your left.

€ Prices 2010	High	Mid	Low	Off
Pitch + 2 & 16A	34.50	29	24.50	21
Water & Dr	6.50	5	4	3.50

Address Caudon par Montfort, Vitrac, 24200 Sarlat

www.soleilplage.fr
email info@soleilplage.fr
Tel 05.53.28.33.33

GPS N 44° 49' 31 E 01° 15' 14

Sarlat, Le Moulin du Roch ****

Location Sarlat 10.5km. Les Eyzies 11km. Souillac 38km. Périgueux 62km. Bergerac 73km.

Open 10th May to 17th Sept

Pitches 196 (128 touring)

As the name suggests this Castels site has been created around an old Perigordian watermill. The services are housed in converted stone faced farm buildings and a pretty stream runs through the site. It is a terraced site laid out in woodland with the best pitches nearer the bottom of the site. The Dutreux family offer a warm welcoming atmosphere which attracts a good mixture of nationalities. The site is an ideal base for visiting all the main attractions of the Dordogne area, the castles, caves and gastronomic restaurants. In July/August an evening trip to Sarlat with its street entertainment is highly recommended.

Site suitable for all ages, particularly those keen to explore the area.

Pitches	Laid out on terraces rising up from pool/bar area. They are flat, grassy and divided by low hedges. Most enjoy a fair amount of shade. The more open pitches overlook the pool, but can be more noisy.
Hook-Up	6 amps - 100 standard pitches. 10 amps, water & drainage - 28 pitches.
Motorhomes	No motorhome service point, and transport required to visit region.
Swimming pools	Attractive pool area 320m^2 in total which includes paddling pool with mini waterslide, good sized almost rectangular-shaped basin for swimming, and generous sun terrace with sun loungers and parasols.
Activities on site	Tennis, volleyball pitch, boules pitch, small fishing lake with carp. Children's play area.
Entertainment	In high season: children's club for 4 -12 yr olds (small charge per session), organised sports tournaments and aquagym, theme evenings with games, dancing and music. The site can book canoe trips on the Dordogne and Vézère rivers, or on a traditional 'Gabare' boat which used to carry merchandise along the Dordogne and organises a guided walk once a week.
Sanitary facilities	Three well-maintained, attractively tiled toilet blocks. Push button temperature control showers with hooks and shelf. Separate wash basins with hot and cold water. Toilets with seats and toilet paper. Good washing up facilities. Only criticism is that they are a bit dark. Disabled facilities. Baby room. Laundry. Chemical waste point.
Services	Small shop - pre-order bread. Bar, take-away and reasonably priced restaurant with pretty terrace. Tourist information point near reception. Barbecues allowed. Dogs not accepted. Internet and Wi-Fi in bar area.
Accommodation	68 mobile homes and chalets, several on terraces at top of site.
Tour operators	None.

Excursions/Places to visit
Sarlat, Les Eyzies, Beynac, Castelnaud, Le Bugue, La Roque-Gaegac. Rocamadour, Gouffre de Proumeyssac, Grotte de Lascaux.

Directions
The site is situated 10km from Sarlat on the road to Les Eyzies (D47) and is well-signposted.

€ Prices 2010	Peak	High	Mid	Low
Pitch + 2	30	25	21	15
Hook Up 6A	4	4	4	4

Address Rte des Eyzies, St-André-d'Allas, 24200 Sarlat

www.moulin-du-roch.com
email moulin.du.roch@wanadoo.fr

GPS N 44° 54' 30 E 01° 06' 54

Tel 05.53.59.20.27

Souillac, Domaine de la Paille Basse ****

Location Souillac 8km. Sarlat 15km. Limoges 136km. Cahors 76km.

Open 15th May to 15th Sept **Pitches** 254 (130 touring)

Set in woodland on top of a hill, this site has been created from a medieval hamlet of three farms and has been beautifully restored to house all the facilities. The cream stone faced Perigordian buildings with terracotta tiled roofs are the focal point of this Castels site. The pitches are spread out on either side of the facilities along a ridge above the valley. Although the buildings and services are maintained to a high standard the grounds could do with a bit more TLC. Access is along a 1km lane leading to the site.

Site suitable for all ages particularly older children.

Pitches	Irregular shaped pitches laid out in terraces, generally about 100m². You can choose from a variety of surroundings, shaded or sunny, on grass or hard standing, close to all facilities or hidden away in a quiet spot towards the end of the site.
Hook-Up	3 or 10 amps - all pitches. Water & drainage - 61 pitches
Motorhomes	Motorhome service point. Not particularly suitable for motorhomes as some distance from nearest town.
Swimming pools	Good swimming pool complex with a large pool excellent for swimming 25m x 10m and a paddling pool 5m x 10m. Four track waterslide coming down into separate basin. Pretty sun terrace with sun loungers and magnificent views over the surrounding hills.
Activities on site	Two tennis courts (free). Large multi-sports area for football, volleyball and basketball. TV room. Table tennis room. Games room with pool and video games. Two children's play areas. Boules pitch. Three short marked out walking routes directly from site.
Entertainment	In high season: Children's club 4 - 12yrs. Aqua gym and sports competitions in the daytime, concerts, karaoke, and other evening entertainment. Disco 3 times a week.
Sanitary facilities	Two toilet blocks in attractive buildings both well appointed and kept clean with good number of individual cabins. Showers are push button, temperature control, with shelf, hook and rail. Individual wash basins. Good quality toilets with toilet paper and washbasin, soap and towel outside. Disabled facilities. Baby room. Laundry. Chemical waste point.
Services	Vival shop, bar with large terrace, take-away/ crêperie. Oak beamed restaurant. All are set out in attractive buildings and open all season. In peak season there is a sound proof night bar open from 11pm until 2 am. Barbecues allowed. Dogs accepted. Internet and Wi-Fi.
Accommodation	Variety of mobile homes - 60 units.
Tour operators	One French company.

Excursions/Places to visit
Canoeing on Dordogne, Souillac, Sarlat, Rocamadour, Lascaux caves, Beynac.

Directions
From Brive. Take the A20 to Souillac. As you come into the town of Souillac, at the first traffic island take the second road on the right to Salignac on the D15 (the site is signposted from here). Follow this road for 5km. You pass through the hamlet of Bourzoles continue on the D62, take the next turning right. The road winds up the hill to the camp and is very well signposted. From the south. Take the N20 to Souillac. Follow signs to Salignac on the D15 and D62 and proceed as above.

€ Prices 2010	High	Mid	Low
Pitch + 2	25.80	21.90	18.60
Hook Up 3A	4	4	4
10A + W & Dr	6	6	6

Address 46200 Souillac-sur-Dordogne

GPS N 44° 56' 41 E 01° 26' 30

www.lapaillebasse.com
email info@lapaillebasse.com
Tel 05.65.37.85.48

EASTERN FRANCE

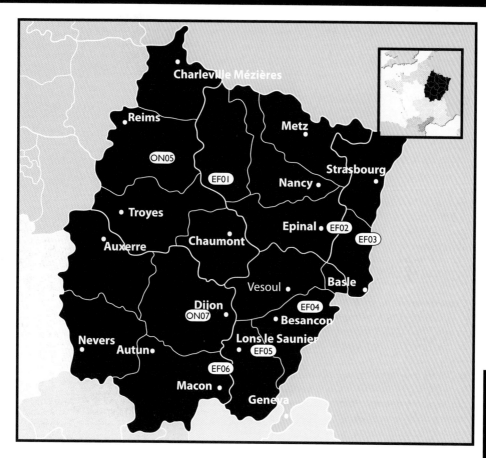

Cascade du Hérisson

Places of Interest - Eastern France

We have included several areas in Eastern France, Vosges, Alsace, Jura and Burgundy.
The Vosges is a mountain range near the Franco-German frontier, 250 km in length and rising to its highest point 1,422m at the Ballon de Guebwiller. It is separated from the Jura Mountains to the south by the Belfort Gap. The hills and rich green country of the Vosges spread fanwise across Eastern France. Visitors have an infinite number of walks to choose from along lush plains decked with wild flowers or shady paths in the forests.

Domrémy and the house where Jeanne d'Arc was born.

Epinal is a city with an attractive basilica and is a centre for spinning, weaving and sawmills.

The spring waters of the **Vosges** have given rise to numerous therapeutic spas and health resorts such as Vittel, Contrexéville and Plombières. The eastern part of the region offers a wonderful blend of mountains, lakes, rivers and waterfalls, and is great for walking and site-seeing.

Lake at Gérardmer

Gérardmer, is the jewel of the Vosges, as it is dominated by a lake and surrounded by forests, rivers, lakes and waterfalls - it is also famous for its textile industry.

Le Tholy, a delightful village about 10km from Gerardmer, extending in terraces up the "Grandes Roches" 950m, is an ideal starting point for numerous hiking tours in the neighbouring forests.

Parc Regional des Ballons des Vosges
The park was created in 1989 and covers an area of 3,000 km². It is named after the famous 'ballons' or dome-shaped mountains and is a hiker's paradise, combining wonderful views in rich natural surroundings.

Alsace which enjoys a border with Germany bears testimony to the influence of its neighbours both in its architecture and its culture. Towns worth visiting include:

Mulhouse whose incredible industrial development can be traced in its eight museums which make up the largest grouping of technical museums in Europe. The Tour de l'Europe, 99m high, contrasts with the old craftsmen's and tradesmen's district, now a pedestrian-only zone. It also has the world's largest car museum consisting of more than 600 motor vehicles and 90 well-known makes.

Strasbourg is a city set on the river Rhine and a major gateway to Europe. Today it abounds with a rich mixture of cultural traditions and along with New York and Geneva, it shares the privilege of being the seat of numerous international organizations without being a capital city. The old city lies around the cathedral on an island formed by two arms of the Ill river. The narrow streets of the old town offer a series of half-timbered houses dating from the 16th and 17th centuries with large inner courtyards and high sloping roofs.

Colmar is the capital of the Alsatian wine-growing region. It is well-known for its historic old town, now a vast pedestrian precinct. The centre is made up of a web of narrow cobbled streets, flanked by medieval half-timbered houses with carved gables, ancient signs, oriel windows and doors with vintage lintels.

Eguisheim - near Colmar

Franche-Comté is one of the smallest regions in France and stretches between the Vosges and Jura mountains. It shares a border with Switzerland and consists of four départements including the Doubs and Jura. It is a region blessed with a wealth of lakes, fascinating caves and small villages. Eight out of ten villages have less than five hundred inhabitants. The Comté bell-towers à l'impériale, a sort of dome which tops more than 400 churches, are signs that religion is everywhere. It is also the centre of French clock-making and birthplace of Peugeot cars. The Doubs offers 1,500km of paths, many of them particularly suitable for mountain-biking and the Jura is best known for its wines and the Lac de Chalain. Places of interest to visit in the region include:

Villersexel with its château de Grammont, built at the end of the 19th century.

Baume-les-Messieurs Caves, near Lons-le-Saunier are 30 million years old. Visitors can explore galleries 120m underground with spectacular lighting effects, rock formations and a beautiful waterfall at the cave entrance.

Osselle Cave, near Quingey regarded as one the most wonderful caves in Europe is renowned for its outstanding natural colours varying from blue to translucent orange.

Three further caves to visit are, **Glacière Cave**, nr Valdahons, and the **Moidon Cave** and **Les Planches Cave** both near Ardois.

Cascade du Saut du Doubs, near Villers-le-Lac on Swiss border is a 27m high waterfall.

Cascade du Hérisson - a magnificent waterfall near Clairvaux-les-Lacs.

Burgundy's natural riches and colourful history have marked the region with some of the finest heritage of European art and architecture. It is a beautiful fertile land of undulating hills, woods and waterways whose wealth is nurtured by farmers, vine-growers and foresters. It has always been on the way to somewhere and is well worth a long stopover. Its strategic location, close to Germany, within easy reach of the Netherlands and a short distance from Switzerland has made its people particularly hospitable and friendly. The reputation of the local cuisine is famous throughout the world, while its wines are a byword for the very best. Some of the most important places of architectural interest are listed below:

Autun with its Roman theatre and gates from the Gallo-Roman period.

Vézelay was one of the most important places of pilgrimage in France on the way to Santiago de Compostela and is famous for its abbey, a masterpiece of Romanesque architecture.

Fontenay's 12th century abbey is one of the earliest and most impressive examples of Cistercian architecture.

Dijon has a wonderful palace and around it stretches the historical centre. The visitor can take a stroll down small streets past half-timbered houses and elegant mansions, through elegant squares and beneath the shadow of its church spires.

Beaune The brightly coloured tiled roofs of the Hôtel-Dieu in Beaune have come to symbolise Burgundy throughout the world. A maze of little streets make up the old town and no visit would be complete without a visit to the town's wine cellars.

Arnay-le-Duc is a charming little city and among its many attractions are its 15th -17th century houses and shaded walks.

Châlon-sur-Saône is a major commercial and industrial centre offering a wide range of tourist attractions.

www.vosges.fr
www.tourisme-alsace.com
www.jura-tourism.com
www.burgundy-tourism.com

Lac de Chalain

Thonnance-les-Moulins, La Forge de Ste Marie ****Map Ref EF01

Location Poissons 4km. Joinville 12km. Neufchâteau 40km. Chaumont 56km. Reims 148km.

Open 24th Apr to 10th Sept   **Pitches** 170 (105 touring)

An old stone-faced forge and mill which overlook a small lake and river are the focal point of this Castels site. Set in the heart of the Champagne hills, it is well placed as a stopover point en route to Eastern France, Germany and Italy. It is also suitable for longer stays to explore this charming unspoilt region. It is a spacious site rich in fauna and flora. Wild orchids grow in abundance, there are numerous rare trees including 200-year old oaks and over 50 different species of birds have been spotted. Narrow entrance for large outfits.

Site suitable for couples and young families who enjoy a quiet rural atmosphere with some entertainment.

Pitches	Grassy pitches ranging from 100m² - 150m², some laid out on terraces and gently sloping. Divided by low hedges and shrubs. Trees give shade on some pitches.
Hook-Up	6 amps, water & drainage - all pitches.
Motorhomes	Motorhome service point. Some hard standing pitches. Need transport to visit area.
Swimming pools	In the old forge attractive medium-sized indoor pool and paddling pool with indoor terrace plus outdoor sun terrace and sun loungers.
Activities on site	A large, open, grassy area for football, volleyball, basketball and badminton. Boules pitch. Table tennis. Archery. Children's play areas dotted round the site. Indoor games room with pool, table football and electronic games. TV room. Category A trout fishing in river with permit available from Poissons 3km. Pony riding lessons.
Entertainment	High season: children's club 4 -12 yr olds and children's discos. Guided walks. Cheese & Wine tasting afternoons. Evening entertainment includes live music once a week, quizzes and barbecue evenings.
Sanitary facilities	Two unisex toilet blocks, which although now 15 years old are still quite respectable and well-maintained. Push button showers, no temperature control, with hooks and shelf. Individual wash cubicles with hot and cold taps. Toilets with toilet paper. Disabled facilities. Baby area. A washing machine and tumble dryer in each block. Chemical waste point.
Services	Small shop. Bar and restaurant are in an attractively renovated stone faced building which is 300 yrs old and has a terrace overlooking site's own fishing lake. Take-away/pizzeria. Barbecues allowed. Dogs accepted. Internet and Wi-Fi in bar area.
Accommodation	35 mobile homes, 15 gîtes.
Tour operators	One British company on 12 pitches and one Dutch company on 10.

Excursions/Places to visit
Grand and its Gallo-Roman amphitheatre, Domrémy-la-Pucelle, birth place of Joan of Arc. Little Switzerland area and Cul du Cerf for walking. Der-Chantecoq lake 30km. Nigloland children's theme park- less than an hour.

Directions
From St Dizier. Take the N67 to Joinville (Chaumont) and exit at Joinville-est. Follow the signs for Poissons and Neufchateau turning right onto the D60 and right again onto the D427. Continue on this road through Poissons and Noncourt-sur-le-Rongeant. The campsite is situated 2km after Noncourt-sur-le-Rongeant on your right. N.B. The entrance to the site is narrow so care should be taken when turning into the site.

€ Prices 2010	High	Low
Pitch + 2	29.90	18.70
Hook Up 6A	Incl	Incl

Address 52230 Thonnance-les-Moulins

www.laforgedesaintemaire.com
email la.forge.de.sainte.marie@wanadoo.fr

GPS N 48° 24' 23 E 05° 16' 16

Tel 03.25.94.42.00

Le Tholy, Camping de Noirrupt ****

Location Le Tholy 1.3km. Gérardmer 10km. Epinal 28km. Colmar 74km.

Open 15th Apr to 15th Oct **Pitches** 82 (70 touring)

A short walk from the village of Le Tholy, this cosy little site nestles in the heart of the Vosges mountains. It offers great views of the village and the surrounding landscape and is beautifully maintained. The flowery entrance is complemented by forty different varieties of tree. You can be sure of a warm welcome from the friendly owners, who are very keen to maintain a quiet peaceful atmosphere. A good mixture of nationalities comes to enjoy the verdant scenery of this pretty mountainous region.

Site suitable for couples and young families, particularly walkers and cyclists.

Pitches	Flat, grassy and laid out on terraces ranging in size from 90m² - 150m². Divided by low trees and shrubs, giving some privacy and some shade. Smaller pitches with views at top of site.
Hook-Up	2 or 6 amps - all pitches. Water & drainage - 30 pitches
Motorhomes	Emptying facilities but no special motorhome service point. Need transport to visit area.
Swimming pools	Good-sized pool for small site 15m x 10m and sun terrace with sun loungers, good for a dip at the end of a day walking or cycling. No paddling pool but shallow area at both ends of pool. Open mid-June to mid-Sept.
Activities on site	Cycle hire. Tennis. Badminton. Table tennis. Boules pitch. Children's play area. Sauna with charge.
Entertainment	No organised entertainment on site itself. Guided mountain walks are arranged every two or three days. Occasional wine-tasting.
Sanitary facilities	Two very well maintained toilet blocks. First block at bottom of the site has recently been renovated with attractive tiling. Separate men's and ladies in this block, second one unisex. Push button showers, no temperature control with hook and shelf. Separate wash cubicles. Toilets with seats and toilet paper. Disabled facilities. Baby room. Separate laundry. Chemical waste point.
Services	Pre-order bread in July/August. No shop. Bar/snack overlooking pool which sells drinks, ice creams and pizzas. Barbecues allowed. Dogs accepted. Internet and Wi-Fi.
Accommodation	12 chalets.
Tour operators	None.

Excursions/Places to visit
Gérardmer. Parc Naturel des Ballon des Vosges. Col de la Schluct and Col du Ballon - mountain passes offering magnificent views.

Directions
From Epinal. Take the N420 exit and after approximately 500m turn right onto the D11 east in the direction of Gérardmer. After approximatey 27km you arrive at Le Tholy. Turn right as you enter the village and follow signs to the site marked Camping & Chalets, turning again after 500m.
From Gérardmer. Take the D417 in the direction of Epinal. After 13km you arrive at Le Tholy. Turn right into the village and follow signposts to the campsite marked Camping & Chalets.

€ Prices 2010	High	Low
Pitch + 2	20.70	14.49
Hook Up 6A	5	5

Address 5 Chemin de l'Etang, 88530 Le Tholy

GPS N48 ° 05' 20 E 06° 43' 42

www.jpvacances.com
email info@jpvacances.com
Tel 03.29.61.81.27

Ste-Croix-en-Plaine, Camping Clair Vacances **** Map Ref EF03

Location Herrlisheim 1.5km. Ste Croix-en-Plaine 2km. Colmar 11km. Mulhouse 36km.

Open 1st Apr to 17th Oct   **Pitches** 135 (125 touring)

Situated in a pretty glade in the middle of a forest just 3km from the motorway and walking distance of two villages, this pretty little site is renowned for its peace and quiet. There is no bar nor evening entertainment making it particularly suitable for young families. The wealth of trees, plants and flowers are well tended and create a welcoming atmosphere that attracts a good cross-section of nationalities. You are well positioned here for visiting the Alsace, a pretty region greatly influenced by its German neighbours.

Site suitable for couples and young families.
American motor homes not accepted.
British twin-axle caravans must book in advance.

Pitches	Flat, grassy, varying in size from 80m² - 110m², separated in groups by hedges with low shrubs between the individual pitches. Far end of site is very spacious but there is no electrical hook up.
Hook-Up	8 or 13 amps. - 65 pitches. X-Large pitch - 35 pitches. Water & drainage - 10 pitches.
Motorhomes	Motor home service point and some hard standing pitches. Walking distance of villages but transport needed for shopping and touring.
Swimming pools	Attractive oval-shaped pool 150m², paddling pool with large cemented sun terrace and sun loungers, all surrounded by pretty flowers and shrubs.
Activities on site	Table tennis. Good children's play areas. Boules pitch. No TV room. Football pitch and clay court tennis court 2km.
Entertainment	In high season, children's activities mostly sport and games are organised. There is a huge open play area by 2nd toilet block. Wine tasting once a week in high season.
Sanitary facilities	Two very well appointed heated toilet blocks maintained to a high standard. Have to remove shoes to go into shower area. The 2nd block at far end of site is more modern and luxurious with showers and washbasins together in spacious cubicles. Push button temperature controlled showers with hooks and rail. Individual wash cubicles. Toilets with seats and toilet paper. Disabled facilities. Baby room. Laundry area in both blocks. Chemical waste point.
Services	No shop, but milk and wine available in reception. Pre-order bread. No bar or restaurant. In high season take-away pizzas two days a week. Butchers and small supermarket in Ste. Croix. Barbecues allowed. Dogs not accepted. Wi-Fi for 50m round reception area.
Accommodation	10 mobile homes.
Tour operators	None.

Excursions/Places to visit
Colmar 10mins, Ribeauvillé and Riquewihr 20mins, Mulhouse and Kayserberg 30mins. Strasbourg -1hr. Eguisheim 7km.

Directions
The site is south east of Eguisheim and due west of Ste-Croix-en-Plaine just off the D1. From A35 South, take exit 27 to Ste Croix-en-Plaine. At the roundabout take the 3rd exit signposted to Herrlisheim and Clair Vacances. The site entrance is on your left after 2km. From A35 North exit 27 to Ste-Croix-en-Plaine and Herrlisheim. Turn right onto the D1 to Herrlisheim and continue as above.

€ Prices 2010	High	Mid	Low
Pitch + 2	20	15	12.50
Hook Up 8A	3.50	3.50	3.50

Address Route de Herrlisheim, 68127 Ste-Croix-en-Plaine

www.clairvacances.com
email clairvacances@wanadoo.fr
Tel 03.89.49.27.28

GPS N 48° 00' 59 E 07° 21' 02

Rougemont, Le Val de Bonnal ****

Location A36 and Baume-les-Dames 13km. Rougemont 3.5km. Vesoul 26km. Besançon 59km.

Open 30th Apr to 5th Sept

Pitches 350 (213 touring)

The major attraction of this Castels site is its position 200m from four lakes and the spacious layout of the pitches along the banks of the River l'Ognon. Two of the lakes are for fishing, one is for private water ski-ing and the nearest lake has a large attractive beach area suitable for swimming and boating. The pretty little hamlet of Bonnal just outside the gates complements the stone-faced buildings and verdant setting. A small island in middle of river is great for picnics. The Franche-Comté region's attractions are within easy reach.

Site suitable for all ages particularly active families.

Pitches	Very generous spacious pitches 140m² - 200m², flat and grassy, separated by low shrubs and trees, some overlook river.
Hook-Up	5 amps - all pitches. 10 amps - 120 pitches. Water & drainage - none.
Motorhomes	Motorhome service point. Everything on site but need transport to visit area.
Swimming pools	Good sized pool area with large irregular shaped basins divided by a bridge. Waterslide, paddling pool. Pretty sun terrace and sun loungers. Open 11 am to 6 pm.
Activities on site	Cycle hire. Two good children's play areas. Football pitch. Badminton. Boules pitch. Indoor games room with table tennis, table football and electronic games. TV in bar. New gym area called the Hexagon after the shape of its glass-sided building. Fishing in river and two fishing lakes with permit. Further lake with beach for supervised swimming, canoe, kayak and pedalo hire. Go-kart track by lake. Golf 8km.
Entertainment	In high season: children's club, tree climbing adventure park as part of organised entertainment for older children as well as sporting competitions, dance and music evenings in the bar.
Sanitary facilities	Four toilet blocks. One nearest reception is modern, spacious, light, attractively tiled, push button temperature controlled showers with hooks, some combined with wash basins. Toilets with seats and paper. Second block opposite bridge over river is older but respectable. Third block is even older and one at far end is modern but only has toilets and washbasins. Disabled facilities. Baby room. Laundry. Chemical waste point.
Services	Reasonably well-stocked shop. Bar/snack/ take-away. Wooden beamed restaurant by lake, only open in evening. All open all season. Barbecues allowed. Dogs accepted. Internet. Wi-Fi around bar area and covering about half of site.
Accommodation	10 chalets and 2 mobile homes.
Tour operators	Two British and two Dutch companies on 125 pitches.

Excursions/Places to visit

Rougemont 20 mins by bike, Villersexel 9km, Vesoul, Besançon, Le Saut du Doubs, Gouffre de Poudre, Grotte de la Glacière.

Directions

From the A36. Take the exit at Baume-les-Dames and head north on the D492 towards Villersexel. After 13km turn left to Rougemont. As you leave the town, turn right to Bonnal and the site entrance is on your right just past the village centre. From Vesoul. Head in the direction of Villersexel along the D919 which turns into the D9 after 2km. After 20km you will arrive at the village of Esprels, turn right here and then left after 3km. The site entrance is 1km on your left hand side.

€ Prices 2010	High	Mid	Low
Pitch + 2	37	28	20.50
Hook Up 5A	7	5.50	4.50

Address 1, Rue du Vieux Moulin, 25680 Rougemont

GPS N 47° 30' 28 E 06° 21' 22

www.camping-valdebonnal.fr
email val-de-bonnal@wanadoo.fr
Tel 03.81.86.90.87

Marigny, La Pergola ****

Location Doucier 2.5km. Lons-le-Saunier 23km. Geneva 97km. Besançon 85km.

Open 8th May to 13th Sept

Pitches 350 (130 touring)

A unique position stretching along the banks of the magnificent Chalain lake in the heart of the Jura mountains makes this site a very attractive holiday destination. It is a great spot for water sports enthusiasts. Just outside the town of Doucier, it is a very well maintained site with fabulous flowers decorating the reception, bar and restaurant area. It is also a very convenient base for visiting the magnificent scenery of the region, the numerous woodland trails, cycle tracks and walking paths.
Clef Verte

Site suitable for all ages particularly active families.

Pitches	Flat, grassy 100m² - 110m² divided by high hedges and laid out in terraces overlooking the lake. Some slope slightly. The pitches near the lake are actually the smallest and there is a large mesh fence protecting the pitches from the beach with several entry gates. The best views are higher up.
Hook-Up	6 or 12 amps water & drainage - all pitches.
Motorhomes	Motorhome service point. Everything on site.
Swimming pools	A large attractive aqua complex 1,200m² including the huge sun terrace with sun loungers. There are three separate pools, a large one 450m² with jacuzzi for bathing, an exercise pool and a paddling pool.
Activities on site	Large games area with football pitch, volleyball, badminton and archery. Boules pitch. Fantastic children's play area. Table tennis. Giant chess. Swimming in lake, but stoney beach (plastic shoes recommended). On lake: hire of windsurfers, catamarans, canoes, kayaks, pedaloes and electric boats (motorboats prohibited). Fishing with permit.
Entertainment	High season: children's club 5 - 12yrs, organised programme of daytime and evening activities including aquagym, sports tournaments, discos, concerts and shows.
Sanitary facilities	Two attractive toilet blocks. One nearest reception is more modern and tiled in red and white. Push button temperature control showers, shelf, hook and rail. Individual wash cubicles. Toilets with toilet paper outside. Laundry in both blocks which are well maintained. Disabled facilities. Baby room. Chemical waste point
Services	Small shop, bar, take-away. Two restaurants with panoramic views, one fast food and one more traditional with good menus. Barbecues allowed. Dogs accepted. Internet. Wi-Fi in bar/restaurant area.
Accommodation	130 mobile homes and chalets.
Tour operators	Three British companies and one Dutch company on 80 pitches.

Excursions/Places to visit
Cirque de Baume valley. Cascades du Hérisson. Lons-le-Saunier. Champagnole. Mountain-biking, hiking in the Jura mountains. Day trip to Geneva.

Directions
From the A39 Motorway. Leave the A39 motorway at junction 8 and follow signs to Lons-le-Saunier. At Lons-le-Saunier take the D471 towards Champagnole and then turn right on to the D27 at Pont-du-Navoy towards Marigny. The campsite is well-signposted to your left from Marigny.

€ Prices 2010	Peak	High	Mid	Low
Pitch + 2	37	32	21	19
Hook Up 6A	Incl	Incl	Incl	Incl

Address Lac de Chalain, 39130 Marigny

www.lapergola.com
email contact@lapergola.com
Tel 03.84.25.70.03

GPS N 46° 40' 38 E 05° 46' 49

Gigny-sur-Saône, Château de l'Epervière ****

Location Sennécy Le Grand 7.5km. Chalon-sur-Saône 23km. Tournus 17km. Dijon 94km.

Open 28th Mar to 30th Sept   **Pitches** 160 (113 touring)

You cannot fail to be impressed by the superb setting of this site. It is situated in the heart of rural Burgundy in the magnificent wooded parkland of an elegant 16th century château. The site is laid out in two spacious areas, one near the château and the other across a small causeway over the pretty fishing lake, overhung with weeping willows. The services are housed in the pretty stone-faced outbuildings. It a good centre for exploring the region and offers a calm relaxing atmosphere. The site is renowned for its delightful gourmet restaurant in the château and wine tastings in the 14th century vaulted cellars three times a week.

Site suitable for all ages, particularly couples and young families.

Pitches	Good-sized, flat pitches, laid out under the trees, most with some shade. Separated by hedges for privacy. Mostly grassy but some hardstanding.
Hook-Up	10 amps - all pitches. Water & drainage - 28 pitches.
Motorhomes	Motorhome service point. Some hardstanding pitches. Nearest services are found in Sennécy 7km.
Swimming pools	Good-sized rectangular pool behind the château with generous sun terrace and sun loungers. Paddling pool in second half of site. Medium sized indoor pool, jacuzzi and sauna.
Activities on site	Children's play area. Bouncy castle. Fishing in small lake - no permit. Fishing in river Saône 500m with permit. Indoor games: pool, table football, video games and TV in bar. Several marked out cycle tracks direct from the site - details in reception.
Entertainment	Wine tasting three times a week. High season: children's club and organised games. Music evenings once a week.
Sanitary facilities	Two toilet blocks well maintained with separate ladies and gents. Attractively tiled well-lit and airy. Push button temperature controlled showers with hooks. Individual wash basins. Toilets with seats and toilet paper. Good washing up area. Disabled facilities. Baby room. Separate laundry. Chemical waste point.
Services	Small shop well stocked with basics. Attractive bar area. Take-away. Beautiful restaurant with covered terrace serving reasonably priced menus. Barbecues allowed. Dogs accepted. Internet, Wi-Fi in bar area.
Accommodation	5 mobile homes and 3 appartments.
Tour operators	Two British companies on 42 pitches.

Excursions/Places to visit

Gigny-walking distance. Chalon-sur-Saône, Tournus, Abbey at Cluny. Beaune. Dijon. Numerous Burgundy vineyards.

Directions

From the north. Exit the A6 motorway at the Chalon-sud exit. Take the N6 travelling south to Sennecey-le-Grand. Turn left here on to the D18 to Gigny-sur-Saône. The campsite is situated to the south of the village and is well-signposted. From the south. Take the Tournus exit from the A6 motorway. Join the N6 travelling north to Sennecey-le-Grand. Turn right here on to the D18 to Gigny-sur-Saône and continue as above.

€ Prices 2010	High	Low
Pitch + 2	28.10	19.90
Hook Up 6A	5.40	3.50

Address Rue du Château, 71240 Gigny-sur-Saône

GPS N 46° 39' 16 E 04° 56' 39

www.domaine-eperviere.com
email domaine-de-leperviere@wanadoo.fr
Tel 03.85.94.16.90

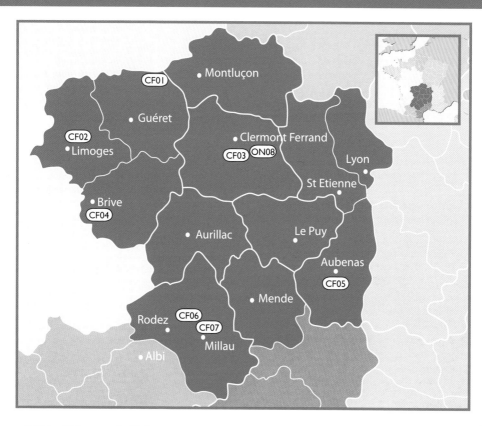

Picture opposite - Craters of the Massif Central

Places of Interest - Central France

In the Central Region we have included two sites in the Limousin area, a site in the Corrèze, one in the Auvergne, one in the Ardèche and two in the Aveyron.

Limousin is a region typified by open countryside, a third of which is forested. It is also one of the lowest populated regions in France. Its capital city Limoges is renowned for its porcelain, whilst Aubusson is famous for its beautiful tapestries. Crozant and Fresslines to the north of the region have long been a centre for artists (in particular Monet), and the river Creuse offers awe inspiring gorges. With the exception of Limoges and a few small towns, the population is scattered among tiny villages and hamlets which pepper the countryside.

Four château in the region worth a visit are the medieval **Château de Boussac**, **Château de Chalus** - the final resting place of Richard the Lionheart, **Château de Villemonteix** between Guéret and Aubusson which is privately owned, and the impressive **Château de Rochechouart** a 15th Century château which houses the area's Centre of Contemporary Art.

Corrèze is an area to the west of the Dordogne region, but still home to a large section of the Dordogne River. It abounds in waterfalls, attractive views and great stretches of water to canoe and kayak. The Dordogne valley between Argentat and Liourdres is exceptionally beautiful and is classed as a "grand site national ".

Over the centuries **Argentat** has been an important trade centre. Wood, leather and oil were transported by boat and the beautiful quayside lined with old turreted houses bears witness to this.

The pretty medieval town of **Beaulieu-sur-Dordogne** has a magnificent Benedictine Abbey, an attractive square and narrow cobbled streets. Several other villages in the region are classified amongst the most beautiful villages in France. These are: **Collonges-la-Rouge, Curemonte, Saint-Robert, Ségur le-Château** and **Treignac.**

Auvergne is a region of vast green open spaces, dotted with lakes, forests and volcanoes, and offers some of the best walks to be found in France. Sculpted by fire, the Auvergne is the largest volcanic region in Europe and has four volcanic massifs, the youngest of which dates back 10,000 years. For the enthusiast it is a veritable open-air geological exhibition. The last volcanic eruption was some 5800 years ago. The Loire, Allier and Dordogne rivers rise in the Auvergne region which along with the lakes is full of rapids and thermal springs including Vichy and Chaudes-Aigues.

The Puy de Sancy is the highest mountain in the Massif Central and a trek to the summit is well worth the effort to enjoy the magnificent views. **Issoire** with its ancient Benedictine abbey and **Saint-Nectaire** with its cathedral-like church on top of Cornadore hill are both worth a visit.

Le Puy de Sancy

Murol is small town with a delightful gothic style church famed for its interior decoration and for its 12th century château.

Vulcania www.vulcania.com, the volcanic theme park helps explain the fascinating universe of volcanoes via satellite images, moving models and audio visual shows.

Walking in Central France

Ardèche is one of the richest natural sites in Europe. It is a region of beautiful unspoilt scenery, rushing rivers, dramatic gorges, wonderful lakes and cultural traditions ranging from prehistoric times to the present day. The Southern Ardèche region is well-known for its Mediterranean climate, beautiful riverside beaches and canoe-kayaking. It is a favourite place for sporting holidays. Mountain biking, paragliding, climbing, potholing, canyoning or simply hiking are also popular.

Cevennes Village

Le Pont d'Arc is a graceful natural arch over the river Ardèche, in the heart of the Ardèche gorge. Little footpaths lead to its base where you will find spectacular scenic routes to explore over 26km of the gorge.

The modernised town of **Vallon Pont d'Arc** has plenty of bars and restaurants.

The beautifully positioned hilltop town of **Largentière** is worth a visit because of its lovely quaint local market.

There are also several wonderful caves to visit in the area including the **Aven d'Orgnac** grotto characterised by a big lava flow looking like an organ case and the **Aven Grotte de la La Forestière,** located on road D217 between Vallon Pont d'Arc and Orgnac, where you can admire the Cave Animal Zoo, and beautiful coral-like stalactites and stalagmites emerging from pools of water.

Le Mont du Gerbier de Jonc not far from Privas rises to 1,550 metres in height and offers superb panoramic views. The **Cascade de Ray-Pic** is a natural waterfall located between Aubenas and Burzet.

Aveyron is a magnificent region of breathtaking scenery with deep chasms in the valleys of the Tarn and Dourbie. Many people visit the area for the canoeing, rafting and hang-gliding. A canoe trip along the Tarn gorges is an unforgettable experience.

Millau is renowned as a shopping centre for leather goods, including gloves but is now equally famous for its fabulous viaduct, designed by British architect Norman Foster. It can be viewed from a visitor's centre just off the A75.

Drive along the valleys and see picturesque villages perched on the top of cliffs like **Peyreleau, Cantobre** and **Saint-Véran.** In the centre of the Causse de Larzac, you will find **La Couvertoirade**, a fantastic Knights Templar town encased in a five-sided outer wall.

Montpellier-le-Vieux is a weird universe of amazing rock formations. Water and wind transformed the grey rocks of the Causse Noir into a wonderful city which has now become the shelter for delicate flora. You can walk on well signed footpaths or take the little green train that will lead you to the heart of this imposing site.

Aven Armand, an extraordinary cave of stalcamites and stalactites, 75m deep, discovered one Sunday afternoon in September 1897 by Louis Armand.

Roquefort, home of the famous blue-veined cheese made from ewes milk, offers a fascinating visit.

Monts d'Aubrac are in the north of the region and are the final volcanic rampart of the Massif Central region. This region is famous for its livestock breeding, and its lakes which are ideal for fishing, swimming and all kinds of watersports. The **Lac de Pont de Salars** and the **Lac de Pareloup** offer 15km of beaches and are the largest in southern France. The towns of **Décazeville, Entraygues, Espalion, Estaing** and **Saint-Geniez d'Olt** are all worth a detour. **Laguiole** is well-known for both its knives and its cheese.

www.the-limousin.co.uk
www.vacances-en-correze.net
www.auvergne-tourisme.info
www.guideweb.com/ardeche
www.ardeche-guide.com
www.tourisme-aveyron.com

Boussac-Bourg, Château de Poinsouze ****

Location Boussac 4km, Montluçon 42km, Guéret 52km. La Châtre 34km. Limoges 136km.

Open 12th May to 11th Sept

Pitches 133 (108 touring)

A very attractively landscaped site in the grounds of a fairy-tale style castle where you can be sure of a quiet relaxing holiday. The charming owners of this Castels site create a warm friendly atmosphere and maintain the grounds and facilities to a very high standard. The pitches overlook a small lake suitable for boating, small inflatables and beginner windsurfers. The site is set in rolling countryside in an undiscovered corner of France that offers a wealth of little châteaux, churches and pretty villages to visit. Due to its remote location, we would recommend combining a stay here with a visit to another region.
Clef Verte

Site suitable for couples and young families. Not suitable for teenagers.

Pitches	Grassy, mostly flat although some slope gently. Very generous in size up to 150m². Divided by low shrubs not heavily hedged giving a spacious feel. Some have lovely view over lake towards the château.
Hook-Up	6 amps - all pitches. Water & drainage - 67 pitches. Possibility of 10 amps, 16 amps or 25 amps on some pitches.
Motorhomes	Motorhome service point. Special area for overnight motor homes at reduced rate. Need transport to visit the region.
Swimming pools	Small swimming-pool with water slide. Paddling pool with baby waterslide. In attractive setting behind château and next to stone-faced outbuildings. Sun terrace with sun loungers.
Activities on site	Cycle hire. Sports area for football, volleyball, basketball and badminton. Table tennis. Children's play area. Small animal park. TV room. Library. Trampoline and bouncy castle. Indoor games room. Fishing in lake. Kayaks, catamaran, canoes, pedalos and sail boards for hire. Annual golf competition 14th June 2010.
Entertainment	High season: children's club, occasional evening entertainment such as dance evenings and quiz nights.
Sanitary facilities	One extremely well-maintained toilet block which has been built to a high specification. Separate ladies and gents. Push button, temperature control showers with shelves and hooks. Individual wash basins. Toilets with seats and toilet paper. Washing up area in middle of block. Disabled facilities. Baby room. Laundry. Chemical waste point.
Services	Small shop, bar, take-away and pretty oak-beamed restaurant - all open all season. Second bar overlooking the pool open according to demand. Barbecues allowed. Dogs accepted only in low season. Internet and Wi-Fi in area near toilet block.
Accommodation	25 mobile homes and chalets and 2 gites.
Tour operators	None.

Excursions/Places to visit
Market and medieval château in Boussac, château in Villemonteix. Aubusson. Limoges.
Vulcania - 2 hours.

Directions
From Montluçon. Take the ring road and follow the N145 towards Guéret. After 16km you turn right onto the D917 towards Boussac. Continue through Boussac on the D917 and the site entrance is on your left after 3km.
From Guéret. Take the N145 towards Montluçon. After 31km turn left towards Boussac on the D997. Then continue as above.

€ Prices 2010	High	Mid	Low
Std Pitch + 2	22	17	13
Confort 6A	29	24	19

Address Route de la Châtre, BP12 23600 Boussac-Bourg

www.camping-de-poinsouze.com
email info.camping-de-poinsouze@wanadoo.fr

GPS N 46° 22' 21 E 02° 12' 06

Tel 05.55.65.02.21

Location A10 2km. Bonnac La Côte 1km. Limoges 12km. Brive 103km.

Open 15 Apr to 20th Sept

Pitches 80 (78 touring)

We have chosen this site because of its unique setting in the grounds of a fabulous medieval château combined with its proximity to the A20 motorway. It is a small site set in the heart of the rolling wooded Limousin countryside and it is said that Victor Hugo found the inspiration for one of his poems here. The reception, bar and restaurant are housed in pretty stone faced outbuildings. There is a peaceful, friendly atmosphere, although we would only recommend it for short stays as there is a large turnover of visitors and the sanitary facilities could do with modernising. The site does not accept credit cards.

Site suitable for couples and recommended for short stays only.

Pitches	Mostly flat and grassy. A few slope gently. Divided by trees and low shrubs giving a spacious open feel.
Hook-Up	10 amps - 72 pitches. Tents only - 6 pitches.
Motorhomes	Motorhome service point. Not walking distance of town.
Swimming pools	Small rectangular pool and paddling pool with small attractive sun terrace and sun loungers.
Activities on site	Tennis. Boules pitch. Children's play area. Table tennis. Small games room with pool and table football. TV in bar. Good sized lake for fishing but not recommended for swimming. Small deer park by château. Walking trails near the site.
Entertainment	No organised entertainment. Classical music occasionally played (through PA system) over meadow in front of the château.
Sanitary facilities	One unisex toilet block in a converted barn. It is now rather dated, with old fashioned tiling and plumbing. However it was originally built to a high standard so it still functions adequately. Push button temperature control showers with hooks. Different parts have been renovated over the years and there is no consistent style. Only two individual wash cubicles. Toilets with seats and toilet paper. The facilities are kept clean. Chemical waste point.
Services	No real shop: pre-order bread. Wine and ice-creams sold in reception. Bar. Good restaurant. Supermarket 2km. Barbecues allowed. Dogs accepted. Internet and Wi-Fi
Accommodation	2 chalets.
Tour operators	None.

Excursions/Places to visit

Limoges, famous for its porcelain 12km. Lac de St Pardoux 14km.

Directions

From the north. Take the A20 towards Limoges, leaving at exit 27 in direction of Bonnac-la-Côte. the site is well signposted. All other directions. Pass through Limoges taking the A20 north in the direction of Châteauroux and the site is well signposted from exit 27 turning to Bonnac-la-Côte, 8km from Limoges.

€ Prices 2009	High	Low
Pitch + 2	24	21
Hook Up 10A	5	5

Address 87270 Bonnac-la-Côte

GPS N 45° 55' 59 E 01° 17' 24

www.leychoisier.com
email contact@leychoisier.com
Tel 05.55.39.93.43

Murol, Camping la Ribeyre ****

Location Murol 1km. A75 37km. St Nectaire 6km. Clermont Ferrand 36km. Issoire 31km.

Open 1st May to 15th Sept   **Pitches** 430 (285 touring)

A very well maintained site hidden in the heart of the Auvergne, 1km from Murol. This is a region of extinct volcanoes where the mountains rise to over 1500m. Although very close to the beautiful Lac Chambon, the site has its own man-made lake ideal for swimming and boating. The site is well positioned for visiting the whole region and is ideal for those who enjoy the mountains, walking and mountain biking. A wealth of beautiful trees and flowers give the site a very verdant feel. There is a good view of the château in Murol from the back of the site.

Site suitable for all ages, particularly active families in high season but good for couples in low season.

Pitches	Flat, grassy, not heavily hedged, divided by trees, up to 100m². Mobile homes are situated round the periphery of site and do not dominate touring pitches.
Hook-Up	6 or 10 amps - all pitches. Water & drainage - 74 pitches.
Motorhomes	No motorhome service point although walking distance of Murol and Lake Chambon.
Swimming pools	Superb aqua parc with total surface area of 1,500m². Outdoor area 400m² includes waterfalls and artificial rocks, geysers and bridges, water cannons, a 4-lane waterslide, a lazy river, a jacuzzi. Paddling pool. 200m covered pool which is excellent for swimming. Large sun terrace with sun loungers.
Activities on site	Tennis. Football pitch, volley ball court. Boules pitch. Children's play area. Indoor games area. TV room. Man-made lake 20,000m² with sandy beach for boating and swimming. Canoe hire on lake. Fishing in nearby river with permit.
Entertainment	High season: children's club, and programme of daytime and evening activities including aquagym, water polo, guided walks, theme evenings in bar with concerts and karaoke. Weekly welcome drink. Visiting craft market.
Sanitary facilities	Three unisex toilet blocks. Adequately equipped and well maintained, but nothing special. Block nearest reception could do with being refurbished as it is very dark. Other two blocks are more modern. Push button showers, no temperature control, with hooks. Individual wash basins. Toilet paper not provided. Disabled facilities. Baby room. Separate laundry. Chemical waste point.
Services	No shop - pre-order bread. Large Bar area with pretty terrace. Snack/pizzeria from 15th Jun. Barbecues allowed. Dogs accepted. Internet and Wi-Fi.
Accommodation	90 mobile homes and chalets.
Tour operators	One French company on 40 pitches and one Dutch company.

Excursions/Places to visit

Lake Chambon (1km on foot, 3km by road). Château in Murol, hike up Puy du Sancy, Saint-Nectaire. Site will arrange transport to top of Puy de Sancy for mountain bikers to then ride back to campsite.

Directions

From Clermont Ferrand. Take A75 south and exit at junction 6 in the direction of St Nectaire. Continue to the town of Murol and turn left and then turn right opposite the Syndicat d'Initiative. La Ribeyre is the second site along just after the entrance to Jassat and is well marked on the left. From Issoire. Take exit 14 from A75 and follow the ring road to the west of the town. Follow signs to Champeix along the D996 then continue as above.

€ Prices 2010	High	Mid	Low
Pitch + 2	25.30	19.80	18.75
Hook Up 6A	2.60	2.40	2.40

Address Jassat, 63790 Murol

GPS N 45° 33' 46 E 02° 56' 18

www.laribeyre.com
email info@laribeyre.com
Tel 04.73.88.64.29

Beaulieu-sur-Dordogne, Camping les Iles ***

Location Beaulieu/Dordogne 300m. Argentat 24km. Brive-la-Gaillarde 45km. Souillac 46km.

Open 17th Apr to 25th Sept   **Pitches** 120 (90 touring)

Staying on an island in the middle of the Dordogne river just 5 minutes walk from the pretty medieval town of Beaulieu makes this friendly family run site a truly unique spot. Access to the site is under a low wooden bridge with 3m high clearance. The fabulous flowery reception area is in a lovely old partly timber framed building and the pitches are laid out along the river amidst a variety of beautiful trees including oaks, beeches and weeping willows. There are numerous places of interest to visit nearby.

Site suitable for all ages, particularly young families and couples.

Pitches	Flat, grassy pitches with shade from trees. Vary in size up from 80m² - 120m², divided by shrubs. Supplement for riverside pitches.
Hook-Up	10 amps - 85 pitches.
Motorhomes	Motor home service point. Ideal as 5-min walk from centre of town.
Swimming pools	Medium sized oval-shaped pool and small paddling pool with generous sun terrace and a few sun loungers – opens in May.
Activities on site	Wide screen TV. Fishing in river. Canoe trips, cycle and walking tours organised by nearby agency. Tennis 600m, aquagym 700km. Archery 1km.
Entertainment	In high season: children's club 3 - 12yrs, music evenings twice a week. Guided walks including one round the town once a week.
Sanitary facilities	Three well-appointed toilet blocks, one of which has recently been refurbished. Push button temperature control showers, with hook. Individual wash basins. Toilets with toilet paper. All very clean and respectable. Disabled facilities. Baby room. Laundry facilities. Chemical waste point.
Services	Pre-order bread in high season. Bar/snack. Restaurant and take-away in high season. Good variety of shops including an Intermarché in the centre of the town. Gas barbecues only. Dogs accepted. Wi-Fi nr reception. Internet in town.
Accommodation	18 mobile homes and 12 tents.
Tour operators	None.

Excursions/Places to visit
Beaulieu itself with its magnificent market place. Annual "fête of the strawberry" on 2nd Sun in May. Collognes-la Rouge, medieval ruins of Turenne, fortress at Castelnau, towers of St Laurent St. Céré, Gouffre de la Fage, Gouffre de Padirac, Argentat. Rocamadour.

Directions
The site is on an island and is accessible from the centre of the town. Follow D940 to the town centre and turn Into the Boulevard-Rodolphe-de-Turenne following signs for the site. Vehicles over 3m high should telephone before arriving in the town to arrange access via a different route.

€ Prices 2010	High	Mid	Low	Off
Pitch + 2	21.90	19.90	17.90	10.90
Hook Up 5A	4	3	3	3

Address Boulevard Rodolphe-de-Turenne,
19120 Beaulieu-sur-Dordogne
GPS N 44° 58' 47 E 01° 50' 26

www.campingdesiles.fr
email info@campingdesiles.fr
Tel 05.55.91.02.65

Vallon-Pont d'Arc, L'Ardéchois ****

Location Vallon Pont d'Arc 1km. Pont d'Arc bridge 2km. Aubenas 35km. Alès 46km.

Open 1st Apr to 30th Sept   **Pitches** 244 (203 touring)

Situated walking distance from Vallon Pont d'Arc and the famous arched bridge cut into the rocks, this site has a spectacular position right on the Ardèche river, where it has its own beach and its own canoes. The friendly site owners have worked tirelessly since 1984 to create what is probably the best site in the area. Everything is beautifully maintained and totally in harmony with the natural verdant surroundings. All services including toilet blocks have been installed in pretty stone-faced buildings with an arched theme and further enhanced by an abundance of well-trimmed hedges and trees. A lively atmosphere in high season.

Site suitable for all ages, particularly canoe and outdoor sport enthusiasts.

Pitches	Flat spacious pitches ranging from 100m² for the standard pitches to 140m² for luxury pitches, divided by hedges giving some privacy. Will need strong pegs for tents and awnings.
Hook-Up	6 amps - 83 pitches. 10 amps with water & drainage (G.C.) - 120 pitches.
Motorhomes	Motor home service point. Walking/cycling distance of Vallon Pont d'Arc.
Swimming pools	Very attractive 400m² heated pool complex with large pool for swimming, a medium-sized basin and further paddling pool. Well-tiled sun terrace with sun loungers and straw parasols.
Activities on site	Tennis. Mini-golf. All weather sports pitch. Football pitch. Boules pitch. Table tennis. Pool and table football in bar area. Good children's play area. TV Room. Canoe hire and beach on river.
Entertainment	From mid-June to Sept, a programme of organised entertainment plus a children's club up to 12yrs, aquagym, sports tournaments, guided walks and music evenings in the bar.
Sanitary facilities	Two magnificent toilet blocks, each with a different theme but equally well appointed and maintained. Separate ladies and gents. Beautifully tiled and great attention to detail with arched doorways, wooden framed doors, fabulous mirrors, children's facilities and baby room. In one block some showers and washbasins together. Push button temperature control showers. Toilets with toilet paper. Disabled facilities. Laundry. Chemical waste point.
Services	Shop, attractive bar and restaurant. Take-away. Gas Barbecues only allowed. Special barbecue area on site. Dogs accepted. Internet and Wi-Fi in reception and bar area.
Accommodation	24 mobile homes.
Tour operators	One British company on 17 pitches.

Excursions/Places to visit
Ardèche gorges and numerous caves including Grottes des Tunnels and Aven d'Orgnac. Largentière 40km.

Directions
The site is situated by the Ardèche river on the D290. From Vallon Pont d'Arc follow signs to Gorges de l'Ardèche and Pont St Esprit. The site is on your right about 1km from the junction with the D978. You are advised to approach the site from Villeneuve-de-Berg to the north or Barjac to the south as the route along the river is twisty and can be very busy.

€ Prices 2010	Peak	High	Mid	Low
Std Pitch + 2	45	35	27	25
GC Pitch + 2	53	42	34	31
Hook Up	Incl	4.50	4.50	4.50

Address Route des Gorges de l'Ardeche, 07150 Vallon Pont d'Arc

GPS N 44° 23' 53 E 04° 23' 56

www.ardechois-camping.com
email ardecamp@bigfoot.com
Tel 04.75.88.06.63

Canet-de-Salars, Le Caussanel ****

Location Pont de Salars 10km. Millau 50km. Rodez 35km. A75 (Exit 44.1) 39km.

Open 10th May to 11th Sept

Pitches 235 (115 touring)

We have included this site because of its fabulous location on the Lac de Pareloup, situated 800m high between the Tarn and the Aveyron valleys. The pitches stretch out in gently rising terraces along the lake with a view from nearly every spot. Most of the services are housed in pretty stone-face buildings and it is a great site for water sports enthusiasts. It has not been chosen for the quality of its sanitary facilities which need to be refurbished, although the small block in the main building is modern and of a good standard.
Clef Verte

Site suitable for all ages, particularly those keen of water sports.

Pitches	Flat, grassy, laid out on terraces, most about 100m². Some of the pitches with water & drainage are more generous. Not hedged but divided by the odd tree, giving very spacious feel, but no privacy.
Hook-Up	6 amps - all pitches. Water & drainage - 45 pitches.
Motorhomes	Motorhome service on nearby farm. Need transport for visiting area.
Swimming pools	One pool 16m x 7m for swimming. Leisure pool with 2 waterslides. Good paddling pool with mini waterslides. Sun terrace with sun loungers.
Activities on site	Tennis. Cycle hire. All weather sports pitch for football and volleyball. Table tennis. Boules pitch. Good children's play area. Electronic games and table football in bar. Sailing, windsurfing, water ski-ing, canoeing and fishing in lake - own equipment required or hire nearby. There are signed walking and cycle tracks direct from the site.
Entertainment	High season: children's club 4 - 10yrs, organised sports tournaments and evening entertainment with music, karaoke and shows.
Sanitary facilities	There are three unisex toilet blocks. Although they are clean and quite respectable, two of them need renovating as the décor, design and plumbing are old. The showers are push button, no temperature control with hook and shelf. They have no dividing wall but are long and thin so clothes do not get damp. Individual wash basins, no mixer tap, so hot water for teeth cleaning. Toilets with paper but no seats. Chemical waste point.
Services	Well-stocked shop, bar, take-away. Attractive oak beamed restaurant, but very small and would recommend pre-booking. Barbecues allowed. Dogs accepted. Internet and Wi-Fi in reception and bar.
Accommodation	120 mobile homes and chalets mostly in one area, where shrubs and trees are too young to make it attractive.
Tour operators	None.

Excursions/Places to visit
Canoe trips in Gorges du Tarn, bungee jumping and quad biking can be arranged. Pont de Salars. Millau and its viaduct. Gorges du Tarn.

Directions
The site is on the Lac de Pareloup near the end of a cul de sac. From D911 Pont de Salars to Millau road take the D933 south towrds Salles Curan. After 6km turn right onto the D538 to Canet-de-Salars and then turn left after 200m following signs to the site.

€ Prices 2010	High	Mid	Low
Pitch + 2	28.50	18.60	14.50
Hook Up 6A	4.50	4.20	3.40

Address Lac de Pareloup, 12290 Le Caussanel

www.le caussanel.com
email info@lecaussanel.com
Tel 05.65.46.85.19

GPS N 44° 12' 53 E 02° 45' 59

Rivière-sur-Tarn, Le Peyrelade ****

Location Rivière-sur-Tarn 2km. Millau and A75 13km

Open 16th May to 12th Sept | **Pitches** 190 (145 touring)

The biggest asset of this site, situated 350m high at the mouth of the Tarn Gorges is its direct access to the river and delightful setting in a wooded valley. The pebbly beach stretches the length of the site and the river is shallow enough to bathe. Do remember to bring rubber shoes. The stunning rocks opposite the site offer magnificent views and are home to nesting vultures. The Peyrelade château towers over the site on the opposite side of the road. It is a great spot for canoeing with some interesting rapids further upstream and a perfect place from which to explore this fascinating region.

Site suitable for all ages, particularly ramblers, nature lovers and canoe enthusiasts.

Pitches	Flat, set out in terraces but varying in size up to 110m². Most have some shade, and are divided by low shrubs. Many tend to be long and thin. The best pitches overlook the river but tend to be smaller.
Hook-Up	6 amps - all pitches. Water & drainage - none.
Motorhomes	Motor home service point, but need transport for visiting area. Local village - 2km and restaurant 500m.
Swimming pools	Attractively laid out pool area, small for size of site. One pool for swimming 18m x 5m, paddling pool and sun terrace but no sun loungers.
Activities on site	Children's play area. TV, games room, table tennis tables, boules pitch, canoe hire. Tennis courts and mountain bike hire - 200m.
Entertainment	In high season: children's club for 5 to 10 yrs, archery, walks from the campsite, aquagym, fossil-hunting outings, boules competitions, bingo, musical evenings several times a week.
Sanitary facilities	Two toilet blocks, one updated more recently. Push button temperature control showers with hooks, some with wash basins combined in one block, no temperature control in older block. Individual wash cubicles. Toilets with seats but no paper. Both kept clean and respectable. Disabled facilities. Baby room. Laundry. Chemical waste point.
Services	Small shop June - Sept. Bar, take-away. Restaurant with attractive covered terrace. Barbecues allowed. Dogs accepted. Internet and Wi-Fi in bar/restaurant.
Accommodation	37 mobile homes, 8 Trigano tents.
Tour operators	None.

Excursions/Places to visit

Tarn and Jonte Gorges. Millau. Roquefort and its famous cheese cellars. Montpellier-le-Vieux, La Couvertoirade. Aven Armand. Les Cevennes.

€ Prices 2010	High	Mid	Low
Pitch + 2	27	20	15
Hook Up 5A	4	4	4
Riverside	8	6	4

Address 12640 Rivière-sur-Tarn

GPS N 44° 11' 27 E 03° 09' 24

Directions

From the North. Exit A75 at junction 44.1 and take the D29 to Aguessac. Then turn left in the direction of the Gorges du Tarn on the D907. Continue through the town of Rivière-sur-Tarn and the site is situated on the right-hand side by the river. The entrance is downhill and steep.
From the South. Exit A75 at junction 45 towards Millau. Then head north on the N9 and turn right at Aguessac. Then continue as above.

www.campingpeyrelade.com
email campingpeyrelade@orange.fr
Tel 05.65.62.62.54

MIDI-PYRÉNÉES

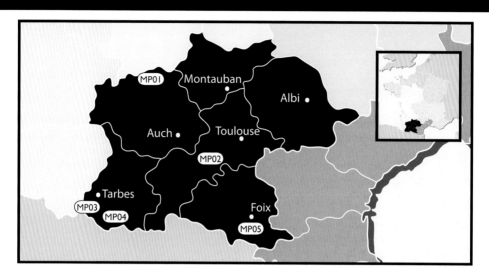

Picture opposite - The Pyrénées

Places of Interest - Midi-Pyrénées

Called Midi after the noonday sun, this region is one of the most varied in France, ranging from warm limestone plateaux to snowy peaks in the Pyrenean mountains. Dozens of medieval towns and fortified villages are scattered along the hilltops and valleys. It is a region of castles, thick-walled houses and rolling farmland with attractive old dovecots. It is also offers great contrasts. Rural Gascony, the land of d'Artagnan, the musketeer and Armagnac is a far cry from the bustling city life of Toulouse, an important aerospace centre, university city and capital of the area. Toulouse also marks the start of the Canal du Midi, a world heritage site linking the Atlantic to the Mediterranean.

Foix The 11th - 15th century castle of the Counts of Foix is made up of three superbly, dissimilar towers from different eras. They create a dramatic view from any angle. The château today is a museum of exhibits of the Ariège across the centuries.

St Girons occupies a unique spot at the confluence of eighteen little Pyrenean valleys. Situated on the rapids of the River Salat, the Pont-Vieux points you into the old commercial centre of the town on the right bank, where there are intriguing old-fashioned shops, whose fronts and fittings have remained unchanged for generations. The nearby hilltop town of **St Lizier** is certainly worth a detour as it is a walled town with arcades, cobbled streets, pretty half-timbered houses and two small cathedrals.

Pontneuf Toulouse

Martres Tolasane, situated on the left bank of the Garonne river has an old town which is circular in shape with half-timbered houses made of stone and bricks. It is also famous as a pottery centre and for its biscuit factory.

Auch is the capital of Gascony. This former Gallo-Roman city contains a monumental staircase (370 steps) leading from the lower to the upper town, where the visitor comes face to face with a statue of the local hero D'Artagnan, the famous musketeer.

Condom is a town of seven churches and the former Bishop's Palace of Bossuet, where the 16th century cathedral, flamboyant cloister and ancient town houses are of particular interest.

La Romieu an ancient walled town on the road to Santiago de Compostella has one architectural gem, a 14th century collegiate church with a mysterious past and rich Gothic paintings.

La Romieu

Lectoure, once a flourishing city in the Gallo-Roman age, then a military town that became the stronghold of the Counts of Armagnac. Lectoure was embellished with large religious buildings and mansions throughout the 15th and 16th centuries and now offers a rich architectural heritage.

Le Parc National des Pyrénées extends over some 120,000 acres, from the Néouvielle massif and nature reserve at the eastern end to the Aspe Valley in the west. The highest peak is the Vignemal summit at 3,298m. Wild mountain goats called izards can be spotted roaming the mountains. Various species of buzzards, eagles and falcons patrol the skies along with vultures including the bearded vulture or lammergeier the largest bird of prey in Europe. A wide variety of Pyrenean flora and wild plants can also be seen on walks in these magnificent mountains. Wild cats, martens and marmots all survive in healthy numbers due to the splendid isolation of the much of the high country.

Hundreds of miles of paths run through the park with refuges to accommodate hikers and mountaineers. They range from the 150km GR10 path which links the Atlantic and the Mediterranean and runs through the park from East to West, to 2-, 3- and 4-hour walks among the peaks, tarns, cirques and corries. Walkers will discover a wealth of wildlife, pure mountain streams, magnificent beech and pine forests and above all glorious views.

Places with access to the mountains include **Luz St Sauveur, Les Cauterets, Saint Lary and Arrens-Marsous.** It is also a superb area to go white-water rafting and canoeing.

From the Pic du Midi

Cirque de Gavarnie is a magnificent glacial cirque, rising to over 1,400m and has been scoured by the ice into a near-perfect semi-circle. It is 800m wide at its lowest point and about 3000m wide at the top. It can be reached via the village of Gavarnie, on foot, by donkey or on horseback. The view on to the Cirque is splendid, steep rock, snow capped peaks and the great waterfall reached by a sign-posted footpath. There is an impressive view from above this waterfall (420m), which is the highest in Europe, over the waters of the ice-covered Lake of Mont Perdu.

Pic du Midi de Bigorre is an extraordinary mountain dominating the neighbouring peaks for miles around, and is a protected heritage site. The observatory was set up in 1878 at 2,878m to take advantage of the clear pure air which is vital for the study of cosmic rays. It can be visited via le Col du Tourmalet either on foot or using a cable car and offers unique views over the whole chain. The steep walk up the mountainside is highly recommended.

The Road over the Passes Numerous passes in the Pyrénées are well known because of the "Tour de France" bike race, including Aspin, Tourmalet, Peyresoude. These mountain roads that run from valley to valley reveal an ever changing landscape at every bend. The Pic du Midi gives way to the Arbizon Massif. You then overlook the valleys of the Upper Adour, Aure and Louron with splendid panoramic views from each pass.

Lourdes' ceremonies and processions attract thousands of pilgrims every year particularly during the summer months. The most important place of pilgrimage is the Massabieille grotto where the Virgin Mary appeared on 18 occasions to local peasant Bernadette Soubirous. In the holy city, you can visit the underground basilica of Saint-Pius-X, one of the largest sanctuaries in the world. Nearby there is the basilica of the Rosary and the Upper Basilica dedicated to the Immaculate Conception. The fortified castle on a rocky cliff overlooking the city now houses a museum of customs, craft and folklore central to the Pyrénées.

Walking in the Pyrénées

Donjon des Aigles, at Beaucens just outside Argelès-Gazost. This "Eagles' Keep" in the grounds of the château offers in-flight displays of Pyrenean birds of prey including falcons, vultures etc.

Gargas Caves, near St Bertrand-de-Comminges are classified as a national heritage monument and rank among the foremost European prehistoric sites. The caves feature the intriguing and unique spectacle of a series of over 200 mutilated hands in silhouette as well as remarkable engravings of deer, antelope, buffalo and other prehistoric animals.

www.pyreneesguide.com
www.lespyrenees.net
www.picdumidi.com

La Romieu, Camp de Florence****

Location La Romieu 500m. Agen 62km. Condom 8km. Lectoure 14km. Auch 49km.

Open 1st Apr to 10th Oct

Pitches 183 (109 touring)

The setting of this site on the outskirts of the pretty bastide village of La Romieu, in the rolling hills of Armagnac makes it an ideal destination for a relaxing outdoor holiday. The village is on the pilgrimage route to St Jacques de Compostella and the region is renowned for its clement climate. The services are housed in pretty stone-faced farm buildings and the bar terrace covered in wisteria and vines is a very attractive feature. The charming Dutch/English owners have created a warm laid-back atmosphere and offer services particularly suitable for children and the disabled.

Site suitable for all ages particularly families with young children.

Pitches	Spacious pitches most a minimum of 100m² with some enormous 180m² pitches at a higher tariff. Flat, grassy, divided by hedges for privacy. Some with shade, some have splendid views. Special hard standing area for 13 motorhomes with pitches at reduced rate.
Hook-Up	10 amps - all pitches. Pitch180m² - 10 Pitches. Water & drainage - 10 pitches.
Motorhomes	Motorhome service point, hardstanding pitches and walking distance of La Romieu.
Swimming pools	Attractive tropical style swimming pool, with fountain, waterfall, and jacuzzi. Large paddling pool with clown fountain and mini-waterslide. Sun terrace pool with sun loungers and parasols. The pool is accessible to all, including physically handicapped - a special swimming pool wheelchair is available free of charge. Opens 1st May.
Activities on site	Road and mountain bike hire. Tennis. Animal park. Bouncy castle. Trampoline. Outdoor table tennis and pool table. Two good children's play areas. Football and volleyball pitch. Boules pitch. Indoor games area in farmhouse with pool, table football, electronic games, darts and wide-screen TV.
Entertainment	In high season children's club and organised sports tournaments. Evening entertainment includes talent shows and discos, barbecues, professional singers, a music quiz, karaoke and line dancing. Various walks are possible directly from site. Road cycling and mountain biking are also popular.
Sanitary facilities	One lovely brand new unisex toilet block with terracotta tiled roof and sensor lights. Spacious push button showers but no temperature control, with shelf and hooks. Individual wash cubicles with stainless steel sinks and toilets with toilet paper. Second block is respectable but with older plumbing. Third block could do with renovation, although acceptable. Disabled facilities. Baby room. Laundry. Chemical waste point.
Services	No shop as only 500m from town, but bread available. Pretty bar/snack with terrace overlooking pool area. Take-away. Excellent restaurant with lift. Barbecues allowed. Dogs accepted. Internet and Wi-Fi in bar area.
Accommodation	28 mobile homes, 2 chalets and 4 tents. 40 pitches with privately owned mobilehomes.
Tour operators	None.

Excursions/Places to visit
The 13th century Collegiate in La Romieu is an UNESCO world-heritage site. Condom, Lectoure. Château de Monluc and Château de Cassaigne.

Directions
From A62, exit 7 direction Agen and follow the D931 Agen to Condom road. Turn left by a television mast onto the D41 to La Romieu just 3km before you reach Condom. The site is situated on the outskirts of the village and is well signposted.

€ Prices 2010	Peak	High	Mid	Low
Pitch + 2	29.90	23.90	17.20	15.50
Hook Up 10A	2	2	2	2

Address 32480 La Romieu

GPS N 43° 58' 59 E 00° 30' 06

www.lecampdeflorence.com
email info@lecampdeflorence.com
Tel 05.62.28.15.58

Martres-Tolosane, Le Moulin ****

Location Martres-Tolosane 2km. Cazères 6.5km. St Gaudens 31km. Toulouse 62km.

Open 1st Apr to 30th Sept

Pitches 99 (63 touring)

A delightful little site not far from the motorway between Toulouse and the Pyrénées, yet in a rural location full of birds and wild flowers. Set in the grounds of 17th century water mill alongside a pretty stream and the Garonne river, the focal point of the site is a magnificent 400 year old plane tree. The reception is situated in the old mill and the impressive 19th century house is inhabited by the friendly family who run the site. Respect for nature and the environment helps to create a happy relaxed and peaceful atmosphere.
Clef Verte

Site suitable for For all ages, particularly couples and young families.

Pitches	Flat, grassy, well hedged and spacious about 100m² with wide alleys.
Hook-Up	6 amps - 41 pitches. 10 amps - 22 pitches.
Motorhomes	Motorhome service point. Good for motorhomes as walking distance of town (2km).
Swimming pools	Good sized heated rectangular pool 22m x 9m. Paddling pool. Generous sun terrace with sun loungers. Surrounded by trees. Open 1st Jun – 15th Sep.
Activities on site	Cycle and tricycle hire. Tennis - free and good well maintained court. Volleyball pitch, basket ball, boules pitch. Trampoline. Children's play area. Indoor games room with table tennis, table football, pool and video games. Fishing with permit.
Entertainment	In high season: programme of organised activities such as canoe trips on Garonne, pony riding, pottery, archery and walking with a professional guide. Music most evenings.
Sanitary facilities	One unisex toilet block, modern and well-maintained, built round a small courtyard. Individual cabins indicated by pretty little paintings on doors. Push button temperature control showers with hook, rail and shelf. Individual wash basins with hot and cold taps. Toilets with toilet paper. Disabled facilities. Baby room. Laundry. Chemical waste point.
Services	In high season, baker comes every morning exc Monday between 8:15 and 8:30. Can also pre-order inc Monday. Basic goods are stocked at the bar inc fair trade food. Bar/snack. Restaurant in high season exc Thursdays when a theme meal evening is often organised. Barbecues allowed. Dogs accepted. Internet. Wi-Fi in bar area.
Accommodation	4 mobile homes, 17 chalets.
Tour operators	None.

Excursions/Places to visit

Medieval town of Martres-Tolosane. Summer palace at Alan 10km. Cloisters at Notre Dame de Lorette. Château St Elix 20km. St Lizier 35km. Cathedral at St Bertrand de Comminges 40km.

Directions

The site is just to the south of Martres-Tolosane on the banks of the Garonne. Exit the A64 at junction 22 and take the D817 towards the centre of Martres-Tolosane. The site is signposted to the right off a roundabout as you approach the town. Continue for about 2km following signs to the site.

€ Prices 2010	High	Mid	Low
Pitch + 2	24	19.20	16
Hook Up 6A	3.80	3.00	2.80
Large Pitch	6.50	5.60	1

Address 31220 Martres-Tolosane

GPS N 43° 11' 26 E 01° 01' 05

www.domainelemoulin.com
email info@domainelemoulin.com
Tel 05.61.98.86.40

Estaing, Pyrénées Natura ****

Location Lourdes 23km. Argelès Gazost 11km. Tarbes 46km. Pau 81km.

Open 24th Apr to 20th Sept   **Pitches** 65 (50 touring)

As the name suggests, this site situated 1000m high in the Pyrenean mountains, is a true paradise for nature lovers. It is a spacious verdant site where chickens roam free and the scenery all round is stunning. It is beautifully maintained with an abundance of trees, plants and flowers. The friendly site owners are keen to share their love of nature and the beauty of their region with all their visitors and maintain a calm peaceful atmosphere. Guided walks allow you to see Pyrenean chamois, marmots, eagles, vultures and lammergeiers. Respect for the environment is a very important aspect of the site's ethos. Your carbon footprint travelling to the site is offset by the proprietors themselves through contributions to a tree planting scheme in Africa.
Clef Verte -Via Natura.
Site suitable for all nature lovers and those keen to explore the Pyrenees either on foot or by bike.

Pitches	Generous sized, flat, grassy pitches divided by shrubs giving a very spacious feel. Only breathable groundsheets are allowed.
Hook-Up	3, 6 or 10 amps - all pitches. Water & drainage - 6 pitches. Tents only - 5 pitches.
Motorhomes	Motorhome service point. 4 hardstanding pitches. If you come with basics, you do not need to leave the site except on foot.
Swimming pools	No swimming pool, but little beach on stream running beside site, good for paddling. Swimming is possible in any of the 20 lakes nearby. There is an open-air heated pool in Arrens Marsous 4km. Reductions for those staying on site and children under 16 free.
Activities on site	Cycle and mountain bike hire. Sauna. Solarium. Relaxation room. Giant chess, draughts and Connect sets. Games room above bar, with pool and TV. Children's play area. Telescope on tripod in middle of site for bird-watching.
Entertainment	Daytime guided walks direct from site. The GR10 route runs near the site. Unforgettable evening walks several times a week with head torches supplied by the campsite - you share your meal with fellow hikers in a mountain shelter. Rafting trips and horse riding in Estaing can also be organised.
Sanitary facilities	Two well-equipped toilet blocks, immaculately maintained. Push button temperature control showers with hook, rail, shelf and stool outside. Individual wash cubicles. Toilets with toilet paper. Disabled facilities. Baby room. Washing machine and tumble dryer. Chemical waste point.
Services	Small shop selling basics and fresh vegetables. Serve yourself and pay at reception. Pre-order bread. Comfortable bar area in lovely stone-faced building with upholstered seats and pretty terrace. Excellent varied take-away menu including set price 3-course meals. Barbecues allowed. Dogs accepted. Internet.
Accommodation	15 mobile homes.
Tour operators	None.

Excursions/Places to visit
Numerous walking and mountain biking circuits. Cirque de Gavarnie. Lourdes. Col d'Aubisque. Col du Tourmalet. Pont d'Espagne. Pic du Midi.

Directions
From Argelès-Gazost take the D102 towards Col d'Aubisque. Stay on this road past Arras-en-Lavedan for 8km and then turn left onto the D13 to Bun. Continue through Bun and turn right at the junction with the D103. The site is a further 4km along this road with the entrance to your right.

€ Prices 2010	High	Low
Pitch + 2	25	16.50
Hook Up 6A	2	2

Address 65400 Estaing

GPS N 42° 56' 29 W 00° 10' 38

www.camping-pyrenees-natura.com
email info@ camping-pyrenees-natura.com
Tel 05.62.97.45.44

Luz St Sauveur, Airotel des Pyrénées ****

Location Luz St Sauveur 1km. Lourdes 38km. Pau 84km. Bagnères-de-Bigorre 50km.

Open 1st Dec to 11th Apr & 1st May to 30th Sep   **Pitches** 155 (78 touring)

This site has been chosen for its accessibility and its proximity to the bustling little town of Luz St Sauveur. Its indoor pool also makes it a good choice if the weather is less clement. Set 700m high in a wooded valley surrounded by mountains, it is an ideal spot for ramblers and nature lovers. The local tourist office arranges guided walks of varying difficulty which can be booked through the site reception. There is a pretty flowery entrance and a very verdant feel to the site. The facilities have all been created at different times and the sites own mobile homes vary in age. Although attractively laid out, the site could occasionally do with a little more TLC and it might feel a bit cramped in high season. Some daytime road noise as on main road from Argelès-Gazost.

Site suitable for all ages, but particularly ramblers, nature lovers and young children.

Pitches	Flat, grassy varying in size from 80m² -120m², divided by low shrubs. Some are amongst the mobile homes. Best pitches are near 2nd toilet block and indoor pool.
Hook-Up	3, 4, 6 or 10 amps - all pitches. Water & drainage - none.
Motorhomes	Motorhome service point. 15-min walk to Luz St Sauveur.
Swimming pools	Three separate pool areas, all small, one attractive indoor pool good for a dip, an outdoor pool with paddling pool and a further pool with waterslides and sun terrace.
Activities on site	Half-court tennis. Table tennis. Climbing wall. Boules pitch. Gym. Children's play area. Spa area with hammam, sauna, jacuzzi and massage.
Entertainment	Guided walks for all levels including a walk to see sun rise over Pic du Midi organised by guiding group www.guides-de-luz.fr. Site can also arrange rafting, canoeing, canyoning etc. In high season: children's club and one music evening a week.
Sanitary facilities	Two unisex toilet blocks, one nearest reception is a strange mixture of styles but is respectable. Second block near indoor pool is more modern with attractive tiling. Push button showers, no temperature control with hooks in both blocks. Individual wash cubicles with hot and cold taps. Toilets without toilet paper, three of which are French style in 2nd block. Disabled facilities. Baby room. Laundry. Chemical waste point.
Services	Pre-order bread 15th May - 15th Sep. Carrefour supermarket 500m. Basic take-away in high season only. Restaurants in town. Barbecues allowed. Dogs accepted. Wi-Fi throughout site.
Accommodation	48 mobile homes, 12 chalets.
Tour operators	Two British tour operators on 17 pitches and in 10 chalets.

Excursions/Places to visit
Luz St Sauveur, Cirque de Gavarnie, Pic du Midi, Pic d'Ardiden, Col du Tourmalet, Lourdes, Tarbes, Pau.

Directions
From Lourdes, take the N21 to Argelès Gazost and then follow the D921 to Luz St Sauveur. The site is on your left as you climb the hill just before the village of Luz St Sauveur and shortly after passing "Camping International".

€ Prices 2010	High	Mid	Low	Winter
Pitch + 2	26	20	14	20
Hook Up 4A	4	4	4	4

Address 46 Avenue du Barège, 65120 Esquièze-Sère

www.airotel-pyrenees.com
email airotel.pyrenees@wanadoo.fr
Tel 05.62.92.89.18

GPS N 42° 52' 48 W 00° 00' 38

Tarascon-sur-Ariège, Le Pré Lombard ****

Location Tarascon 500m. Foix 18km. Ax-les-Thermes 27km. St Girons 62km. Toulouse 104km.

Open 27th Mar to 14th Nov   **Pitches** 185 (90 touring)

This site has been included because of its proximity to the pretty, little town of Tarascon and its delightful setting on the banks of the Ariège river 470m high in the heart of the Pyrénées. It is an ex-municipal site and laid out in straight lines stretching along the river bank. The beautiful wide tree-lined alleys give it a spacious feel. The site is called Pré Lombard as its field or 'pré' is where an army of Lombards from Italy stayed prior to a battle in 788. It is a great starting point for numerous walks and cycle rides in the area.

Site suitable for all ages, particularly families who prefer a livelier atmosphere in high season.

Pitches	Flat, grassy 100m² - 120m, divided by trees but not hedged. The best ones overlook the river.
Hook-Up	10 amps - all pitches. Water & drainage - none.
Motorhomes	Motorhome service point. Half price for overnight area.
Swimming pools	Swimming pool complex is attractively laid out with banana trees and plants surrounded by hedges with a grassy area next to the sun terrace. The rectangular swimming-pool is heated and 20m x 8m. The paddling-pool is divided into two parts : 0.2m deep and 0.4m deep. Open 1st May - 30th Sept.
Activities on site	All weather sports pitch for football, volleyball and basketball. Table tennis undercover. Boules pitch. Children's play area. Games room with pool, table football, electronic games and TV. Fishing with permit.
Entertainment	In high season: children's club 6 - 12 yrs, programme of daytime sporting activities, organised evening entertainment includes concerts, shows, cabarets and a nightly disco.
Sanitary facilities	Five toilet blocks, separate ladies and gents, one heated in low season. All respectable and well maintained but nothing special. Push button showers no temperature control with hook and shelf. Individual wash cubicles. Toilets with toilet paper. Showers and washbasins together in one block. Disabled facilities and laundry in two blocks, baby room in one. Chemical waste point.
Services	Shop sells bread and basic provisions inc regional products. Supermarket 300m. Excellent tourist information in the "Chalet Montagne" next to reception. Pretty wooden-beamed bar/restaurant "La Guinguette" and pizzeria/take-away by the river. Barbecues allowed. Dogs accepted. Internet Point.
Accommodation	60 mobile homes, chalets and tents.
Tour operators	One French and one Dutch tour operator on 35 pitches.

Excursions/Places to visit
Walking, rafting, climbing, canyoning, "Via Ferrata". Numerous prehistoric caves. Foix and its fairytale château. Andorra.

Directions
The site is situated to the south of the centre of Tarascon-sur-Ariège on the banks of the river. Fom Foix take the N20 to Tarascon. As you enter the town stay on the N20 and the site is well-signposted to the left. The route takes you towards the town centre and then turns right to follow the river. The site entrance is on your right just after you cross the river where it takes a sharp bend.

€ Prices 2010	Peak	High	Mid	Low	Off
Pitch + 2	32	28	20	17	15
Hook Up 10A	Incl	Incl	Incl	Incl	Incl

Address BP90148, 09400 Tarascon-sur-Ariège

GPS N 42° 50' 23 E 01° 36' 43

www.prelombard.com
email leprelombard@wanadoo.fr
Tel 05.61.05.61.94

ALPS

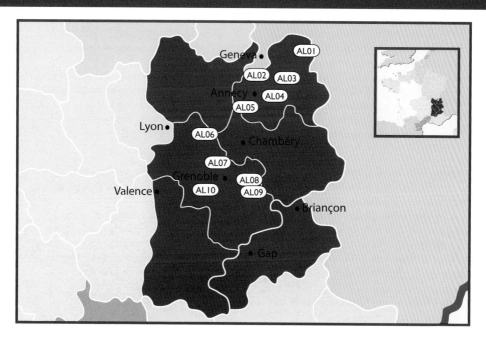

Picture opposite - Waterfall from Le Champ du Moulin

Places of Interest - Alps

The Alpine region is divided into 3 'départements': **Savoie, Haute Savoie, Isère.**
They share the same Alpine territory with its glaciers, deep gorges, mountain passes and lakes. A haven for tourism both in winter and summer, they have the same distinctive life style, rooted in their montagnard heritage. It is a region of natural contrasts ranging from the magnificence and majesty of the Mont Blanc massif to the solitude and unspoiled natural beauty of the nature reserves and the pleasant green plains round its many famous lakes. The mountain ranges rise majestically to a height of 4,800m. Mont Blanc is the highest peak in western Europe. The region has an excellent road network system, fully maintained in all types of weather conditions. Access to ski resorts is guaranteed at all times. It has 180 kms of motorway and all ski resorts are within 40 kms of motorway exits. The region has 5 major National Parks, **Vanoise, Massif des Bauges, Chartreuse, Ecrins and Vercors.**

Walking With its lakes mountains and varied terrain, the Alps region offers a wide range of cross-country walks and alpine treks. They have several hundred kilometres of graded footpaths and Grand Randonnées - GRs. The tour of Mont Blanc is perhaps the best known trek in the region. However other lesser known trails cross the Chablais, Bornes and Aravis mountain ranges. Treks across Haute-Savoie's G.R.s enable hikers to discover some of the region's finest scenery. They avoid built-up areas and link up with resting places and supply points on the way.

Walking in the Alps

Country hikes across the valleys and plains can take place from May onwards. Treks in the medium-range mountains start in June and continue throughout the season until late November. Always ask for advice at the tourist offices to check on the accessibility of the footpaths and check the weather forecast before setting off.

There are three levels of difficulty:
Green is an easy hiking circuit between and 1½ and 3 hours long with generally an altitude difference of less than 350m.
Blue is an average hike 3 to 4 hours long between 350m and 650m altitude.
Red is for accomplished hikers and involves 4 to 6 hours of walking at an altitude difference of more than 650m.

Cycling Although the region is best known by cyclists for its prestigious high mountain passes and its long and acrobatic mountain bike descents, there are other spots to be discovered on your bike. It is full of quiet little roads in the valleys, middle mountain paths, undulating vineyards, lakeside scenery and especially breathtaking alpine panoramas.

Cycling by Lake Annecy

White water sports In the heat of the summer, white-water sports will refresh all of those who crave strong sensations. The rivers Isère and the Doron in the Savoie area are ideal for rafting, kayaking and hydrospeed. Whatever the level of difficulty, adventure is guaranteed.

Para-gliding and **Hang-gliding** is available in many resorts for those who want to see things from higher up.

The Alpine lakes are always worth a visit and are good for all manner of water sports - sailing, wind surfing, water-skiing and underwater diving.

Lake Geneva or Lac Léman, the largest lake in Western Europe, 70km long and 14km wide is crescent shaped and forms a natural border with Switzerland. Thonon-les-Bains and Evian are the most important towns on the French side.

Le Bourget is the largest natural lake in France, 18km long and 3.5 km across at its widest part. Aix-les-Bains situated on the edge of the lake is a busy spa town renowned for its balneotherapy.

Caravaneige at Camping l'Oustalet

Lake Annecy is a deep blue lake surrounded by majestic mountains, and covers an area of 27km². The shores of the lake offer a succession of magnificent views and pretty towns including **Annecy** town at the northern end of the lake with its impressive 12th century castle, arcaded streets and cathedral. **Doussard** is set back from the southern shore of the lake and **Talloires** is probably the most famous resort after Annecy. It nestles at the foot of the Roc de Chère and was for centuries a major pilgrimage centre.

Aiguebelette good for fishing, rowing and swimming as no motorboats are allowed.

Col de Forclaz at a height of 1,150 metres offers magnificent panoramic views over lake Annecy and is a centre for hang-gliding.

Chamonix Mont Blanc - Aiguille du Midi is the one of highest cable cars in Europe and transports passengers to the Aiguille du Midi 3,942m high in 20 minutes. At the top there is a breathtaking panorama of Mont Blanc and the surrounding peaks, the Swiss and Italian Alps and the valley of Chamonix.

Les Deux Alpes lies at the boundary between the North and South Alps, and at the gateway to the Ecrins National Park. It offers a unique ski area with snow all year round on the glacier at the top, at a height of 3,600m, as well as magnificent views in summer.

Alpe-d'Huez 1860 m high is a popular winter and summer sports resort renowned for its exceptional micro-climate, a vast paradise for lovers of skiing, pure air and wide open spaces.

Oisans Region Allemont is a small village in the Eau d'Olle Valley, at the heart of the Oisans on the shores of Lac Verney. It combines the delights of water and mountains all year round.

Bourg d'Oisans capital of the six valleys of the Oisans, is the gateway to the Ecrins National Park and offers a wide range of cross-country skiing activities in winter.

Venosc is an authentic, charming, peaceful mountain village, just an 8-minute cable-car ride away from the resort of Les Deux Alpes.

Vercors Regional Park has deep caves and gorges cutting into vast wooded plateaux and lush green valleys. Although cross-country skiing is popular in the winter, it attracts lovers of climbing, caving and hiking in summer.

Chartreuse Abbey

Chartreuse The Chartreuse Massif looks out over Grenoble to the south and Chambery to the north. **St Pierre-de-Chartreuse** is famous for its Carthusian monastery and unique liqueur.

Autrans was used for some of the 1968 Olympic Games and is most famous for cross-country skiing, but is also popular for downhill ski-ing, dog-sled rides and snowshoeing. The Aventure Parc located in Autrans, is the world's strangest amusement park: 752 obstacles built in a dense forest at an altitude of 1,201m. Thrills guaranteed! Children must be at least 8 years old, or one metre tall.

Pont-en-Royans This village, originally a prosperous centre for the wood trade, is famous for its picturesque houses clinging to the rock face above the river - an ingenious feat of construction.

www.savoiehautesavoie.com
www.lac-annecy.com
www.isere-tourisme.com

Châtel, l'Oustalet ****

Location Châtel 1.5km. Thonon-les-Bains 38 km. Geneva 72km. Martigny 45km.

Open 19th Dec to 25th Apr & 20th Jun to 6th Sept   **Pitches** 100 (78 touring)

Situated 1200m high, two minutes from the Swiss border between Mont Blanc and lake Geneva, this site is perfect for summer and winter holidays and for those who appreciate a real Savoyard atmosphere. It is in the heart of the mountains and the fabulous Portes du Soleil ski-ing area, 450m from the nearest cable car. In the summer it is a centre for walking, mountain biking, rafting and pony riding. It is right on a tributary of the river Dranse, and is well-loved by trout fishermen. The site is 1.5km below the centre of the village in a verdant valley and the pitches are laid out on two sides of a quiet mountain road. In summer you can't fail to be impressed by wealth of beautiful flowers throughout the site.

Site suitable for all ages, particularly those who enjoy a peaceful ambiance.

Pitches	Flat and grassy up to 100m², not hedged. Pitches on side opposite reception are more generous and better for large outfits. Breathable groundsheets are essential.
Hook-Up	10 amps - all pitches. Water & drainage - none.
Motorhomes	Motorhome service point. 15 hard standing pitches. Ideal as walking distance of all services.
Swimming pools	An attractive and well maintained indoor pool, large enough for swimming. Paddling pool outside with sun terrace and sun loungers. Sauna.
Activities on site	Tennis. Basket-ball. Table tennis. Boules pitch. Children's play area. Fishing with permit. Pretty picnic tables by river.
Entertainment	Daily sports and leisure programme includes guided mountain walks, archery, meals in an alpine chalet and rafting. Activity centre 100m away offers mini-golf and mini go-karts. In winter: access to cross country ski pistes, winter footpaths, and snow shoe walks. Beginners' slopes and ski school for young children. No evening entertainment.
Sanitary facilities	Two very attractive and immaculately maintained blocks, on each side of the road. Unisex showers and wash cubicles but separate ladies and gents toilets with paper outside. Push button temperature controlled showers with shelf and rail. Disabled facilities. Baby room. Drying room for ski gear. Washing machine and tumble dryer. Chemical waste point.
Services	No services on site, but just 150m away bakery, snack bar, small local grocery store, ski hire shop and a bar/restaurant. In both summer and winter, regular free shuttle buses will ferry you around the area - bus stop right outside the campsite. Barbecues allowed. Dogs accepted. Wi-Fi throughout site.
Accommodation	10 chalets. 12 residential pitches.
Tour operators	None.

Excursions/Places to visit

Châtel, Abondance, Thonon-les-Bains, Gorges du Point du Diable. Numerous mountain walks and lakes.

€ Prices 2009	High	Mid	Low
Pitch + 2	23.50	19	16
Hook Up 5A	5.90	5.90	5.90
Winter +2 & 6A	240/wk	31.30	8.30

Directions

From Thonon-les-Les Bains take the D902 towards Morzine. After 11km turn left onto the D22 to Abondance and Châtel. After 27km you arrive on the outskirts of Châtel. Fork right onto the D230 after 4.5km you will see a chair lift in front of you turn left here then left again into Rue des Freinets and the site entrance is on your left.

Address 1428, Route des Freinets, 74390 Châtel

GPS N 46° 15' 28 E 06° 49' 47

www.oustalet.com
email contact@oustalet.com
Tel 04.50.73.21.97

Les Gets, La Grange au Frêne ***

Location Les Gets 2km. Thonon-les-Bains 39km. Bonneville 42km. Geneva 69km.

Open 23rd Jun to 6th Sep

Pitches 32 all touring

We have decided to include this site because we simply fell in love with the views. It is 1300m high and on a clear day you will be rewarded with an excellent view of Mont Blanc and the surrounding mountains. We discovered the site by accident and were pleasantly surprised by its unique location. It is an unsophisticated site, as it has nothing but a toilet block, but these sanitary facilities are very comfortable. The site is in a totally rural location 2km up a steep narrow road from Les Gets and it is a haven for nature lovers and mountain bikers. There are numerous marked out trails in the mountains and forests around. A perfect spot for those who enjoy complete peace and quiet. The reception and toilet block are decorated with flowers.

Site suitable for smaller outfits only because of access. Also not recommended for young children.

Pitches	Terraced site. Flat, grassy pitches varying in shape and size, some up to 90m². divided by low shrubs. Not suitable for outfits over 6m.
Hook-Up	2 or 4 amps - all pitches. Water & drainage - none.
Motorhomes	No service point and not suitable for very large motorhomes.
Swimming pools	No swimming pool on site.
Activities on site	Small games room with pool table. In les Gets 2km away: 18 hole golf course and leisure centre on lake suitable for swimming. There are numerous marked out trails in the mountains and forests around.
Entertainment	None.
Sanitary facilities	Two very respectable and well maintained heated toilet blocks. One mixed, the second with separate areas for ladies and gents. Push button showers with hooks, shelf and good hot water. Individual wash cubicles but no cold water for cleaning teeth. Toilets with seats but no paper. Good washing up area. Chemical waste point.
Services	Nothing on site. Bread van comes each morning about 8 am. Drinks machine outside toilet block. Barbecues allowed. Dogs accepted. Internet at reception.
Accommodation	None. Owner has hotel in Les Gets and some chalets.
Tour operators	None.

Excursions/Places to visit
Les Gets, 180km of footpaths and mountain bike tracks. Lifts open in peak season take mountain bikes.

€ Prices 2010	All Dates
Pitch + 2	17
Hook Up 4A	5

Directions
The site is situated 2km from Les Gets overlooking the valley. From Bonnière take the D902 to Les Gets. As you enter the village you arrive at a roundabout. Take the third exit almost doubling back on yourself onto Route des Perrières. After 700m fork right into Route des Cornuts following signs for the campsite. Continue to climb on this road until you arrive at the site.

Address Les Cornuts, 74260 Les Gets

www.alpensport-hotel.com
email info@alpensport-hotel.com
GPS N 46° 09' 03 E 06° 38' 35   **Tel** 04.50.75.80.60 (high season) 04.50.79.70.64 (low season)

Neydens, La Colombière****

Location Geneva 8km. Annecy 30km. Easy access from A40 and A41.

Open 1st Mar to 11th Nov   **Pitches** 120 (88 touring)

This site has a unique setting just on the edge of the pretty little village of Neydens with fabulous views over the mountains behind Geneva. Neydens is on the pilgrimage route to Santiago de Compostela. The pitches are attractively laid out in an orchard and it is perfect for visiting this part of the Alps with a regular bus service 700m from the site to Geneva and Annecy. You can expect a warm welcome from the Bussat family who also own the nearby vineyard. The site is managed in an eco-friendly way using sustainable energy facilities and eco-friendly products for cleaning.
Clef Verte

Site suitable for all ages, particularly couples and young families.

Pitches	Flat, grassy pitches 95m² -130m² set between trees and divided by low hedges, some shady and some sunny.
Hook-Up	6 amps - all pitches. 10 amps - 50 pitches. Water & drainage - 63 pitches.
Motorhomes	Motorhome service point. Special one-night rate for motorhomes. Bus stop for Geneva 700m from site.
Swimming pools	Rectangular outdoor pool 13.5m x 7.5m, paddling pool with sun terrace and sun loungers, attractively laid out, open 15th Jun - 15th Sep. Small indoor swimming pool and jacuzzi. Further large public pool complex 900m.
Activities on site	Boules pitch. Volleyball. Table tennis. Children's play area. Giant chess set. Indoor games area.
Entertainment	Monday afternoons, a visit to the site's own vineyard is followed by a welcome drink and Savoyard evening in the restaurant with a "raclette". Tuesday afternoons a guided visit of Geneva. In high season: children's club, archery, organised games and music evenings in the bar.
Sanitary facilities	Two modern toilet blocks. The block furthest from reception is the better of the two. Separate ladies and gents. Push button, temperature control showers, hooks, shelf and rail. Individual wash cubicles. Toilets with seats, toilet paper and washbasin. Disabled facilities. Baby room. Separate laundry. Chemical waste point.
Services	Pre-order bread, baked on site. Farmers market every Thursday evening in Neydens. Typical Savoyard style wooden-beamed bar and restaurant overlooking pool. Barbecues allowed. Dogs accepted. Internet. Wi-Fi nr reception Fridge hire.
Accommodation	14 mobile homes, 8 chalets, 2 tents. 8 private pitches.
Tour operators	None.

Excursions/Places to visit

Geneva and Annecy both accessible by bus. Mont Salève on foot or by cable car for panoramic view. Annemasse 20 mins and St Julien-en-Genevois 10 mins A41 Exit 13, direction Cruseilles and Annecy.

Directions

The site is on the eastern outskirts of the village. From A40. exit junction 13 St Julien-en-Genevois and follow directions for Annecy on the N201. Then follow signs for Neydens, continue through the village carefully following signs for the campsite. The campsite entrance is clearly visible on your right hand side.

€ Prices 2010	High	Mid	Low
Pitch + 2	26	20	16
Hook Up 5A	5	5	5

Address 166 Chemin Neuf, 74160 Neydens

GPS N 46° 07' 13 E 06° 06' 19

www.camping-la-colombiere.com
email la.colombiere@wanadoo.fr
Tel 04.50.35.13.14

Le Grand Bornand, Camping l'Escale ***

Location In Le Grand Bornand. Annecy 30km. Bonneville 26km.

Open 4th Dec to 18th Apr & 21st May to 26th Sept   **Pitches** 149 (126 touring)

Set 935m high amidst stunning mountain scenery and only 200m from the pretty Alpine town of Le Grand Bornand with its lively bars, restaurants and shops. The site is run by the charming Baur family who create a warm welcoming atmosphere. The pretty wooden-beamed bar/restaurant is located in a 200-year old building or 'alpage', decorated in traditional style and offering excellent Alpine dishes. It is a great area for ski-ing in the winter and para-gliding in summer.

Site suitable for all ages and those who enjoy mountain activities in lively surroundings.

Pitches	Not huge, majority 80m² -90m², 80 on a gravelled surface and the rest on grass. Good strong pegs are needed. Not divided by hedges. In summer there are a few 100m² pitches available.
Hook-Up	2 -10 amps - all pitches. Water & drainage - 30 pitches.
Motorhomes	Motorhome service point. Ideal for motorhomes as in town.
Swimming pools	Aqua complex 240m², of which 80m² is indoor. It is attractively laid out with artificial rocks and bridges and includes a paddling pool, two jacuzzis, water jets and a lagoon. Good for a dip but not swimming. Outdoor pool open mid-June to end Aug. There is a public swimming pool next door to the site.
Activities on site	Tennis - free. Table-tennis. Indoor games room with pool, video games, table football. Children's play area. In town mini-golf, adventure park, archery and trampoline.
Entertainment	No organised entertainment. Town organises many activities throughout the season.
Sanitary facilities	Three toilet blocks, the largest in centre of site needs modernising, as it has very old tiling and plumbing. It is however acceptable and clean. Small showers, push button, no temperature control with shelf, hook and rail. Individual wash cubicles. Toilets with toilet paper outside. Other blocks have temperature control showers and are more modern. Disabled facilities. Baby room. Laundry. Chemical waste point.
Services	No shop, pre-order bread Jun to end Aug. Pretty wooden beamed bar and excellent restaurant open to public. Take-away/pizzeria. Short walk to shops in town. Drying rooms for skis and outdoor gear in winter. Barbecues allowed. Dogs accepted. Internet and Wi-Fi connection throughout site.
Accommodation	19 mobile homes. 4 private pitches. 32 appartments and studios.
Tour operators	None.

Excursions/Places to visit

Special prices if booked at reception for Aiguille du Midi cable car to top of Mont Blanc and Mer de Glace in Chamonix. Annecy. 150km of marked and maintained trails for walking and mountain biking in the vicinity.

€ Prices 2010	High	Mid	Low
Pitch + 2	22.50	19.50	16
Hook Up 6A	5.70	5.70	5.70
Pitch + 2 Winter	23.80		18.50
Hook Up 6A	7.10		7.10

Directions

From Geneva. Follow the A40 towards Chamonix and exit at Bonneville. Turn right onto the D12 to La Clusaz and when you arrive at the T-junction just before St Jean de Sixt turn left onto the D4 signposted towards Le Grand Bornand. As you arrive at the village follow signs to the site. From Annecy. Take exit Annecy Nord from A41 and follow D16 and then D909 to Thones. Continue as above from St Jean-de-Sixt. Larger caravans are recommended to approach the campsite via Annecy.

Address Route de la Patinoire, 74450 Le Grand Bornand

GPS N 45° 56' 24 E 06° 25' 42

www.campinglescale.com
email contact@campinglescale.com
Tel 04.50.02.20.69

Doussard, La Ravoire ****

Location Doussard 3km. Annecy 18km.

Open 15th May to 7th Sept

Pitches 108 (79 touring)

Although only 800m from the lake, this delightful little site is renowned for its quiet peaceful atmosphere. Situated on the western side of Lake Annecy near Doussard, it enjoys stunning views of the surrounding mountains. The site is very well maintained by the friendly family who own it. The profusion of flowers and well trimmed hedges create a good first impression and it attracts a good cross-section of nationalities. A cycle track next to the site will take you to the town of Annecy which is a bonus as the roads are very busy in high season. There are good beaches along the lakeside and plenty of places to visit in the area by bike, on foot in the mountains, or for day trips by car.

Site suitable for all ages, but particularly for those who prefer a quiet ambiance.

Pitches	Flat, grassy divided by low hedges. Not enormous, up to 100m² but good size for area.
Hook-Up	5, 10 amps - all pitches. Water & drainage - 21 pitches.
Motorhomes	No motorhome service point, but suitable if you have bikes.
Swimming pools	Pretty pool area by bar which includes a rectangular pool 17m x 6m, paddling pool 4m x 4m, and separate basin for a waterslide. Grassy sun terrace.
Activities on site	Table tennis. All weather sports pitch for basket ball and volleyball. Boules pitch. Children's play area. Indoor games area with pool and table football. TV room above bar.
Entertainment	No organised entertainment. Plenty to do in the area: swimming in lake 1km, fishing, canoeing, sailing, windsurfing, cycling, mountain biking, walking in mountains. Mini-golf 1.5km. Rafting 7km.
Sanitary facilities	One excellent toilet block, attractively tiled and kept immaculately clean. Separate ladies and gents. Push button temperature controlled showers with hooks. Individual wash basins. Toilets with toilet paper. Good washing up area with stainless steel sinks. Disabled facilities. Baby room. Laundry. Chemical waste point.
Services	Small shop with basics, pre-order bread. Bar/snack. Shops in Doussard and St Jorioz. Barbecues allowed. Dogs accepted. Wi-Fi connection for 2010.
Accommodation	4 wooden chalets.
Tour operators	One British tour operator on 25 pitches.

Excursions/Places to visit
Talloires 13km, Annecy 18km, Le Grand Bornand and la Clusaz, Geneva 60km, Chamonix a day trip.

Directions
From A41. Exit at junction 16 signed Annecy and Albertville. Then take the N508 to Albertville along the western shore of the lake. After the village of Duingt continue for 1½ km until you arrive at traffic lights in the centre of Bredannaz where you should turn right. Follow signs for the site. The entrance to the site is on your left after a further 400m. From Albertville. Take the N212 north to Ugine and then the N508 in the direction of Annecy past Doussard village. The turning to the campsite is on your left just after the hamlet of Bout du Lac. The site is signposted from here.

€ Prices 2010	High	Low
Pitch + 2 & 5A	30	24
Water & Dr	3.50	2.80

Address Route de la Ravoire, Bredannaz, 74210 Doussard

www.camping-la-ravoire.fr
email info@camping-la-ravoire.fr

GPS N 45° 48' 09 E 06° 12' 35

Tel 04.50.44.37.80

Les Abrets, Le Coin Tranquille ****

Location Chambéry 26km. Grenoble 40km. Easy access from A43.

Open 1st Apr to 1st Nov

Pitches 192 (178 touring)

Situated in the rolling foothills of the Alps with lovely views all around, this family-run site always offers a warm welcome. The site has a pleasant spacious feel, is well maintained and enhanced by an abundance of flowers by the reception and outside the restaurant. The site is well known for its excellent restaurant and here you can savour the specialities of the Chartreuse region including its famous liqueur and Savoyard fondue. It is also a region rich in green valleys, lakes and medieval villages. There is plenty to keep you occupied and on arrival the site give you a welcome pack full of information on all the activities and attractions in the Western Alps.

Site suitable for all ages but particularly couples and young families.

Pitches	Flat, grassy, divided by hedges and shrubs and a good size up to 120m². Pitches at the back of site have the best views but a long way from the sanitary block.
Hook-Up	2, 3 and 6 amps - all pitches. Water & drainage - none.
Motorhomes	Two motorhome service areas. Need transport to visit area.
Swimming pools	Rectangular pool 180m². Small paddling pool. Attractively laid out with good sun terrace and sun loungers. Terrace of restaurant overlooks the pool.
Activities on site	Cycle hire. Football pitch. Volleyball pitch. Table tennis. Children's play area. Bouncy castle. Table football. Boules pitch. Canoe/kayak and fishing with permit 7km.
Entertainment	Guided walks on Wednesdays starting in July. In high season: children's club, archery, organised volleyball and games in the pool, two dance and music evenings per week. Occasional barbecues. Walking routes with maps ranging from 3.5km to 20km available in reception.
Sanitary facilities	Two toilet blocks, an excellent one in middle of site and a smaller older one towards back of site, which is still in good condition. Separate ladies and gents. Push button temperature control showers with hooks, shelf and rail. Toilets with toilet paper outside. Disabled facilities. Baby room. Separate laundry. Chemical waste point.
Services	Small well-stocked shop. Bar, attractive restaurant, also open to public, and take-away open all season. Barbecues allowed. Dogs accepted. Internet.
Accommodation	14 chalets.
Tour operators	None.

Excursions/Places to visit
Lac Paladru-Charavines 12km, Lac d'Aiguebelette 18km, Walibi theme park 12km. Château de Vireu 12km, Lac du Bourget 45km. Annecy - an hour on the motorway.

Directions
From Lyon. Take the A43 in the direction of Chambéry. Exit at Chimilin and follow the D592 to Les Abrets. In the village turn left at the roundabout in the direction of Chambéry Pont de Beauvoisin onto the N6. Turn left again after 1km, before you cross the railway line. The campsite is well-signposted from here.

€ Prices 2010	High	Mid	Low
Pitch + 2	29	18	15
Hook Up 6A	3	3	3

Address 6 Chemin des Vignes, 38490 Les Abrets

GPS N 45° 32' 29 E 05° 36' 27

www.coin-tranquille.com
email contact@coin-tranquille.com
Tel 04.76.32.13.48

St. Pierre-de-Chartreuse, Camp de Martinière *** Map Ref AL07

Location St Pierre-de-Chartreuse 3km. Grenoble 23km. Voiron 26km. Chambéry 39km.

Open 1st May to 11th Sept   **Pitches** 100 (95 touring)

This small family-run site 900m high in the heart of the Chartreuse National Park offers exceptional panoramic views. The Chamechaude a wonderful grey rocky mountain peak 2,082m high presides majestically over the site. It is located between Grenoble and Chambéry, in the grounds of an old Carthusian farmhouse. You are welcomed to this peaceful, relaxing site by a pretty flowery entrance and a variety of different trees. The roads are pebbled not tarmaced. St. Pierre occupies a unique spot at a crossroads to four pretty valleys and is a starting point for numerous hikes and walks.

Site suitable for nature lovers and walkers.

Pitches	Flat, grassy pitches, divided by trees. Pitches round edge of site are larger and hedged up to 130m². In the middle, the pitches are smaller but more open.
Hook-Up	2, 3 4, 6 or 8 amps - 87 pitches. Water & drainage - none.
Motorhomes	Motorhome service point, 5 hardstanding pitches. Need transport to visit area.
Swimming pools	Attractive good-sized pool for swimming. Paddling pool. Sun terrace with sun loungers - open June to Sept.
Activities on site	Boules pitch. Children's play area which is looking a bit old. Games room with table tennis and table football. Adventure park in the trees, tennis and mini-golf 1.5km.
Entertainment	No organised entertainment. Nearby in village: paragliding training, via ferrata, mountain biking and caving.
Sanitary facilities	Two modern well maintained toilet blocks in pretty stone-faced building, attractively tiled. Separate ladies and gents toilets but unisex push button temperature controlled showers and wash cubicles. No disabled facilities. Baby room. Chemical waste point.
Services	Small shop selling basics and local artefacts. Attractive bar/snack with lovely hand carved wooden surfaces. Library. Barbecues allowed. Dogs accepted. Hotel/Restaurant 50m.
Accommodation	Four mobile homes.
Tour operators	Dutch tour operator on 10 pitches.

Excursions/Places to visit
270km of marked out walking paths. Magnificent Carthusian monastery of La Grande Chartreuse in St. Pierre. The wonderful waterfalls in the Cirque de St Même. Voiron with its medieval churches and the Chartreuse liqueur distillery.

Directions
From the A48 take exit 12 or 13 at Voreppe and follow the D520A and then D520 towards Saint Laurent du Pont. In St Laurent turn right onto the D520B to Saint Pierre-de-Chartreuse and at "La Diat", take the D512 to Col-de-Porte. The campsite entrance is on your right in the hamlet of "La Martinière".

€ Prices 2010	High	Mid	Low
Pitch + 2	19	16	15
Hook Up 6A	3.90	3.90	3.90

Address Route du Col de Porte -
D512, 38380 St Pierre-de-Chartreuse
GPS N 45° 19' 34 E 05° 47' 51

www.campingdemartiniere.com
email camping-de-martiniere@orange.fr
Tel 04.76.88.60.36

Bourg d'Oisans, A la Rencontre du Soleil ****

Location Bourg d'Oisans 500m. Grenoble 50km. Lyon 150km.

Open 1st May to 30th Sept   **Pitches** 73 (48 touring)

On the edge of the pretty little town of Bourg d'Oisans at the foot of the road to Alpe d'Huez, this is a very well tended site, with a profusion of flowers, shrubs and trees. It is a south-facing site at the heart of six beautiful valleys and ideally placed for exploring the Alps and the Ecrin National Park. The friendly site owners have created a warm peaceful atmosphere and will help you organise hiking, mountain biking tours, summer ski-ing, rock-climbing and rafting. This is truly a land of cycles and mountain biking. From the celebrated 21 hairpin bends of Alpe d'Huez to the rocky paths for maniac mountain bikers, there are routes for all. Bourg d'Oisans regularly hosts the Tour de France. Clef Verte

Site suitable for couples and young families particularly nature lovers and cyclists.

Pitches	Flat, grassy, divided by hedges and not overly generous, 80m² - 100m². As the turning circle is quite narrow we do not recommend it for outfits over 6.5m.
Hook-Up	2, 6 or 10 amps - all pitches. Water & drainage - none.
Motorhomes	Two points, one to empty and one for water. Ideal as walking distance of Bourg d'Oisans.
Swimming pools	One small almost rectangular pool good for a dip. No paddling pool. Attractive sun terrace with sun loungers.
Activities on site	Tennis. All weather sports pitch for handball, basketball and volleyball. Table tennis. Children's play area. TV room. Cycle hire in town. www.bike-oisans.com
Entertainment	High season: Children's club, party evenings with variety shows and concerts once a week. The site can help organise or advise on any of the numerous mountain activities available in the region including walks with a guide once a week. See site's web under 'activities' at top.
Sanitary facilities	One beautifully tiled toilet block. Separate ladies and gents. Push button showers, no temperature control, fabulous wooden doors, hooks shelf and soap dish. Individual wash cubicles. Toilets with seats and toilet paper. Baby room. No disabled facilities. Washing machine and tumble dryer. Chemical waste point.
Services	Pre-order bread. No shop as plenty within walking distance. Bar and small restaurant with pizzeria and take-away, shaded terrace. Restaurant serves local specialities and traditional recipes. Barbecues allowed. Dogs accepted. Internet point.
Accommodation	13 mobile homes, 10 chalets, 2 roulottes - gypsy style caravans.
Tour operators	None.

Excursions/Places to visit

Bourg d'Oisans, Adventure Park at Venosc 15km. Les Deux Alpes and Alpe d'Huez ski resorts. Grave cable car to top of Meije massif to visit ice caves. Numerous pretty villages round about including St. Christophe-en-Oisans and la Bérarde.

Directions

The site is situated almost opposite Camping La Cascade on the Alpe d'Huez road from the N91 just east of the town of Bourg d'Oisans.

€ Prices 2010	High	Mid	Low
Pitch + 2	27	25.35	15.45
Hook Up 6A	4.30	4.20	4

Address Route de l'Alpe d'Huez, 38520 Bourg d'Oisans

www.alarencontredusoleil.com
email rencontre.soleil@wanadoo.fr

GPS N 45° 03' 56 E 06° 02' 22   **Tel** 04.76.79.12.22

Venosc, Le Champ du Moulin ***

Location Venosc 1km. Bourg d'Oisans 15km. Grenoble 65km

Open 15th Dec to 25th Apr & 29th May to 15th Sept   **Pitches** 84 (69 touring)

This little site is in a fabulous location 960m high at the foot of the Oisans mountain range and on the banks of the river Vénéon. It is also just a 300m walk from a cable car that takes you up to Les Deux Alpes ski resort in summer and winter, and on further to the glacier right at the top. It is a pretty well maintained site offering a quiet but welcoming ambiance with a good mixture of nationalities. Mountain enthusiasts will find numerous activities nearby including winter and summer ski-ing. Venosc is just a short walk and has several restaurants and two shops selling local produce and artefacts.
Clef Verte

Site suitable for nature lovers and mountain sports enthusiasts.

Pitches	Flat, some grass, but quiet hard, so need good pegs, 80² - 90m². Not hedged, divided by the occasional tree, so open feel. Best pitches overlook river which is not fenced off.
Hook-Up	6 or 10 amps - all pitches. Water & drainage - none.
Motorhomes	Motorhome service point. Walking distance to cable car and village.
Swimming pools	No swimming pool on site, but pretty municipal pool with waterslide next door, open 10am - 7pm., adults 3 euros, children 2 euros. Swimming in the river is not allowed.
Activities on site	Table tennis. Boules pitch. Sauna 6pm – 9pm. Indoor games room, library and TV room heated in winter. Children's play area and tennis, just outside site near pool. Trout fishing with permit.
Entertainment	No organised entertainment, but numerous daytime activities available nearby including walks (the GR54 goes past the site), cycling, mountain biking, rafting, paragliding, via ferrata and donkey riding.
Sanitary facilities	A very clean toilet block, a bit old but very comfortable and heated in winter. Separate ladies and gents. Three shower and wash cubicles together, six further very spacious showers with push button temperate control water, hooks and shelf. Nine individual wash basins. Toilets with seats and toilet paper. Drying room for ski gear. Baby room. Disabled facilities. Separate laundry. Chemical waste point.
Services	No shop, but pre-order bread and croissants baked on site. Basic provisions in reception- milk, ham eggs, wine, camping gaz and walking maps. etc. Bar and take-away (15/6 – 23/8), but all meals must be ordered by midday. Barbecues allowed. Dogs accepted. Internet and Wi-Fi on central part of site.
Accommodation	Chalets mobile homes, caravans and furnished appartments.
Tour operators	None.

Excursions/Places to visit
Adventure Park in woods, donkey riding, cable car to Les Deux Alpes and Venosc: all walking distance. St Christophe-en-Oisans 6km. Bourg d'Oisans 15km. La Bérarde 18km. Tour de France cycle routes: Col du Lauteret and Col du Galibier. Lauvitel and Muzelle lakes.

Directions
From Grenoble. In Grenoble follow signs to Vizille,"stations de l'Oisans" or Briançon. In Vizille take the N91 towards Briançon. About 5km past Bourg d'Oisans turn right onto the D530 towards Venosc, La Bérarde. The campsite is 8km along this road on the right, 300 metres after the cable-car arrival point from Venosc - Les 2 Alpes.

€ Prices 2010	High	Mid	Low	Off	Winter
Pitch + 2	19.40	17.30	15	13.60	16.90
Hook Up 6A	4.30	3.30	4.30	4.30	6.40

Address Bourg d'Arud, 38520 Venosc

GPS N 44° 59' 11 E 06° 07' 12

www.champ-du-moulin.com
email info@champ-du-moulin.com
Tel 04.76.80.07.38

Autrans, Au Joyeux Réveil **** Map Ref AL10

Location Autrans 300m. Grenoble 37km. Lyon 128km. Valence 82km.

Open 1st Dec to 31st Mar & 1st May to 30th Sept   **Pitches** 104 (73 touring)

Situated 1050m high in the heart of the Vercors National Park just 300 metres from the pretty village of Autrans, this site is a lovely spot for a quiet relaxing holiday. You can't fail to be impressed by the fantastic views over the surrounding mountains which includes an old Olympic ski jump. It is an area renowned for downhill and cross-country ski-ing in the winter and for hiking, pot-holing and mountain biking in the summer. There is a short ski-lift near the site with a shuttle bus in winter to longer runs 5km away. You can expect a warm welcome from the friendly couple who run the site. Autrans offers a full range of shops and activities.

Site suitable for couples and young families.

Pitches	Flat, grassy and laid out in straight lines, not hedged but divided by trees. Good size but very little shade.
Hook-Up	2, 4 or 6 amps - all pitches. Water & drainage - none.
Motorhomes	No service point, but ideal as walking distance of village.
Swimming pools	Three separate pools: a fun pool with water slides, a paddling pool with baby slide and an indoor swimming pool. Sun terrace with sun loungers.
Activities on site	Table tennis. Children's play area. Table football and TV in bar. Library. Fishing, cycle hire and riding 300m. 150km of marked out trails for walking.
Entertainment	High season: children's club. Organised activities, such as rock-climbing, pot-holing and canyoning. One music evening per week.
Sanitary facilities	A modern toilet block heated in winter, attractively tiled and well maintained. Push button temperature controlled showers with hooks shelf and rail. Individual wash basins. Toilets with toilet paper. Disabled facilities. Baby room. Laundry. Drying room in winter for ski gear. Chemical waste point.
Services	No shop as so close to town. Attractive, spacious bar/snack and take-away in July/August. Several restaurants and hotels within walking distance. Barbecues allowed. Dogs accepted. Internet. Wi-Fi in bar and on terrace.
Accommodation	20 mobile homes. 11 privately-owned mobile homes.
Tour operators	None.

Excursions/Places to visit

Autrans. A bus goes from town to Villard-de-Lans 16km and Grenoble. Meaudre. Route de Vercors. Pont-en-Royans. Grottes de Chorande, Col du Rousset.

€ Prices 2010	High	Mid	Low
Pitch + 2	33	30	20
Hook Up 6A	4	4	6
Pitch + 2 Winter	22		20
Hook Up 10A	7		7

Directions

Easy access on well made up roads with steady climbs and no sharp bends.
From Grenoble take the RN 531 in the direction of Villard-de-Lans via Sassenage and Lans-en-Vercors or the RD 106 in the direction of St-Nizier and Lans-en-Vercors.
From Lyon. Exit A48 at Pont-de-Veurey in the direction of Villard-de-Lans via Sassenage.
The site is well signed as you enter Autrans.

Address Le Château, 38880 Autrans

GPS N 45° 10' 31 E 05° 32' 53

www.camping-au-joyeux-reveil.fr
email camping-au-joyeux-reveil@wanadoo.fr
Tel 04.76.95.33.44

PROVENCE & CÔTE D'AZUR

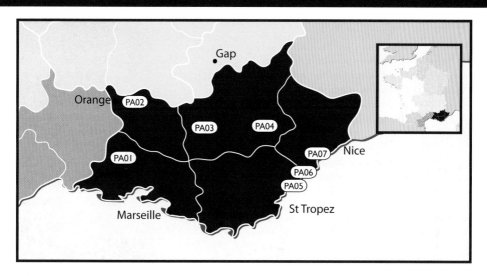

Picture opposite - Les Gorges du Verdon

Places of Interest - Provence & Côte d'Azur

The towns listed below situated in an area just north of the Mediterranean are important places to visit in Provence.

Aix-en-Provence is a magnificent example of the Provençal art of living so admired by the rest of the world. The boulevards shaded by majestic sycamores, the streets bordered by rich private residences, the discreet squares ornamented with beautiful fountains and garnished with welcoming sidewalk cafés, inevitably seduce those who take the time to linger. Cézanne made it his city, and the surrounding countryside inspired some of his greatest impressionist masterpieces.

Avignon is an ancient riverside fortress city situated on the Rhône river. The famous bridge of the nursery rhyme - Sur le Pont d'Avignon - projects oddly into the river, its broken arches stretching just half way across. The uninhabited and immense Palais des Papes or Papal Palace is the most important landmark after the bridge. Today, elegant designer boutiques and jewellers, famous restaurants and fine mansions stand just a few steps away from crowded squares, cheap brasseries and cobbled backstreets.

Gordes is built on the foothills of the Monts of Vaucluse, facing the Luberon, and is one of the best-known hilltop villages in the region, and one of the most beautiful in France. Its houses and buildings of white stone root themselves into the sharp cliff of the mountain, and its labyrinth of "calades" (narrow cobblestone streets) give the village a special charm.

Le Pont du Gard, at Remoulins, two thousand years after its construction, is still a veritable masterpiece, as much for the technical prowess involved, as for its simple beauty. This monument has been registered as a World Heritage of Man site since 1985.

Le Pont du Gard

Arles is famous for its Roman Arena and Theatre which are unique as they are integrated into the houses and buildings of the town. The streets of this city are truly medieval in character: narrow and winding between ancient buildings. Van Gogh stayed here for 14 months, during one of his most prolific periods, when he produced 200 paintings.

Arles

St Rémy de Provence a small town located at the foot of the Alpilles, has kept its traditions and personality. The festive events give rhythm to the town: the bull fights and other bull related events, the sheep migrating festival, the horse fair, concerts and exhibitions. The lively streets of the town centre have private residences with magnificent facades dating from the 17th and 18th centuries.

Vaison-la-Romaine lies at the foot of Mont Ventoux, the "giant of Provence", 1912m high, and enjoys a Mediterranean climate. The town is recognised as one of the Plus Beaux Détours de France and owes its reputation to its heritage both ancient and medieval. It is the site of an ancient Roman colony. Floors in mosaics, marble statues, ponds, atriums, and private thermal baths, all show life in Roman times. It is complemented by a panorama of medieval churches.

Forcalquier is a picturesque town built around the slopes of a steep conical hill, dominated by an octagonal 19th century chapel where a 10th century citadel once stood. Walking through the steep narrow streets, you'll see ancient doorways and wrought iron balconies, some dating from the 12th to 16th centuries.

Côte d'Azur or French Riviera is a region of sun-drenched beaches, luxury hotels and towns full of the highlife. It has 120km of coastline, a succession of well known resorts, 40km of sandy or pebbled beaches, many note-worthy sites, superb capes and islands, and 33 sailing ports allowing thousands of boats to moor all year long. Take a trip along the coast and allow yourself to be captivated by the beauty of the scenery and enjoy the coastal footpaths that contour the capes and the rocky bays.

Cannes, Antibes and **Menton** draw energy from the thriving city of **Nice**. Antibes boasts a network of pretty narrow streets either side of the Marché Provençal. The tropical peninsulas - Cap Ferrat and Cap Martin - frame the tiny principality of Monaco famous for its glamour and for the Grimaldi family who have ruled the principality for 700 years. Just behind the coast, medieval villages mushroom out of the nearby hills, offering the visitor a taste of old Provence. There are more than 120 hill-top villages, villages perchés, scattered all over the Côte d'Azur. Each has its own particular charm and merit.

Grasse, is renowned for its perfume factories, galleries and souvenir shops.

Fayence a definitive 18th century Provençal town, offers superb views.

Mougins, St Paul, Vence and Le Bar-sur-Loup medieval villages perched on top of a rock, are all worth a visit.

Gourdon, opposite Le Bar-sur-Loup, higher up on the mountain, on an even steeper rock, is visible from just about everywhere from Cannes to Nice.

Roquebrune-sur-Argens, is an ancient town sitting amidst bunches of new villas. It is located in an expansive pine forest, accentuated by the beautiful red cliffs of the Rocher de Roquebrune, and cooled by the Argens river. From the village there's a panoramic view out across the Argens plain to the north, with low mountains in the distance. Roquebrune retains a lot of charm with narrow streets between the old buildings and a 16th century church.

Fréjus, a mixture of Roman and medieval architecture, is a large sprawling town. The old Roman harbour now lies well inland and it still has its Roman arena. The Cathedral is built of lovely old stone and is set in a pretty square.

Saint Tropez is still very popular with tourists. It remains famous for the line of yachts along the quayside, the rows of terraced cafés overlooking the bay, the parades of strolling tourists and the slow cruising expensive cars. Behind the cafés, the small streets and old buildings are very picturesque.

Gorges du Verdon is one of France's most spectacular natural wonders, a Grand Canyon-style chasm roaring with milky-green water and edged by one of Europe's most hair-raising drives. The drive goes along part of the Route Napoléon.

The Côte d'Azur

Castellane is located part of the away along this beautiful but winding drive in the heart of the Gorges du Verdon. Castellane's main feature is a chapel, built on top of a 300m high rock that goes straight up from behind the town hall in the old centre. It is floodlit at night.

Moustiers Ste Marie on the other side of the Gorges du Verdon is a gorgeous village on the edge of a small stream in a steep narrow ravine. It is famous for its ceramic "faiences" and has narrow medieval streets and vaulted passages.

Nice Market

www.frenchriviera-tourisme.com
www.provenceweb.fr
www.beyond.fr

St Rémy-de-Provence, Monplaisir ***

Location 1km north-west of St Rémy. Nimes 44km. Arles 26km. Avignon 20km.

Open 6th Mar to 31st Oct   **Pitches** 130 (120 touring)

A truly delightful site with a lovely family atmosphere, maintained to a very high standard and walking distance of the centre of St Rémy. The pitches and hedges are well trimmed and the wealth of trees and plants give it a very verdant, rural feel. The beautiful cypress trees and pretty flowers throughout the site are a particular highlight. The quiet caring ambiance is created by three generations of the friendly Daniel family who are always on hand and are very helpful. There is a good mix of nationalities and it is a real pleasure to stay there. Already well booked for 2010.
Clef Verte

Site suitable for couples and families who appreciate a quiet atmosphere.

Pitches	Flat, well-hedged pitches varying in size up to 100m². Pre-book giving exact dimensions if you have a large outfit. Laid out in straight tree-lined alleys with tarmaced roads giving shade to most pitches. One hard standing pitch for disabled and wheelchairs.
Hook-Up	10 amps - all pitches. Water & drainage - none.
Motorhomes	Two motorhome service points, ideal for motorhomes because of proximity to town and shops.
Swimming pools	Very attractive pool area fenced round with pretty flowers and trees and floodlit at night. Good-sized basin for swimming 18m x 10m. Good-sized paddling pool. Sun terrace but no sun loungers. Open May - Oct.
Activities on site	Children's play area. Table tennis. Boules pitch. Library.
Entertainment	In high season mid July to 20/8: children's club. No other organised entertainment but plenty to do in town.
Sanitary facilities	Five well-appointed toilet blocks scattered throughout the site, all kept immaculately clean. Main blocks have separate ladies and gents and are heated in low season, but two are unisex. They are spacious, attractively tiled with push button, temperature control showers and hook, shelf and rail. Some individual wash cubicles but mostly open. Toilets with toilet paper. Disabled facilities. Baby room. A family room in larger block. Washing machines. Chemical waste point.
Services	Small shop with bread, cakes, fruit and vegetables, cold drinks and ice creams. Intermarché supermarket 500m. Attractive bar/snack area. Very reasonably-priced snack meals including wonderful salads served on terrace in July/August. Gas barbecues only allowed. Dogs accepted. Internet and Wi-Fi in library and on some nearby pitches.
Accommodation	10 mobile homes and chalets.
Tour operators	None.

Excursions/Places to visit
Avignon, Les Baux, Les Alpilles, Fontvieille, Abbaye de Frigolet- within 20km radius. Arles, Nimes, Pont du Gard, Gordes, Isle-sur-Sorgue – within 40km radius.

Directions
Follow the D99 which is the ring road to the north of the town. Take the D5 north towards Maillane and Graveson then fork left after 150m and the site entrance is on your left.

€ Prices 2010	High	Low
Pitch + 2	24.20	14.80
Hook Up 10A	3.80	3.80

Address Chemin de Monplaisir, 13120 St. Rémy de Provence

www.camping-monplaisir.fr
email reception@camping-monplaisir.fr

GPS N 43° 47' 49 E 04° 49' 26   **Tel** 04.90.92.22.70

Vaison-la-Romaine, Camping du Théâtre Romain ***Map Ref PA02

Location Centre of Vaison-la-Romaine 500m. Nyons 16km. Orange 30km. Avignon 51km.

Open 15th Mar to 5th Nov   **Pitches** 75 (69 touring)

This lovely little site has been included because of its excellent facilities and its unique position 500m from the beautiful town and amphitheatre of Vaison-la-Romain. The town is also well known for its superb medieval cathedral, cloisters and chapel. The fields around are full of vines and lavender, and towering over them 1912m high about 30km away is the magnificent Mont Ventoux. The friendly owner runs the site to a very high standard and maintains a quiet peaceful atmosphere. There is no organised entertainment at all. Arrival before midday or reservation is recommended throughout the season.

Site suitable for couples and families keen to explore the area and stay in a very quiet spot.

Pitches	Good-sized flat pitches, minimum 100m² all surrounded by hedges giving good privacy. All are hard standing.
Hook-Up	5 or 10 amps with water & drainage - all pitches.
Motorhomes	Motorhome service area. Excellent for motorhomes due to proximity to town.
Swimming pools	Pretty rectangular pool, quite small but good for a dip. Sun terrace with sun loungers. No paddling pool.
Activities on site	Children's play area. Table tennis. Table football. Pool table - free. Boules pitch.
Entertainment	None, but lots of activities, concerts etc. in town.
Sanitary facilities	Two immaculately clean and well maintained unisex toilet blocks. One of them is attractively tiled in the shape of a courtyard with a flower bed as the central point. The other is heated. Push button, temperature control showers with hooks and shelf. Individual wash cubicles and toilets with toilet paper and washbasins. Disabled facilities. Baby room. Laundry. Chemical waste point.
Services	Pre-order bread. All shops in town. Small bar overlooking pool selling beer, wine, cold drinks and ice-creams. Barbecues allowed. Dogs accepted. Wi-Fi Point near reception.
Accommodation	6 mobile homes.
Tour operators	None.

Excursions/Places to visit
In the heart of one of most beautiful regions of France, you will find, within a radius of 80km, many and varied tourist attractions including Nyons, Orange and Avignon as well as walking and cycling circuits. Information is available and free at reception.

€ Prices 2010	High	Low
Pitch + 2	21	15
Hook Up 5A	3	3

Directions
The site is in the north east of the town near the ancient roman theatre.
From the A7 take exit 4 and follow the D950 towards Carpentras. After 4.5km turn onto the D977 to Vaison-la-Romaine. On arrival at Vaison cross over the river and take the D938 towards Nyons. Continue along the D938 following signs to the site and at the roundabout take the third exit along Ave Pierre Brossolet. Turn left at the T-junction into Chemin du Brusquet.

Address Quartier des Arts, Chemin du Brusquet, 84110 Vaison-la-Romain
GPS N 44° 14' 41 E 05° 04' 47

www.camping-theatre.com
email info@camping-theatre.com
Tel 04.90.28.78.66

Niozelles, Camping Moulin du Ventre **** Map Ref PA03

Location A51 11km, Forcalquier 9km. Niozelles 3km. Aix 74km. Toulon 157km.

Open 3rd Apr to 30th Sep   **Pitches** 124 (105 touring)

Tucked away in a verdant Provencal landscape with fields of lavender all round, this site is a haven of peace and quiet. It is located on a lovely lake suitable for pedalos and little boats. The pitches are set out in a variety of mature trees along 1.5km of river where you can paddle in rock pools. It is well placed for visiting Forcalquier an old provencal town with a pretty church, Franciscan convent and square, and the magnificent Gorges du Verdon are definitely worth a day trip. Shade for the terrace of the attractive wooden beamed bar/restaurant is provided by lovely weeping willows.

Site suitable for all ages, particularly couples and young families. No entertainment for teenagers.

Pitches	Grassy and laid out in terraces and divided by low hedges and trees giving good shade. Mostly flat, some slope slightly. Average 100m², although pitches at far end of site more spacious but long way from toilet block.
Hook-Up	10 amps - 88 pitches. Water & drainage - 16 pitches.
Motorhomes	Motorhome service point. Need transport to visit region.
Swimming pools	Good-sized pool for swimming 200m², paddling pool and excellent spacious sun terrace, open mid-May to mid-Sep. Swimming forbidden in lake.
Activities on site	Table tennis. Volleyball area. Children's play area. Bouncy castle. Library and TV room. Trout, carp and tench fishing in Category 2 river with permit. Pedalos on lake.
Entertainment	In high season: some organised entertainment for children and occasional music evenings.
Sanitary facilities	Three toilet blocks. The one nearest reception has recently been revamped and is more modern. The other two are older but quite respectable. Push button, temperature control showers with hook and shelf. Two showers and washbasins together in first block. Individual wash basins. Toilets with toilet paper. Baby room. Washing machine and tumble dryer. Chemical waste point.
Services	Pre-order bread. Basic provisions only sold in reception. Supermarket 3km. Bar/snack/take-away in pretty old provencal building. Serves basic menus and pizzas. Gas barbecues only allowed. Dogs accepted. Internet. Wi-Fi in bar and on terrace.
Accommodation	14 mobile homes, 5 chalets, 2 appartments.
Tour operators	None.

Excursions/Places to visit
Numerous walks in area. La Brillane 3km, Oraison 5km, Forcalquier 9km, Manosque, Sisteron, Digne. Gorges du Verdon for day trip.

Directions
The site is just off the N100 8.5 km south-east of Forcalquier.
From the A51 take exit 19. Follow the N100 through la Brillane towards Forcalquier and the site is on your left 2.5km from the town.

€ Prices 2010	High	Low
Pitch + 2	23	16
Hook Up 10A	6	4

Address 04300 Niozelles

GPS N 43° 55' 59 E 05° 52' 05

www.moulin-de-ventre.com
email moulindeventre@aol.com
Tel 04.92.78.63.31

Castellane, Domaine du Verdon ****

Location Castellane 1.2km. Digne 53km. Grasse 64km. Draguignan 66km. Nice 114km.

Open 12th May to 15th Sep

Pitches 500 (200 touring)

This large Castels site is situated in a pretty valley right on the edge of the Gorges du Verdon and walking distance of the pretty town of Castellane. This site has been included because of its wonderful setting, its attractive stone-faced buildings and spacious areas by the River Verdon. The river is very low most of the time but the dam is opened twice a week and it fills up for canoeing and kayaking. It is probably the best in the area, but some of the sanitary blocks could do with updating and the grounds could do with a little more TLC. The lively atmosphere and good programme of entertainment make it an ideal spot for active families.

Site suitable for families who enjoy a lively atmosphere, good for teenagers in high season.

Pitches	Flat on hard ground, separated by low hedges. They vary in size but most are a minimum of 100m². They are nearly all in one area.
Hook-Up	6 amps - all pitches. Water & drainage - 80 pitches.
Motorhomes	Motorhome service point. Good for motorhomes as walking distance of town.
Swimming pools	Swimming pool complex with two medium-sized rectangular shaped pools. Two waterslides come down into half of one of the pools. Small paddling pool. Good sun terrace but no sun loungers. Swimming area not large enough for size of site.
Activities on site	Mini-golf. Archery. Volleyball, basket ball. Lots of table tennis tables outside. Boules pitch. Fitness circuit. Two children's play areas. Two ponds: one for boating, one for children to fish. Fishing in river with permit. Indoor games area with electronic games, pool and table football.
Entertainment	In high season: an entertainment team provide a full programme of activities both on and off site. Children's club. Sporting competitions on site. Guided walks, horse-riding, rafting, canyoning and kayaking off site. Evening entertainment includes music, concerts and a disco three times a week. Camp fire for teenagers every evening at 11pm on river bank well away from pitches.
Sanitary facilities	Five fully equipped toilet blocks, one block with toilets and washing up sinks only. They are a mixture of old and new and all different. One block has been completely modernised. All have push button temperature controlled showers with hooks, individual wash basins and toilets with toilet paper. In the new block, there are family showers with showers and wash basins together. Disabled facilities. Baby room. Large laundry. Chemical waste point.
Services	Supermarket, bar, restaurant, take-away/pizzeria – open all season. Fridge hire. Gas barbecues only allowed. Dogs accepted. Internet. Wi-Fi in bar/restaurant area.
Accommodation	220 chalets and mobile homes.
Tour operators	British and Dutch companies on 80 pitches.

Excursions/Places to visit
Castellane with its market place. Gorges du Verdon. Lac de Castillon, Lac de Chaudanne. Lac de Ste Croix. Moustiers Ste Marie. Draguinan.

Directions
The site is situated 1.2km south-west of Castellane on the N952 and well signposted.

€ Prices 2010	High	Low
Pitch + 2	33	20
Hook Up 6A	8	5

Address 04120 Castellane

GPS N 43° 50' 21 E 06° 29' 38

www.camp-du-verdon.com
email contact@camp-du-verdon.com
Tel 04.92.83.61.29

Roquebrune-sur-Argens, Les Pêcheurs ****

Location Roquebrune-sur-Argens 800m. Exit 37 from A8 7.5km. Fréjus 12km. St Aygulf 12km.

Open 1st Apr to 29th Sep

Pitches 220 (150 touring)

Located in a unique position at the foot of the magnificent Roquebrune rock and immediately opposite a fabulous lake, renowned for its beautiful sunsets, this site has a welcoming flowery entrance and offers high class well maintained facilities. Canoeing is possible on the lake, but the water ski-ing and boating are private. It is also just a 10-minute walk from the pretty little village of Roquebrune with its picturesque gates and squares. A cycle ride will take you to the nearest beach. Founded in 1968 by the Simoncini family, the site has constantly been improved and the recently installed spa area is a lovely spot to relax and pamper yourself. Please note that the pitches are heavily shaded.

Site suitable for all ages, particularly young families as ambiance is quiet.

Pitches	Flat, heavily shaded and divided by high hedges. The pitches are set out in straight narrow alleys giving a very tight turning circle to get on to the pitches, therefore not recommended for outfits over 6.5m long.
Hook-Up	10 amps - all pitches. Water & drainage - none.
Motorhomes	Motorhome service point. Walking distance of Roquebrune. Cycling distance of beach.
Swimming pools	Good sized heated pool excellent for a good swim, paddling pool and attractive sun terrace with sun loungers, surrounded by verdant hedging. New spa area with charge: sauna, massage jet stream pool and a swimming pool 6m x 12m with jacuzzi.
Activities on site	On site itself: archery, boules pitch, children's play area, fishing. On the lakeside accessible via an underpass: mini-golf, half-court tennis, canoes - all free and pedalo hire with charge. TV and games in bar.
Entertainment	High season: children's club 4 -12yrs, aquagym, jogging, family theme evenings with live music. Guided walks including one up to top of the Roquebrune, worth the effort for the views.
Sanitary facilities	Three unisex toilet blocks, one large modern one decorated in true Provençal style, beautifully tiled and laid out round a courtyard. Other two blocks older but acceptable. Push button showers in all the blocks, no temperature control. No cold water in individual wash cubicles. Toilets with toilet paper. Well maintained. Disabled facilities. Baby room. Laundry. Chemical waste point.
Services	Small quite well-stocked shop. Bar/restaurant with very pretty terrace shaded by plane trees trained over a pergola. Reasonably priced menu. Take-away. All open all season. Further snack bars on lakeside. Fridge hire. Gas barbecues only allowed. Dogs accepted. Internet and Wi-Fi.
Accommodation	Mobile homes.
Tour operators	One British company.

Excursions/Places to visit
Roquebrune-sur-Argens 1km. Beach at St. Aygulf 12km, Gassin, Ramatuelle. St Tropez, St Raphael, Cannes, Monaco. Gorges du Verdon for day trip.

Directions
The site is just north of Roquebrune on the D7. From A8 motorway exit at Le Muy and then take the N7 east following signs for Roquebrune-sur-Argens. The campsite is approximately 2km south from the N7 turning before you come to the town of Roquebrune and is signposted.

€ Prices 2010	Peak	High	Mid	Low
Pitch + 2	37.50	32	23	17.50
Hook Up 10A	5.50	5.50	5.50	5.50

Address 83520 Roquebrune-sur-Argens

GPS N 43° 27' 04 E 06° 38' 00

www.camping-les-pecheurs.com
email info@camping-les-pecheurs.com
Tel 04.94.45.71.25

St Aygulf, L'Etoile d'Argens **** Map Ref PA06

Location St Aygulf 3km, Fréjus 7km. Cannes 84km. St Tropez 33km. Nice 120km.

Open 1st Apr to 30th Sep   **Pitches** 493 (200 touring)

Although this is a large site, it is unusually spacious for an establishment in this coastal region. It has a privileged position on the banks of the Argens river surrounded by vineyards and is only 3km from the beaches at St Aygulf. One of the site's greatest assets is the free shuttle service by boat along the river to the beach allowing you to avoid the traffic in this busy area in high season. You can also get access to the beach with your own boat. The site is attractively laid out and maintained to a high standard. It is also renowned for its good range of daytime and evening activities, so ideal for those seeking a lively ambiance. The pitches are laid out in long straight tree-lined alleys behind the reception and other services.

Site suitable for families who enjoy a lively atmosphere.

Pitches	Flat, divided by high hedges and trees giving reasonable privacy and shade, although not too heavily shaded. Set out in spacious alleys. Vary in size from 100m² to 250m² and priced accordingly. Largest pitches are luxurious but expensive.
Hook-Up	10 amps - standard pitches. 16 amps - luxury pitches with water & drainage.
Motorhomes	Motorhome service point. Ideal as everything on site and transport provided to beach.
Swimming pools	Very attractive heated aqua complex, laid out with palm trees and 500m² of basins. A good sized pool for swimming, a further medium-sized pool, waterfall, spa area with jacuzzi and a large paddling pool. Large sun terrace with sun loungers which fill up quickly in high season and grassy area round pool.
Activities on site	Four floodlit tennis courts. Mini-golf. Archery. Cycle hire. Four basket/volleyball courts. Outdoor table tennis tables. Boules pitches. Excellent children's play area. Pool, table football and TV in bar. Fishing in river with permit.
Entertainment	In high season a full range of daytime and evening activities including a children's club, organised sports activities and music evenings with cabarets, visiting bands and discos.
Sanitary facilities	About 20 small unisex toilet blocks, one at the end of each alley, all with toilets, washbasins and showers. Two have recently been refurbished and a 3rd is planned for 2010. No individual wash basins in older blocks, which have squeaky doors. Temperature control water in some blocks. Toilet paper provided. Disabled facilities. Baby room. Separate laundry. Chemical waste point.
Services	Vival supermarket. Hypermarket 5-min drive. Spacious bar and restaurant with terrace that overlook pool, but quality of food variable. Take-away. Shuttle boat carrying 44 people runs every 40mins to beach at St Aygulf 15th Jun - 15th Sep. Barbecues not allowed. Dogs accepted. Internet and Wi-Fi.
Accommodation	220 mobile homes.
Tour operators	One British company on 50 pitches. One French company on 20 pitches.

Excursions/Places to visit
Aqualand and go-karting 3 mins from site. St Tropez, St Raphael, Cannes, Monaco. Gorges du Verdon for day trip.

Directions
The site is midway between Fréjus and St Aygulf about 3km from the sea. From A8 take exit 37 and follow D7 to Roquebrune-sur-Argens. From Roquebrune continue on D7 for 7km and turn left onto D8 following signs to the site.

€ Prices 2009	High	Mid	Low
Std Pitch + 2 & 10A	38	21	14
Confort + 2 & 10A	52	22	18

Address Chemin des Etangs, 83370 Fréjus-St Aygulf

GPS N 43° 24' 57 E 06° 42' 19

www.etoiledargens.com
email info@etoiledargens.com
Tel 04.94.81.01.41

La Colle-sur-Loup, Les Pinèdes****　　　Map Ref PA07

Location La Colle 1km. Cagnes-sur-Mer 7km. Cannes 27km. Vence 8km. Nice 26km.

Open 15th Mar to 30th Sept　　　　　　　**Pitches** 150 (123 touring)

We think that this is one of the best sites near the Côte d'Azur coast because of its unique position, its small size and the lovely friendly atmosphere. It is situated in a wooded valley between the sea and the mountains just a 15-minute drive from the Mediterranean beaches and the magnificent scenery of the Gorges du Loup. The pitches are set out on terraces on the side of a south facing hill and reached by fairly steep flights of stone steps throughout the site. There is a good mixture of nationalities and a quiet ambiance. A daily shuttle bus in July/August takes you to La Colle-sur-Loup. There is also a cycle track going to the beach 500m from the site entrance. Reservations Sat - Sat in high season.

Site suitable for all ages, although no on-site entertainment for teenagers.

Pitches	Flat, terraced, divided by low shrubs varying in size up to 100m². Shade from 30 varieties of tree. Good pegs needed as ground is hard.
Hook-Up	3, 6 or 10 amps - all pitches. Water & drainage - 60 pitches.
Motorhomes	Motorhome service point. Need transport to visit region.
Swimming pools	Attractive pool complex decorated with palm trees. Rectangular pool, good size for swimming. Paddling pool. Generous sun terrace with sun loungers. Opens 15th April.
Activities on site	At top of site, all weather sports pitch for basketball, volleyball and football. Archery. Table tennis. Boules pitch. Children's play area. Donkey rides on site's own donkeys. Indoor games area with table football and TV. Library. Fishing in river Loup with permit 50m. Nearby a range of activities on offer including climbing, white-water rafting, canyoning and via ferrata.
Entertainment	In high season: children's club, organised sporting activities and guided walks. One dance evening per week in restaurant.
Sanitary facilities	Two modern unisex toilet blocks. They are bright, beautifully tiled and maintained to a high standard. Push button temperature controlled showers with hook, shelf and rail. Individual wash basins. Toilet paper outside toilets. Disabled facilities. Baby room. Laundry. Chemical waste point.
Services	Small shop in middle of site for basics. Bar/restaurant at bottom of site near reception open to public serving reasonably priced menus. Fridge hire. Gas barbecues only allowed in high season, charcoal in low season. Dogs accepted. Internet and Wi-Fi in reception and restaurant.
Accommodation	27 chalets and mobile homes.
Tour operators	None.

Excursions/Places to visit
Cagnes-sur-Mer 7km, St Paul-de-Vence, the artists town 6km, Grasse and its perfume factories 12km, Gorges-du-Loup 10km, Nice 16km, Cannes 25km, Monaco 45km.

Directions
From A8. Take exit 47 Cagnes-sur-Mer. Follow D2 towards Vence and follow signs to La Colle-sur-Loup. At the roundabout in La Colle-sur-Loup take the D6 towards Grasse and the site entrance is on your right after 3.5km just past the site restaurant.

€ Prices 2010	Peak	High	Mid	Low
Std Pitch + 2	26	23	18	16.50
Large Pitch + 2	31	25.50	19.50	18
Hook Up 6A	4.20	4.20	4.20	4.20

Address Route du Pont de Pierre, 06480 La Colle-sur-Loup

GPS N 43° 40' 55 E 07° 05' 01

www.lespinedes.com
email campinglespinedes06@aol.com
Tel 04.93.32.98.94

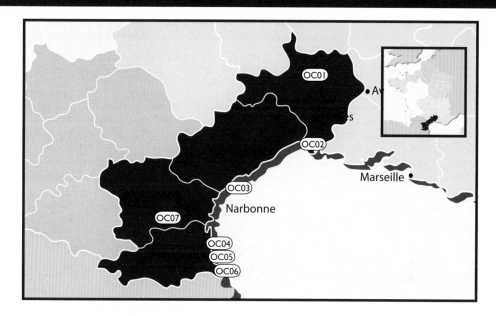

Picture opposite - Collioure

Places of Interest - Languedoc Roussillon

This region stretches from the Pyrénées-Orientales on the Spanish border to Provence. It is bathed in the warm Mediterranean climate which boasts an average 300 days of sunshine per year. You are rarely far from both mountains and sea. On the western side, the foothills of the Pyrénées fall down to meet the sea at Argelès-sur-Mer and on the eastern side the majestic river Rhône flows through Provence before finally exiting to the sea near Marseilles. The coastline offers a kaleidoscope of interesting scenery.

Nîmes is renowned for its magnificent Roman arena. A panoramic view over the town's roof tops from the Tour Magne shows the history of Nîmes at a glance. The 12th century St Pastor cathedral dominates the narrow streets of the old town and still bears witness to their medieval past. The boulevards which encircle the town show the site of the medieval defences and the ancient city limits.

Carcassonne on the eastern edge of the Pyrénées region is a wonderful medieval walled city and one of the most amazing sights in France. Seen from a distance it looks almost like a model, dreamlike with its turrets and crenellations. The oldest parts date from the Roman period and the Cité is defended by 52 sturdy towers and huge heavily fortified entrance gates. In the 13th century it was a stronghold for the Cathars. Inside the walls there are houses, shops, restaurants and cafés which spill out on the square, giving the town a fabulous bohemian atmosphere. There are many "bastides" towns to visit near Carcassonne including **Mirepoix** and **Montségur**.

La Côte Vermeille stretching from Argelès to Sète has steep, rugged cliffs tumbling to the sea. It offers miles of sandy beaches and provides glorious cruising grounds and coves to explore. It is a haven for marine wildlife and thus a very popular destination for divers. This coastline has been home to many famous painters such as Dali and Picasso who were drawn there by the exceptionally bright and clear light. This region also known as French Catalonia, has a fascinating cultural and gastronomic mix of French and Spanish.

Argelès Beach

Argelès a gateway to Spain, is situated in the southernmost part of the region at the foot of the Pyrénées. There are 7km of beaches and 3km of creeks. There are supervised beaches from June till September, children's clubs, sailing schools, windsurfing, bobskiing, deep-sea diving, boat hiring, sea-trips, sea-kayak, waterskiing, pedalos and balneotherapy.

Collioure is the jewel of the coast. This Catalan fishing village has for centuries impressed travellers and traders, artists and invaders with its simple beauty. The little harbour is protected by sea walls and a fortified village church on one side and a 12th century castle on the other. Beside the church with its curious round lighthouse there are small secluded beaches. Behind the waterfront is a delightful maze of narrow streets lined with artists' shops, restaurants and cafes.

Carcassonne

Céret about 25 km inland from Collioure was also a favourite spot with many great modern artists including Picasso and Braque. In the 1910's Céret was regarded as the 'Capitol of Cubism'. There is a surprising Museum of Modern Art with several cubist paintings, a Picasso collection and works by Chall, Dali, Miro, Matisse and Juan Gris as well as the Catalan sculptor Manolo. There is regular open-air Sardana dancing and bullfighting here.

Le Pic du Canigou

Perpignan the largest city in the region stands on the river Tet, but the much smaller river Basse which flows through the centre has pretty gardens along its banks. The main streets are lined with palms and mimosa and there is also the cathedral to visit and lots of intricate narrow shopping streets to explore.

Canet-en-Roussillon has a huge stretch of sandy beach and crystal-blue seawater. The resort offers a wide range of sporting activities, including 4 small activity parks with children's play areas, sports grounds and tennis courts.

Sérignan, a delightful old town about 4km from one of the most beautiful beaches in the area offers a network of small alleys and winding streets, where you can see the remnants of ramparts, Renaissance doors and old wells. The collegiate church of the Notre Dame-de-Grâce, built in stages from the 12th to 15th century dominates the town.

Le Cap d'Agde benefits from an exceptional natural environment. Its basalt sea beds, unique on this coast, are a true marvel. A wealth of sub-marine life can also be seen at the aquarium, an authentic underwater world of 30 pools teeming with Mediterranean and tropical fish, sharks and coral.

Sète cannot be accessed without crossing one of its 14 bridges, bridges made of stone, of iron, rigid ones, swing ones, bascule bridges, they cross the canals and docking bays and lead you right into the centre of the town. Sète was founded three centuries ago around the port, which was constructed by royal decree to open the Languedoc onto the Mediterranean. Despite the number of cargo ships, trawlers and sailing boats, the port is only small and is still at the heart of the town.

The Camargue is a major world heritage wetland and is host to a diversity of habitats and many fragile ecosystems. Ponds and marshes cover a large proportion of the river delta and are habitats of choice for both migratory and sedentary birds. Egrets, night herons, bitterns, mallards and wagtails are common visitors. Pink flamingos are now the emblem of the Camargue. It is one of the few spots around the Mediterranean where they nest. The flamingo population here can reach 20,000 couples grouped into flocks.

Aigues Mortes

Saintes-Maries-de-la-Mer is the largest village in the Camargue. Located on the western tip of the delta on a thin strip of sandy ground still exposed to the unpredictable assaults of the Mediterranean, it is a well-known seaside resort, with a fortified church, built in the 12th century. The statue of the Egyptian servant, Sara, patron saint of the Gypsies is preserved in the crypt. It is covered with a huge pile of dresses and coats. During the last week of May 8,000 gypsies come to the village for an annual festival to worship their patron saint.

Aigues-Mortes St Louis left for the crusades from this impressive walled town. Rising out of the marshes and lakes, its 13th century fortifications have been perfectly preserved.

www.sunfrance.com
www.languedoc-france.info.

Allègre-les-Fumades, Château de Boisson **** Map Ref OC01

Location Alès 16km. St Ambroix 11km. Nimes 65km. Vallon-Pont-d'Arc 28km. Orange 75km.

Open 3rd Apr to 25th Sept   **Pitches** 178 (63 touring)

A top quality Castels site in the grounds of beautiful 15th century château at the heart of a pretty hamlet, dominated by a church tower. It is laid out in three flat terraces on the side of a hill, with the reception at the bottom and the swimming pools and bar/restaurant at the top. Cream-coloured stonework and lovely arches are the predominant features of all the restored buildings. The well tended trees and shrubs give the site a lush verdant feeling. You can enjoy a Mediterranean climate and use it as centre for exploring the many attractions of Provence. The Cevennes, the Camargue, the Pont du Gard and the Gorges de l'Ardèche are all within striking distance. A good low season choice as most services are open and there is a superb indoor pool.

Site suitable for All ages particularly couples and young families.

Pitches	Vary in size from 90m² to 150m². Most have good shade and are divided by hedges and trees. Good pegs are needed. Water & drainage pitches average 130m², and pitches at top of site near château are 120m². Prices vary accordingly.
Hook-Up	10 amps - all pitches. Water & drainage - 39 pitches. Private toilet facilities - 7 pitches.
Motorhomes	Motorhome service point. Need transport to visit region.
Swimming pools	An excellent sized rectangular outdoor pool 25m x 15m with a good waterslide. Paddling pool with mushroom shower. Attractive sun terrace but no sun loungers. Heated indoor pool 14m x 8m.
Activities on site	Two tennis courts. Tennis wall. All weather sports pitch for volleyball, basketball and football. Boules. Table tennis. Children's play areas. Pool and table football. TV in bar.
Entertainment	In high season, children's workshops 4 -12 yrs old, which include painting, drawing, DIY, sculpting, plus a variety of evening entertainment ranging from crazy games in the pool to karaoke nights and family discos which always finish by 11pm. Canoe trips organised on the Cèze.
Sanitary facilities	Two very well appointed toilet blocks, both attractively tiled. Temperature control showers with hook, shelf and rail. Individual wash cubicles and toilets with paper. Disabled facilities and baby room in the block at the top. Laundry facilities in the block the bottom. Chemical waste point.
Services	Small shop. Bar/snack with pizzeria and take-away open from end of May to start of Sept. Terrace overlooks pool. Attractive and beautifully arranged restaurant with covered patio open early Apr to end Sep. This area at top of site is decorated with pretty plants and flowers. Fridges for hire. Gas barbecues only allowed. Dogs accepted in low season only. Internet and Wi-Fi on whole site.
Accommodation	65 mobile homes. 17 appartments.
Tour operators	Two Dutch companies and one British company on 55 pitches.

Excursions/Places to visit
Alès 16km, Vallon-Pont-d'Arc 30km, Uzès 30km, Nîmes 45km, Avignon 65km.

Directions
The site is off the D16 North East of Alès. Exit the A7 at junction 19, take the D994 to Pont-St-Esprit then the N86 to Bagnols-sur-Cèze. Turn west onto D6, following signs to Alès. After 35km turn right onto the D7 to Brouzet and Navacelles. After 10km at the roundabout connecting the D37 and D16, take the D16 and the campsite is on your right.

€ Prices 2010	Peak	High	Mid	Low
Pitch + 2	34.50	25.50	20	19
Hook Up 6A	Incl	Incl	Incl	Incl

Address 30500 Allègre-les-Fumades

www.chateaudeboisson.com
email reception@chateaudeboisson.com

GPS N 44° 12' 34 E 04° 15' 24   **Tel** 04 66 24 85 61

Sommières, Domaine de Massereau ****

Location Sommières 2km. Nîmes 36km. Montpellier 37km. Arles 67km. Aigues-Mortes 40km.

Open 28th Mar to 11th Nov (for pitches)   **Pitches** 120 (58 touring)

Situated between the Mediterranean sea and the Cévennes hills just 2km from the delightful medieval town of Sommières, this site has been created in the grounds of a vineyard. It is an estate that has belonged to the family since 1804. Visits to the vineyard opposite the site and wine-tasting are a pleasant distraction. It is a spacious site with large open areas and offers a quiet ambience with well maintained modern facilities. Not only is it an ideal spot for visiting the Camargue and other areas in Provence but it is only a half hour drive from the Mediterranean coast at Aigues Mortes. A further asset is the superb cycle track, built on an old railway line, which runs from Sommières via the site to just outside Nîmes.

Site suitable for couples and young families and particularly good for short stays.

Pitches	Variety of quality of pitches 100m² - 120m² in size, divided by low shrubs. Some slope gently and some are mixed up with the on-site accommodation. Mixture of sun and shade. Good pegs needed.
Hook-Up	16 amps, water & drainage - all pitches.
Motorhomes	Motorhome service point, although transport needed to visit the region.
Swimming pools	Attractive pool complex with good sized basin for swimming, waterslides and tiny paddling pool. Large sun terrace with plenty of sun loungers.
Activities on site	Mini-golf. Half court tennis. Cycle and mini go-kart hire. Fitness circuit. Children's mountain bike track. Boules pitch. Children's play area. Childrens' room. Two trampolines. Volleyball. Table tennis, pool and electronic games. TV room. Jacuzzi, sauna, hammam with charge for 45-min session.
Entertainment	No organised entertainment except activities for children 5 – 13 yrs in July/August.
Sanitary facilities	One large modern toilet block, built round a quadrangle. Recently built and well-maintained. Good number of showers and wash basins together, push button temperature control showers, with hook and rail. Individual wash cubicles and toilets with paper. Disabled facilities. Baby room. Separate laundry. Chemical waste point.
Services	Well-stocked shop. Bar and restaurant with attractive terrace overlooking the pool, serving reasonably priced meals, take-away, all open all season. Gas barbecues only allowed. Dogs accepted. Internet. Wi-Fi on half the site.
Accommodation	35 mobile homes and 24 chalets.
Tour operators	Two British companies on 27 pitches.

Excursions/Places to visit

Sommières 2km, Nîmes 25km, Montpellier 24km, Aigues-Mortes 30km. Arles 53km. The Camargue.

€ Prices 2010	Peak	High	Mid	Low	Off
Pitch + 2	32	28	23.70	17.50	15.40
Hook Up 16A	6.40	4.50	4.50	4.50	4.50

Directions

The site is 2km south of Sommières on the D12. From A9 take exit 26. Follow signs through through the village of Gallargues-le-Montueux to Sommières along the D12. The site is signposted to your right after 8km.

Address Les Hauteurs de Sommières, Route d'Aubais, 30250 Sommières

www.massereau.fr
email info@massereau.fr

GPS N 43° 45' 57 E 04° 05' 51

Tel 04.66.53.11.20

Sérignan-Plage, Camping Aloha****

Location Agde 26km. Béziers 18km. Sète 63km. Perpignan 105km. Montpellier 72km.

Open 24th Apr to 12th Sep

Pitches 450 (190 touring)

A very well-run lively site with direct access to a beautiful stretch of sandy beach that shelves gently into the sea, so very suitable for younger children. It is also supervised from 15th Jun to 15th Sept. Although a large site, it has been run by the same family for two generations and they are keen to encourage traditional camping. 'Aloha' in the Hawaiian language means 'welcome' and a friendly atmosphere is exactly what the family provides. The site is spread over two sides of a small coast road, the quieter and more shady side is opposite the reception. It is an attractive verdant site, full of trees and palms with access to the pitches via wide alleys, giving a spacious feel.

Site suitable for all ages, particularly families who enjoy a lively atmosphere.

Pitches	Set out in straight lines, divided by pretty shrubs and trees, flat and at least 100m². Not too heavily shaded.
Hook-Up	10 amps - all pitches. Water & drainage - none.
Motorhomes	Motorhome service point. Ideal as right on beach and everything provided on site.
Swimming pools	Large aqua-complex, which caters for everybody. A 25m long pool, good for doing lengths, a huge paddling pool with a mini-slide and mushroom shower and a separate area for two 75m long waterslides. The site organise a championship slide each week! All heated all season. Attractive sun terrace and sun loungers.
Activities on site	Cycle hire. Tennis. All weather sports pitch for volleyball, basketball and football. Table tennis. Boules pitch. Two children's play areas. Gym. Indoor games area and TV. Bathing, sailing and windsurfing on beach.
Entertainment	Throughout season: children's clubs 5 - 7yrs and 8 - 12 yrs, range of sporting activities including aquagym, aerobics, diving, sailing, windsurfing and riding lessons, archery and sports competitions. In evening cabarets karaoke, dance nights and shows.
Sanitary facilities	Seven unisex toilet blocks scattered throughout site. All maintained to a high standard. Push button temperature controlled showers with hooks, shelf and rail. Individual wash cubicles, toilets with paper. Disabled facilities. Baby room. Laundry in two blocks. Chemical waste point.
Services	Supermarket, bakery, butcher, two bars, restaurant overlooking pool. Snack bar/pizzeria/take-away. Cash machine, hairdressers. Fridge hire. Barbecues allowed. Dogs accepted. Internet. Wi-Fi near reception.
Accommodation	166 mobile homes and chalets. New very attractive mobile home park.
Tour operators	Two British companies on 90 pitches.

Excursions/Places to visit
Sérignan with its pretty market place 6km. Béziers 16km, Pézénas 34km, Sète 60km. The Camargue.

Directions
Take exit 35 from the A9. Follow the D612 towards Agde. After 2km at the roundabout take 2nd exit onto D64 to Valras-Plage. After 4.5km turn left onto D37 to Sérignan-Plage. Take the right hand fork in the centre of the village and the site entrance is on your right.

€ Prices 2010	Peak	High	Mid	Low	Off
Pitch + 2	46	42	34	26	18
Hook Up 10A	Incl	Incl	Incl	Incl	Incl

Address Allée du Grand Large, 34410 Sérignan Plage

www.yellohvillage-aloha.com
email info@alohacamping.com
Tel 04.67.39.71.30

GPS N 43° 16' 03 E 03° 20' 05

Canet-Plage, Le Brasilia **** Map Ref OC04

Location Canet 2km. Argelès 23km. Perpignan 14km. Carcassonne 126km. Béziers 107km.

Open 24th Apr to 25th Sep   **Pitches** 753 (472 touring)

The quality of everything on this site and its location right on a beautiful stretch of sandy beach and next to the River Tet make it one of the best in the guide. Although a large site, it is still family run with extraordinary attention to detail in the design and decoration. On arrival you are immediately struck by the superb quality. A very attractive entrance leads to a huge courtyard of shops, dominated by a Catalan tower and adorned with exotic plants and flowers. There is a wonderfully relaxing atmosphere on the site created by spacious pitches with a profusion of palm trees, aromatic pines, shrubs and lawns all blending perfectly with the terracotta shades of the provencal style buildings.

Site suitable for all ages.

Pitches	Flat sandy good-sized pitches up to 120m² laid out in spacious tarmaced tree-lined alleys. Divided by low shrubs with some shade from trees.
Hook-Up	6 or 10 amps - all pitches. Water & drainage - 263 pitches.
Motorhomes	Motorhome service point. Good for motorhomes as everything on site and right on beach and river.
Swimming pools	New 4000m² aqua complex planned for 2010 (see site's web) which will include huge leisure lagoons against a backdrop of granite boulders, cascades, wooden bridges and coconut trees, waterslides for all ages, a paddling pool, a swimming pool for adults, hydrotherapy pool and a superb sun terrace and sun loungers. It is supervised.
Activities on site	Cycle hire. Two tennis courts. Football pitch. All weather sports pitch for basket ball, handball, hockey. Volleyball pitch. Boules pitch. Good children's play areas. Games room with pool, video games and table football. Water sports on beach and jet ski hire.
Entertainment	A programme of entertainment throughout the season which changes each day and is organised daily according to the climate and numbers on site but includes three children's clubs, 5 - 7 yrs, 8 - 12yrs and 13 - 17yrs for sports activities and competitions. Evening entertainment includes music evenings and cabarets, the Brasilia Club for over 15s, and a soundproof disco from 11pm - 1am in high season only.
Sanitary facilities	Nine superbly well appointed toilet blocks, all decorated in an individual style. Two have recently been renovated to 4-star hotel standard with arched entrances, louvred doors beautiful tiling, set off by an abundance of palms, plants and flowers. Family rooms in two new blocks. Baby room. Toddler facilities. Disabled facilities. Separate laundry. Chemical waste point.
Services	Shopping complex with supermarket, bakers, butchers, hairdressers etc. Bar overlooking pool. Attractive bar/restaurant area. Take-away. Cash point. Gas barbecues only. Dogs accepted–special dog exercise area. Internet. Wi-Fi on some pitches.
Accommodation	139 mobile homes and chalets.
Tour operators	Three British companies on 142 pitches.

Excursions/Places to visit
Collioure, Port Vendre, Banyuls, Font Romeu. Not far from Spanish border. A day trip to Cadaquès, Figueras and the Dali museum and the Pyrénées.

Directions
The site is located to the north of Canet. From the A9 take exit 41, Perpignan Nord / Rivesaltes and head towards le Barcares and Canet on the D83 for 10km, then towards Canet on the D81 for 6km. On arrival at Canet, go right round the first big roundabout towards Saint Marie, then follow the signs to le Brasilia on the right.

€ Prices 2010	Peak	High	Mid	Low	Off
Pitch + 2 + 6A	47	45	38	25	19
+ Water	2	2	2	2	Incl

Address 66141 Canet-en-Roussillon

www.brasilia.fr and **www.yelloh.village-brasilia.com**
email camping-le-brasilia@wanadoo.fr

GPS N 42° 42' 30 E 03° 02' 08   **Tel** 04.68.80.23.82

Palau-del-Vidre, Camping Le Haras ***

Map Ref OC05

Location Argelès 7km. Perpignan 20km. Canet Plage 21km. Montpellier 179km.

Open 20th Mar to 20th Oct

Pitches 130 (100 touring)

Located in the small village of Palau-del-Vidre, 7km from the beaches at Argelès, this is a fabulously verdant site and a haven of peace and quiet. It is set in the grounds of an old hunting lodge designed on the lines of a small Italianate palace with a lovely weeping willow hanging over the little duck pond. The pitches are laid out in an amazing assortment of trees and shrubs. The owners' passion for gardening allows you to appreciate over a hundred species of Mediterranean and tropical plants with their wonderful fragrances and colours. It is a family run site with a warm friendly atmosphere. Very occasional noise from trains but not at night.

Site suitable for couples and young families and those who prefer a quiet ambiance.

Pitches	Flat, grassy, varying in size from 80m² to 100m², divided by pretty trees and shrubs. Good shade on most pitches. Mobile homes do not predominate.
Hook-Up	6 amps and 10 amps. Water & drainage on 18 pitches.
Motorhomes	Motorhome service point. Shops and restaurant in the village.
Swimming pools	Attractive pool area with rectangular 20m x 10m basin and semi-circular paddling pool 12m in diameter in a lush green setting with spacious sun terrace and sun loungers.
Activities on site	Boules pitch. Volleyball area. Children's play area. Library. Fishing in lake 100m. Horse-riding 1.5km.
Entertainment	Children's club twice a week, archery, sporting competitions. Concerts twice a week from 10/7 – 22/8.
Sanitary facilities	Two unisex toilet blocks in attractive buildings and well maintained. Push button temperature controlled showers with hooks. Hot and cold taps in wash basins, no individual cubicles. Toilets without seats and no paper. Baby room. Separate laundry. Chemical waste point.
Services	Very basic shop - pre-order bread. Wooden beamed restaurant also open to public, closed two evenings week. Bar/snack with terrace overlooking pool. In village of Palau-del-Vidre 100m away there are two restaurants, a bakers, butchers, small food shop and garage. Fridge hire. Gas barbecues only allowed. Dogs accepted. Internet. Wi-Fi in bar and restaurant.
Accommodation	16 mobile homes. 14 privately owned mobile homes.
Tour operators	None.

Excursions/Places to visit
Argelès sur Mer 6km, Adventure park in trees 7km. Collioure 20km, Aqualand 20km, Figueras in Spain 40km. Pyrénées and Le Pic du Canigou.

Directions
The site is near the centre of the village. From A9 take exit Perpignan Sud and follow directions for Argelès-sur-Mer on the D914. Take exit 9 onto the D11 signposted for Palau-del-Vidre. The campsite is on the left as you enter the village.

€ Prices 2010	High	Mid	Low
Pitch + 2	27	19	15
Hook Up 6A	4	4	4

Address Domaine Saint Galdric, 66690 Palau-del-Vidre

www.camping-le-haras.com
email haras8@wanadoo.fr

GPS N 42° 34' 33 E 02° 57' 53

Tel 04.68.22.14.50

Collioure, Les Criques de Porteils ****

Location Collioure 2km. Argelès 5km. Perpignan 29km. Carcassonne 146km. Béziers 127km.

Open 3rd Apr to 16th Oct   **Pitches** 248 (199 touring)

A site that benefits from a unique position between the Mediterranean sea and the foothills of the Pyrénées. There are stunning views from one side of the site over the creeks from which the site gets its name, with access to the pebbly beaches down steps built into the rocks. On the other side a view of hills and vineyards gives the site a rural feel. You are also just a 30-minute walk from the delightful artists' town of Collioure, a great bonus as access by car in the high season can be difficult. This is a terraced site with a huge variety of pitch sizes. The ones that benefit from beautiful sunsets over the sea are very small and are only suitable for tents and small motorhomes. A quiet atmosphere, good for coastal walks but the bar/restaurant is not recommended.

Site suitable for couples and families with older children. Not suitable for small children.

Pitches	Flat, hard and laid out in narrow terraces and alleys. Can be dusty. Good pegs needed. Not divided by hedges. Beach facing area has no shade and is not verdant. Only about 20 pitches suitable for larger outfits up to 6.5m and reservation is essential.
Hook-Up	6 or 10 amps - 180 pitches.
Motorhomes	Motorhome service point. 5 hard standing pitches for overnights. Good choice as walking distance of Collioure (2km) along coastal path.
Swimming pools	Two small rectangular pools near reception with wooden decking for sun terrace and sun loungers, suitable for a dip.
Activities on site	Tennis. Golf pitch & putt. Volleyball. Basketball. 4 table tennis tables. Small children's play area and small duck pond. Swimming in sea, but access not suitable for small children or disabled. Several coastal walks in the area.
Entertainment	Tennis and boules competitions. A guided walk once a week. Occasional paella or couscous soirées in the restaurant.
Sanitary facilities	Three newly equipped and modern unisex toilet blocks. Attractively tiled in green and terracotta colours and well maintained. Temperature control taps in showers and wash cubicles, hooks and shelf. Toilets with toilet paper. Baby room and toddlers area. Laundry. Chemical waste point.
Services	Small Vival shop. Bar/snack, not a proper restaurant and more like a transport café. Take-away/pizzeria. Barbecues forbidden. Dogs accepted. Wi-Fi in restaurant.
Accommodation	25 mobile homes.
Tour operators	One French company on 24 pitches.

Excursions/Places to visit

Collioure, Port Vendre, Banyuls, Font Romeu. A day trip to Cadaquès, Figueras and the Dali museum in Spain. Pyrénées and the Pic du Canigou.

€ Prices 2010	Peak	High	Mid	Low
Pitch + 2	38	36	25.50	20.50
Hook Up 5A	6	6	4.50	4.50

Directions

The site is situated just north of Collioure off the coast road. From the A9 take exit 43 le Boulou and follow signs to Argelès-sur-Mer. Turn onto the D914 Collioure - signed "Collioure par la Corniche". After 800 metres turn right at the Hotel du Golfe and follow signs to the campsite.

Address Corniche de Collioure 66701 Argelès-sur-Mer

www.lescriques.com
email contact@lescriques.com
Tel 04.68.81.12.73

GPS N 42° 32' 06 E 03° 04' 07

Montclar, Domaine d'Arnauteille ****

Location Carcassonne 14km. Limoux 10km. Easy access from A61.

Open 1st Apr to 26th Sep   **Pitches** 198 (111 touring)

A spacious family-run site included because of its proximity to the magnificent fairy tale city of Carcassonne, its superb panoramic views over the surrounding Malepère and Corbière hills and its huge Roman baths style aqua complex. The site is surrounded by open land giving it a very spacious feel. Access to the site is through a narrow entrance and up a fairly steep hill to the pitches, but it is suitable for large outfits with a good towing vehicle. It is an ideal spot for those who wish to combine a quiet atmosphere with a visit to the Cathar castles of the Aude region. We recommend it for a few days stopover, particularly if you are on the way to Spain.

Site suitable for couples and young families.

Pitches	Laid out in terraces all with views. Generally flat and grassy, though some slope slightly. The more mature pitches are divided by trees and shrubs. Average 100m².
Hook-Up	6 or 10 amps - all pitches. Water & drainage - 50 pitches.
Motorhomes	Motorhome service point, but transport essential for going anywhere.
Swimming pools	A Greco-Roman amphitheatre style aquatic centre with 4 basins including a 25m swimming pool not heated, a lazy river with counter current, a jacuzzi, a spa and a paddling pool, surrounded by 3000m² of tiered sun terraces, but very few sun loungers. Can look a bit bleak as there are no decorative plants and cement getting rather grey but magnificent setting.
Activities on site	Horse riding. All weather sports pitch for volleyball, basket ball and football. Boules pitch. Children's play area. Games room with table tennis and table football. There are walks and cycle tracks all round the site ranging from 3km - 24km.
Entertainment	In high season: children's club 4 - 12yrs, sporting competitions in the afternoons. Music evening once a week. In low season occasional guided walks.
Sanitary facilities	Two unisex toilet blocks. The one nearest reception continues the Roman theme built round a quadrangle decorated with statues and plants. It is well appointed, attractively tiled and maintained to a high standard. Spacious showers and washbasins together, push button showers but no temperature control. Toilets with paper. Disabled facilities. Baby room. Washing machines and tumble dryer. Second block is respectable. Chemical waste point.
Services	Small shop, pre-order bread. Attractive wooden beamed bar/restaurant in converted stable with terrace. However the restaurant is not recommended as meals and service are poor quality. Take-away. Fridge hire. Gas barbecues only allowed. Dogs accepted. Internet.
Accommodation	70 mobile homes and chalets.
Tour operators	One Dutch company on 11 pitches.

Excursions/Places to visit

Carcassonne - 15 mins. Limoux 10km. Four castles in Lastours, medieval town of Mirepoix, Cathar castles in Puylaurens, Quéribus and Peyreperteuse.

€ Prices 2010	Peak	High	Mid	Low	Off
Pitch + 2	36	32	27	25	19
Hook Up 6A	incl	incl	incl	incl	incl

Address 11250 Montclar

GPS N 43° 07' 27 E 02° 15' 40

Directions

From Carcassonne take the D118 south from Carcassonne and by-pass the small village of Rouffiac d'Aude. Continue on the small section of dual carriageway but before coming to the end you will need to turn right to Montclar. Continue up the narrow road for 2.5km and the site is signposted sharp left and up the hill before the village.

www.camping-arnauteille.com
email arnauteille@mnet.fr
Tel 04.68.26.84.53

Suggestions for overnight stops near the ports.

Jumièges,
Camping de la Forêt ***
Map Ref ON01 page 37
Location Le Havre 80km. Dieppe 74km.
Open 1st Apr to 31st Oct
Pitches 111 (70 touring)
Small site in the heart of the Brotonne National Park, walking distance of the pretty little town of Jumièges, famous for its ruined Romanesque abbey and position on a large loop of the Seine river. This site has been included because of its proximity to Le Havre and Dieppe. Grassy pitches, divided by hedges, which vary in size from 80m² - 150m². 10 amps - all pitches. Water & drainage - none

Directions From north: A29 exit 9 on to N29 towards Yvetôt, taking ring road to south. After 7km left on to D131 towards Pont de Brotonne. Just before bridge left on to D982 towards Jumieges and Rouen. After 10km turn right to Jumieges and site is well signposted. From south take exit 25 at Bourg Achard on to D313 toward Yvetot. Turn right just after Pont de Brotonne and continue as above. Access via small toll-free ferry possible for cars, small trailer and small motorhomes only.

Address rue Mainberte, 76480 Jumièges
www.campinglaforet.com
email info@campinglaforet.com
Tel 02 35 37 93 43
GPS N49° 26' 08 E 00° 49' 49

Quelmer,
Domaine de la Ville Huchet ****
Map Ref ON03 page 49
Location St Malo 6km, Rennes 80km.
Open 10th Apr to 12th Sep
Pitches 194 (124 touring)
Although only a few minutes from St. Malo port, the site has a very rural feel. It is situated in the grounds of a château which although not renovated is still very attractive. The site has spacious verdant feel and a good swimming pool area with waterslides. A new toilet block and bar area in the shape of a boat have recently been installed. Pitches re flat, grassy and vary in size, on average 100m². 6 amp electricity on 80 pitches, 16 amps with water & drainage on 4 pitches

Directions. From St Malo. As you approach St Malo take the exit from the dual carriageway towards 'St Malo Centre'. Join the filter onto the main road and continue to the first roundabout where you turn right following signs to Camping de la Ville Huchet. Stay on this road which bends round and eventually leads under the road you have just come along. The site entrance is 200m after the bridge on your right.

Address Route de la Passagère, Quelmer 35400
www.lavillehuchet.com
email info@lavillehuchet.com
Tel 02 99 81 11 83
GPS N48° 36' 54 W 01° 59' 12

Bénouville,
Les Hautes Coutures ***
Map Ref ON02 page 37
Location Ouistreham Ferry Port 6km, Caen 9km.
Open 1st Apr to 31st Oct
Pitches 272 (112 touring)
A few minutes from the port and an ideal stop if arriving late from afternoon crossing or returning on morning ferry. Walking distance of Pegasus Bridge. Site has been greatly improved recently. A new pool complex with waterslides, a covered pool and all weather sports pitch have been installed. One toilet block modernised. Best pitches by canal. Large number of privately owned mobilehomes. Bar open all season. Snack June - Sept. Pitches 90m² - 100m². 6 or 10 amps. Water & drainage - none.

Directions The site is situated to the North of Bénouville just off the D35 and is well-signposted. From the D514 dual carriageway leave at the first exit (D35) signposted to Saint-Aubin d'Arquenay and ZA de Bénouville. Turn right at end of the slip road, then left at the T- junction. The site is 200m along this road on your right. From Caen. Take the D514 towards Ouistreham and continue past the exit towards Cabourg and Pegasus Bridge. Take the next slip road off the D514 on your right which will take you to the campsite entrance.

Address Route de Ouistreham, 14970 Bénouville
www.campinghautescoutures.com
email info@campinghautescoutures.com
Tel 02 31 44 73 08
GPS N49° 14' 59 W 00° 16' 19

St Pol de Léon,
Camping Ar Kléguer ***
Map Ref ON04 page 49
Location Roscoff 8km.
Open 3rd Apr to 25th Sept
Pitches 173 (125 touring)
A small family-run site, a 20-minute drive from the port at Roscoff which enjoys magnificent views over the estuary to Carantec. Attractively laid out with flowers and shrubs. Site is divided in two with the sea on one side and views over the countryside on the other. Good pool complex with waterslides and walking distance of sandy beach and St Pol de Léon. Three toilet blocks getting old but well maintained. Pitches 80m² -100m², some gently sloping. 10 amps electricity. Water & drainage - none.

Directions. From Roscoff stay on the D58 until you are south of St Pol and head towards th etown centre on the D58a Route de Morlaix. Turn right at the T- junction into rue du Port. Turn left when you arrive at the sea and the site entrance is 800m ahead.

Address Plage Sainte-Anne, 29250 St. Pol de Léon
www.camping-ar-kleguer.com
email info@camping-ar-kleguer.com
Tel 02 98 69 18 81
GPS N48° 41' 30 W 03° 58' 02

Suggestions for en-route stops and short stays.

St. Georges-les-Baillargeaux,
Camping le Futuriste***
Map Ref ON05 page 99
Location Near Poitiers 5 mins from A10 and N10.
Open All year
Pitches 112 (102 touring)
A very well run site with friendly owners ideally placed for visiting Futuroscope as well as for overnight stops on the way south and to Spain. There is a good-sized pool with waterslides, small bar/snack, an all weather sports pitch and a new children's play area. An open site with views over the Futuroscope park. Flat, grassy pitches divided by low hedges up to 100m². 82 pitches with 6 amps electricity and 62 with water & drainage.

Directions. From A10 Motorway. Exit the A10 motorway at the Futuroscope exit (exit 28). From N10. Take Futuroscope exit. The campsite is east of both roads, off the D20 to St Georges-les-Baillargeaux. From all directions follow signs for St Georges. The site is on a hill, turn by the water tower and the site entrance is on the left.

Address 86130 St Georges-les-Baillargeaux
www.camping-le-futuriste.fr
email camping-le-futuriste@wanadoo.fr
Tel 05 49 52 47 52
GPS N46° 39' 52 E 00° 23' 40

Vandanesse-en-Auxois,
Camping Lac de Panthier ****
Map Ref ON07 page 123
Location South of Pouilly-en-Auxois. Dijon 48km.
Open 3rd Apr to 9th Oct
Pitches 207 (150 touring)
In a pretty setting on the banks of the Lac de Panthier, this site is particularly suited to overnight stops as it is only 10 minutes from the A6 going south with easy access also from A38. Small indoor and outdoor pool. Bar/terrace overlooking the lake. Pitches are grassy and slope slightly, divided by hedges, but not very generous. Older style toilet blocks but respectable. Good lakeside beach. 6 amps electricity. Water & drainage - none.

Directions. From A6 Motorway. Leave the A6 motorway at the exit for Pouilly-en-Auxois and take the road in the direction of Créancey, then in the direction of Vandanesse-en-Auxois. Turn left in the village and then left again following signs to the site. The site is well-signposted from the autoroute.

Address 21320 Vandanesse-en-Auxois
www.lac-de-panthier.com
email info@lac-de-panthier.com
Tel 03 80 49 21 94
GPS N47° 14' 13 E 04° 37' 42

Châlons-en-Champagne,
Camping Municipal ****
Map Ref ON06 page123
Location South of Reims, 12km from A26 and A4.
Open 1st Apr to 31st Oct
Pitches 131 (all touring)
An ideal spot for an overnight stop on the way east or south with easy access from motorways. Only 2km from the centre of Châlons and within walking distance of a bakers and grocers shop. There is a spacious feel to the site. Small bar/snack near reception. No pool but tennis and mini-golf. Old style but well-maintained toilet blocks. 80 pitches hard standing and 51 on grass, all a good size, at least 100m², divided by low hedges with shade from trees. 10 amps electricity. Water & drainage - none.

Directions. The site is south of Chalons. From the A4 autoroute take exit 28 connecting with the N44 ring-road following signs to Vitry-le-François. Exit to St. Memmie and then drive slowly watching carefully for signs to the campsite.
From the south take exit 18 from the A26 and head towards the centre of Chalons on the N77. Turn right after crossing the river onto Avenue Charles de Gaulle. Proceed down this road and where it turns to the left continue straight on along Avenue des Allies on the D60. Then follow signs for "Camping".

Address rue de Plaisance, 51000 Châlons-en-Champagne
www.chalons-tourisme.com
email mairie.chalons@wanadoo.fr
Tel 03 26 65 17 89
GPS N48° 56' 09 E 04° 22' 59

Issoire,
Camping La Grange Fort ***
Map Ref ON08 page 133
Location South of Clermont Ferrand just off A75.
Open 1st Apr to 31st Oct
Pitches 100 pitches (80 touring)
Just 10 mins from A75, this site is worth an overnight stop just to see its magnificent 15th century château and extensive grounds. The pretty pool is in the courtyard and the services and facilities are housed in the stone-faced outbuildings. Direct access to the Allier river and views over the Massif Central hills. The sanitary facilities are adequate but water tends to be tepid. Also very Dutch clientele as run by friendly Dutch family. The pitches are not huge, maximum 100m² and varying in shape.
6 amps electricity. Water & drainage - none.

Directions. Leave A75 at exit 13. Take D996 to Sauxillanges, then turn onto D999 to Les Pradeaux and right onto D34 following signs to the campsite.

Address 63500 Les Pradeaux,
www.lagrangefort.com
email camping@lagrangefort.com
Tel 04 73 71 02 43 (site) 04 73 71 05 93 (château)
GPS N45° 30' 32 E 03° 17' 05

Riverside pitch at Le Soleil Plage

Index of campsites listed by town